CB082233

GLOBAL CHANGER

TEACHER'S BOOK

3

LOUISE POTTER

CAMBRIDGE
UNIVERSITY PRESS

CAMBRIDGE
UNIVERSITY PRESS

University Printing House, Cambridge CB2 8BS, United Kingdom

One Liberty Plaza, 20th Floor, New York, NY 10006, USA

477 Williamstown Road, Port Melbourne, VIC 3207, Australia

314–321, 3rd Floor, Plot 3, Splendor Forum, Jasola District Centre, New Delhi – 110025, India

103 Penang Road, #05–06/07, Visioncrest Commercial, Singapore 238467

Avenida Paulista, 807 conjunto 2315, 01311 -915, São Paulo, Brazil

Cambridge University Press is part of the University of Cambridge.

It furthers the University's mission by disseminating knowledge in the pursuit of education, learning and research at the highest international levels of excellence.

www.cambridge.org
Information on this title: www.cambridge.org/9781009277662

© Cambridge University Press & Assessment 2022

This publication is in copyright. Subject to statutory exception and to the provisions of relevant collective licensing agreements, no reproduction of any part may take place without the written permission of Cambridge University Press.

First published 2022

20 19 18 17 16 15 14 13 12 11 10 9 8 7 6 5 4 3 2

Printed in Great Britain by CPI Group (UK) Ltd, Croydon CR0 4YY

A catalogue record for this publication is available from the British Library

ISBN 978-1-009-27766-2 Global Changer Teacher's Book with Digital Pack Level 3

Additional resources for this publication at www.cambridge.org/globalchanger

Cambridge University Press has no responsibility for the persistence or accuracy of URLs for external or third-party internet websites referred to in this publication, and does not guarantee that any content on such websites is, or will remain, accurate or appropriate. Information regarding prices, travel timetables, and other factual information given in this work is correct at the time of first printing but Cambridge University Press does not guarantee the accuracy of such information thereafter.

Contents

Welcome to *Global Changer*

You can be a Global Changer!

With its fresh and fun approach to global real-world topics, *Global Changer* is designed to help teachers prepare stimulating and easy-to-teach lessons that will ensure your students are motivated and engaged throughout the whole school year. Our global focused reading topics, in-context language presentations, scaffolded speaking and writing tasks, and the latest digital resources are guaranteed to develop learners' global awareness and encourage a learning mindset.

While developing *Global Changer*, we spoke with a number of teachers and students all over Brazil to identify their top priorities in the Ensino Fundamental 2 English classroom, and we translated these into our key features.

Real-Life Contexts for Language Presentation

We present grammar and vocabulary in a clear context through dynamic reading and listening texts in a wide variety of genres. This, combined with topics that are relevant and authentic, ensures students see the purpose of their learning and feel motivated to explore and use the language.

Global Cultural Topics

Global Changer explores a variety of global topics through its reading and listening pages and in a dedicated *Around the World* spread in every other unit. This helps students broaden their understanding of other people and places, preparing them for life in a diverse, multicultural environment.

Easy-to-teach

Global Changer Teacher's Book includes all the Student's Book and Workbook pages, with the Answer Key integrated on each page. Teacher's Notes and extra tips make it easy to identify each section. Flipped classroom ideas provide useful suggestions for activities that students could do at home to consolidate in-class learning.

All your digital tools together!

With Cambridge One everything you need to teach with *Global Changer* is at your fingertips with classroom presentation, audio and video, additional practice, games, and an innovative digital collaboration space for students.
For more information see page XV.

English is an International Language

Learners of English now outnumber speakers of English as a first language. Students are therefore far more likely to use English to communicate with people whose first language is not English. This has significant implications for traditional English teaching because an understanding of the language is now only *part* of successful communication, and we cannot underestimate the role of cross-cultural understanding. For this reason, *Global Changer* does not elevate one type of English above others and instead embraces different varieties of English, featuring a range of voices and language varieties.

Teen-Friendly Videos

Global Changer documentary videos reinforce and extend the Student's Book content. The topics of the videos are authentic, fresh, and fun with a global scope, presenting ways of life and ideas from different cultures around the world.

Cross-curricular Pages

Global Changer includes a variety of Cross-curricular lessons, with a dedicated Across the Curriculum spread in every other unit. This reinforces and extends students' learning in other areas across the broader curriculum. The attractive and colorful spreads provide a stimulating alternative to the more skills-focused core pages in each unit.

Project Work

We know that it is important for you as a teacher to include projects and collaborative work in your planning and that it is especially motivating for students. That's why we have included two easy-to-teach projects at the back of each Student's Book. These projects recycle and review the language learned in the previous semester, providing a fun and stimulating way to keep students practicing their language skills.

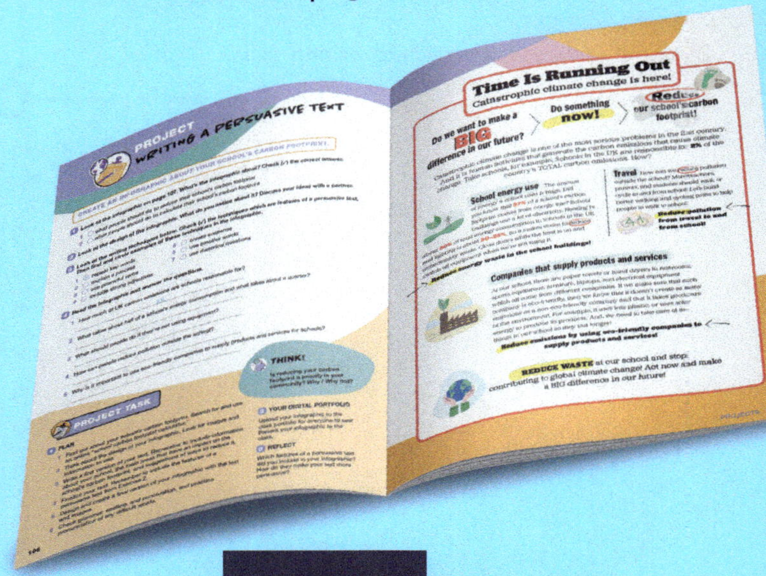

Designed specifically for Brazil

In *Global Changer*, we developed a syllabus that not only includes all the language requirements outlined in the **Base Nacional Comum Curricular** (BNCC), but also reflects its core values. Take a look at the chart below to see the key features we have incorporated into *Global Changer* to address BNCC requirements.

BNCC	Global Changer
Develop intercultural competence: reflect on the role of English in our globalized world and the relationship between language, identity, and culture.	Global topics, documentary videos with a culture focus, and dedicated *Around the World* pages.
Present English as a *lingua franca*, exposing learners to different varieties of English from around the world.	A broad range of accents in our audio, *Living English* functional language feature on each Speaking page.
A focus on the development of effective oral communication.	Staged communicative tasks in *Use it* activities and dedicated Speaking pages with scaffolded productive activities and a functional approach to communication.
Encourage learners to reflect critically on different ways of seeing and analyzing the world around them.	*Think!* critical thinking questions, documentary videos and real-world global topics.
Develop a broad range of reading skills and exposure to different genres of text.	Diverse real-life genres in reading, listening, and writing texts and activities to develop reading skills including genre recognition strategies.
Encourage learners to discover grammar rules and patterns.	Grammar presented in context and shown clearly in accessible grammar charts.
Develop a process approach to writing skills.	Dedicated Writing pages with Plan, Check, and Edit stages

For a chart mapping the BNCC competences for this level, visit www.cambridge.org/gamechanger or scan the QR code to the right.

Cambridge Life Competencies

A framework to develop skills for life

How can we prepare our students to succeed in a world that is rapidly changing? We need to help students develop transferable skills that allow them to work with people from around the world, think creatively, analyze sources critically, and communicate their views effectively. How can we teach these skills alongside language?

In response to these questions, we have developed the *Cambridge Life Competencies Framework*. This Framework informs the syllabus for the *Think!* activities in *Global Changer*, helping teachers recognize and assess the many transferable skills that the course develops.

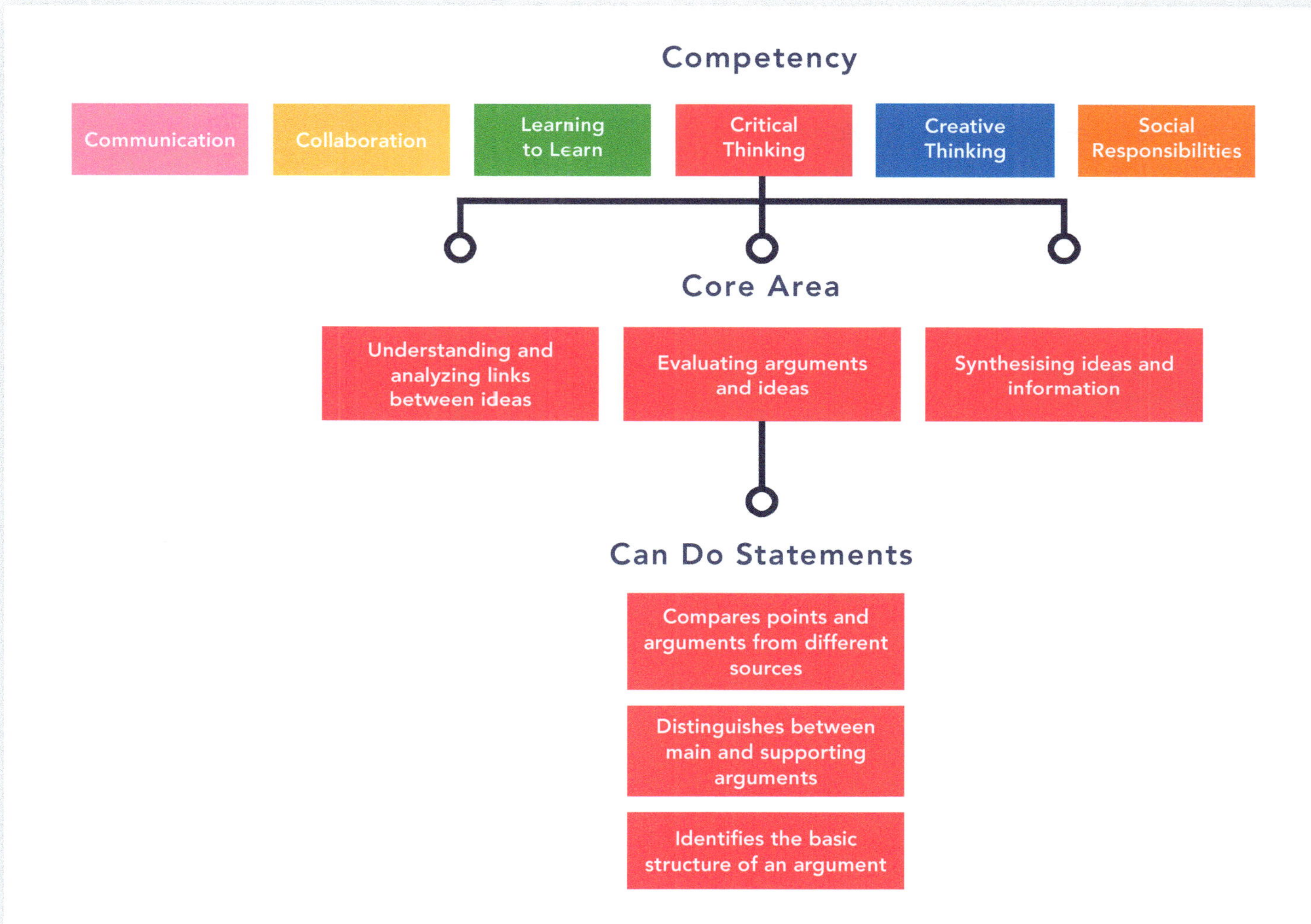

For a chart mapping the Cambridge Life Competencies for this level, visit www.cambridge.org/globalchanger or scan the QR code to the right.

Student's Book Visual Guide

Every unit in *Global Changer* takes the student on a carefully staged journey. Students are gradually introduced to the topic and target language through a variety of scaffolded activities that build their confidence as they progress. Language is presented in context via a rich variety of real-world topics and each unit culminates in a creative writing or speaking task.

Unit Goals

The Unit Goals show the unit aims at a glance.

Attractive Unit Opener photo

A picture is worth a thousand words, and in today's culture, there are images everywhere. This means that visual literacy—the ability to "read" images—is an essential skill. In *Global Changer*, the unit openers provide an opportunity for students to interpret meaning from pictures related to the unit topic.

Think! Questions

We often "read" images before we read words. This happens every day with what we see on television, advertisements, internet memes, emojis, or other media. By encouraging different responses to visual stimuli, you can help your students critically analyze and interpret what they see and develop a deeper understanding of topics. The *Think!* questions in the Unit Opener and throughout each unit encourage students to think beyond the photo or topic and articulate their opinions, developing their critical-thinking skills.

Opener Video

The opener documentary video provides a fun and engaging introduction the unit topic.

Vocabulary in Context

Vocabulary is presented in a real-life context making it easier to understand and more meaningful for the students.

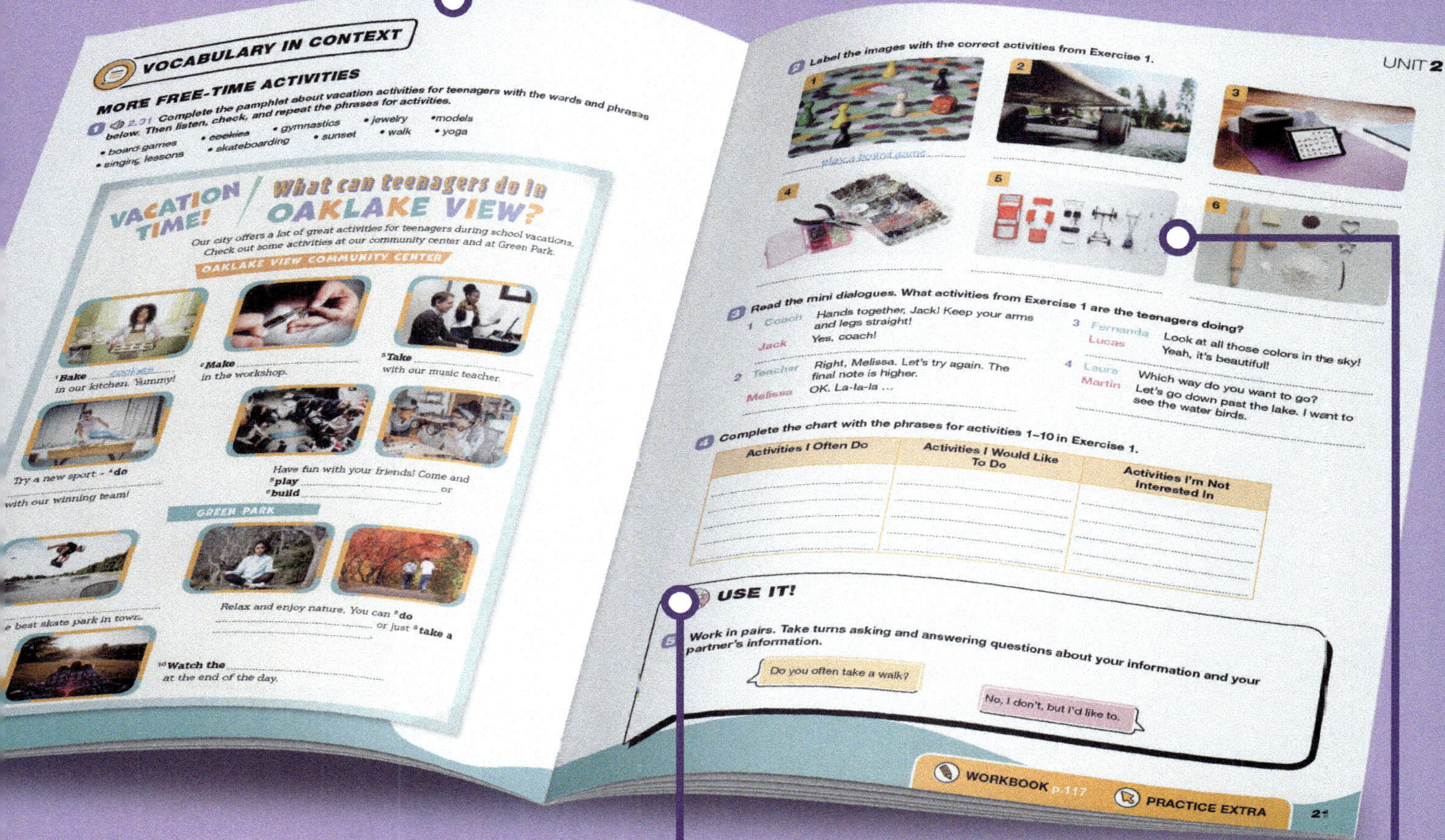

Use It!

Communicative activities give the students a personalized communicative purpose, encouraging them to internalize the language in a fun and motivating way.

Learning to Learn

Activities that ask students to categorize the vocabulary encourage students to develop their own learning skills and so become more motivated, independent learners.

Real-Life Genres

Texts in a range of different genres present the language in a realistic context. Up-to-date and authentic global topics motivate students to read and learn more.

Grammar Chart

Example sentences from the reading and listening texts presented clearly in a grammar chart allow students to easily see the target structures, and encourage them to think about the rules.

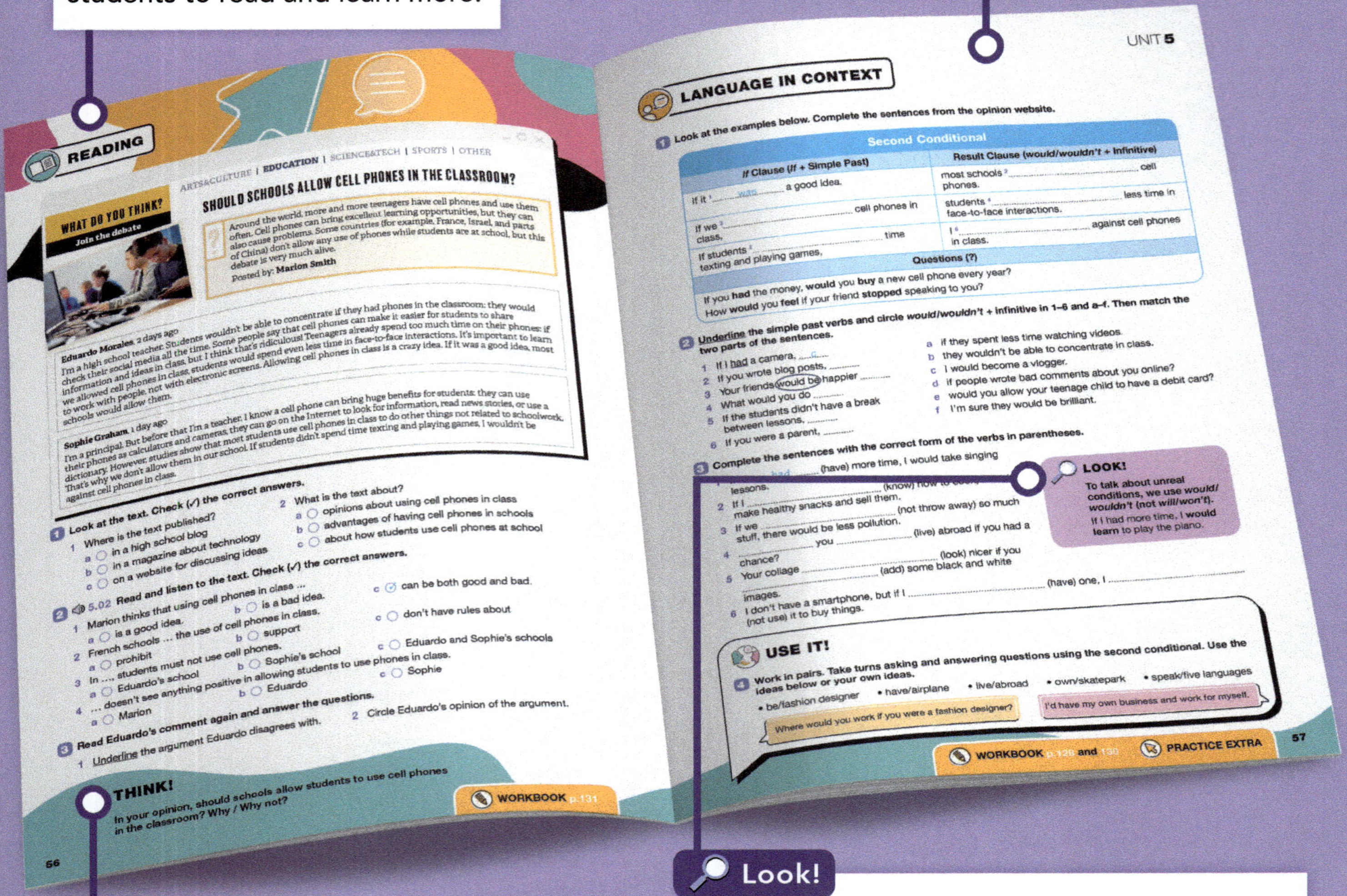

Look!

Look! boxes help students to avoid common Portuguese speakers' errors as identified by the *Cambridge Learner Corpus*.

Think!

Think! questions encourage students to engage with the text in a personal way and develop their critical-thinking skills as well as their awareness of global topics.

Language in Context

Students hear the target language in a real-life context in the listening activity, before they identify the key structures when filling in the grammar chart.

Grammar Charts

Students are encouraged to actively engage with the target grammar structures before they tackle the carefully staged grammar practice activities.

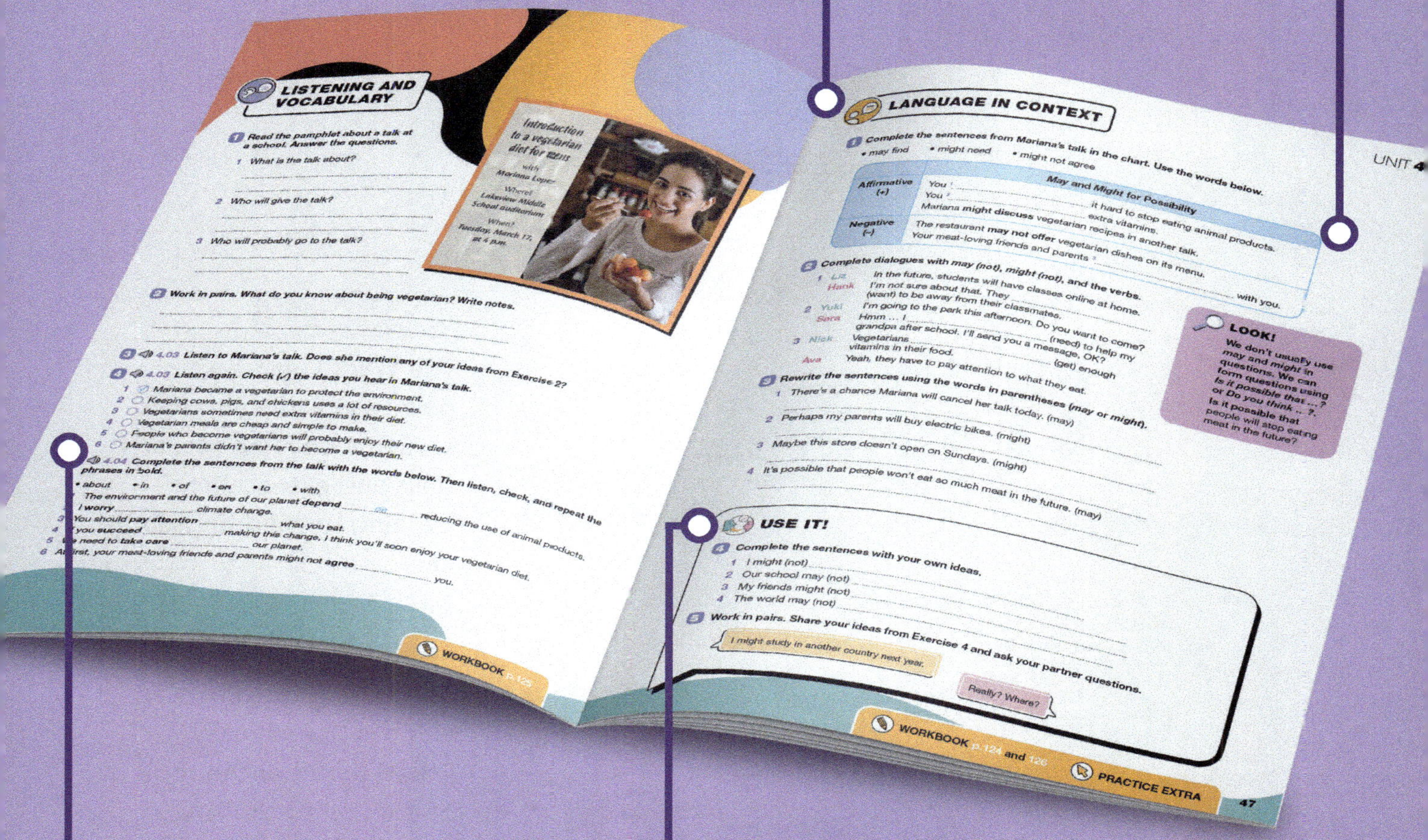

Vocabulary

Vocabulary learning is consolidated with attractive images and follow-up activities.

Use It!

Use it! gets students practicing and producing the target language, often in a personalized way. These activities build students' confidence by giving them the opportunity to prepare what they want to say before speaking.

Around the World

The *Around the World* pages, which appear in Units 1, 3, 5, and 7, introduce students to different people and cultures from around the world, encouraging critical thinking and raising cross-cultural awareness.

Words in Context

The Words in Context activities encourage students to work out meaning from context and to recognize similarities.

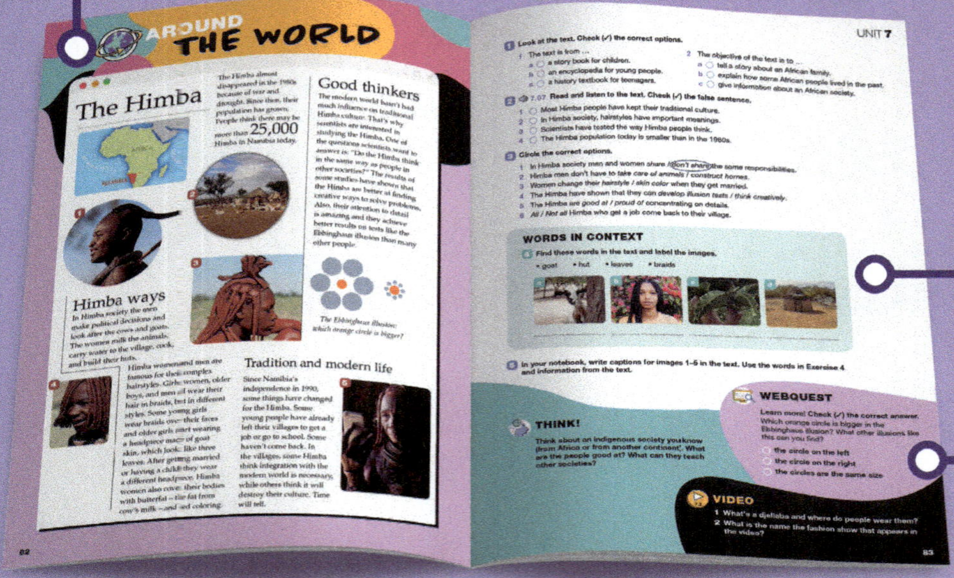

WebQuest

The WebQuest is a fun quiz-type activity to help students develop research skills and extend their learning beyond English.

Closing Video

The closing documentary video is thematically linked to either the topic of the unit or the *Around the World* or *Across the Curriculum* page. These videos contextualize the language in the unit and extend students' interest in the topic.

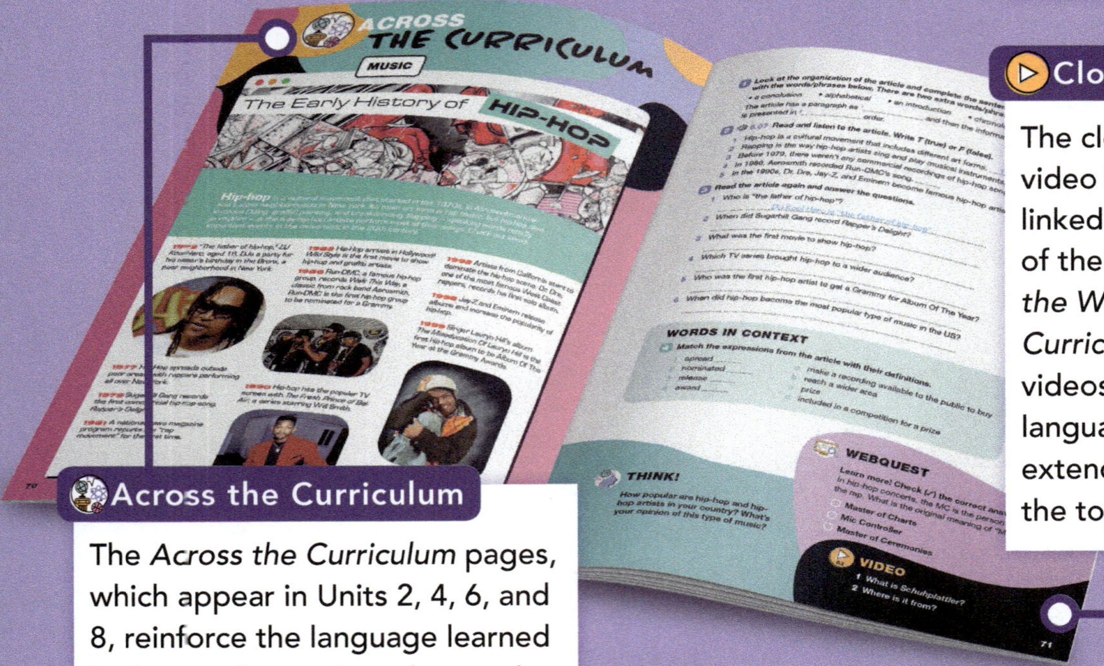

Across the Curriculum

The *Across the Curriculum* pages, which appear in Units 2, 4, 6, and 8, reinforce the language learned in the previous unit and extend students' learning in other areas across the broader curriculum.

Speaking and Writing

The **Speaking** pages, which appear in Units 1, 3, 5, and 7, introduce students to conversation strategies, and encourage learners to practice their speaking in a guided and structured way.

Living English

Living English activities introduce students to common everyday phrases, as identified by the *Cambridge English Corpus*.

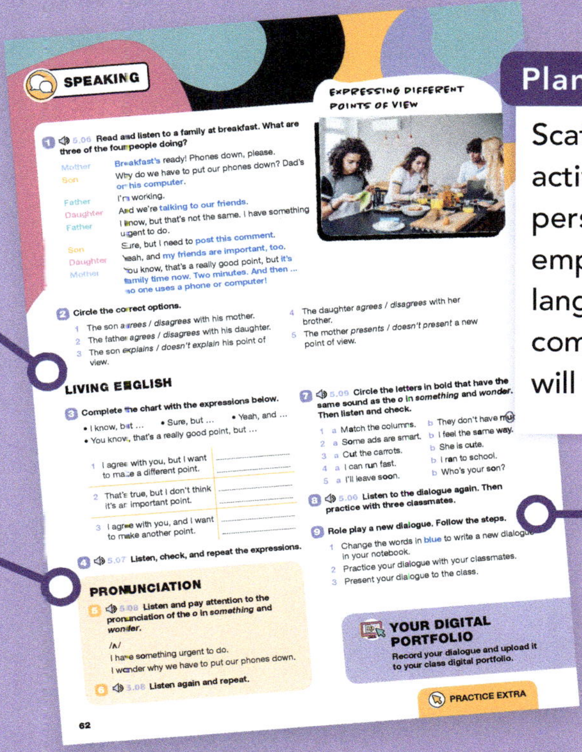

Plan, Practice, and Present

Scaffolded speaking activities allow students to personalize the dialogue and empower them to use the language they've learned in a communicative task, which they will then present to the class.

Pronunciation

The Pronunciation activity models correct pronunciation for students to practice before they speak, and draws students' attention to differences between English sounds and those of their native language.

The **Writing** pages, which appear in Units 2, 4, 6, and 8, introduce students to different genres of model texts and allow them to develop their writing skills in guided way.

Plan, Write, and Edit

The scaffolded approach of the writing pages builds students' confidence by giving them time to prepare before they write. The Check stage encourages self-assessment, a key step toward learner independence.

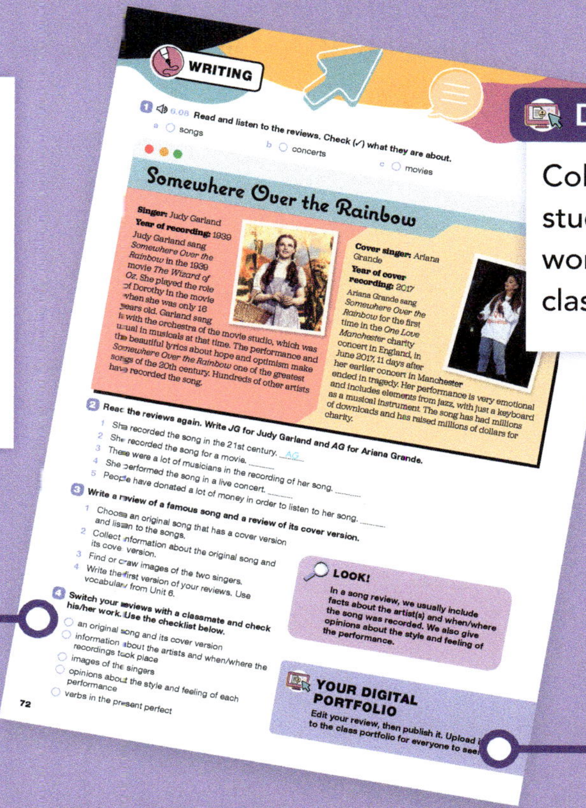

Digital Portfolio Space

Collaboration Plus allows students to upload their final work and share it with their classmates and teacher.

An additional Speaking or Writing page for each unit is also available to download online on Cambridge One.

Workbook

The full-color Workbook with Language Reference, dedicated Vocabulary and Grammar practice pages, and extra Reading is ideal for homework.

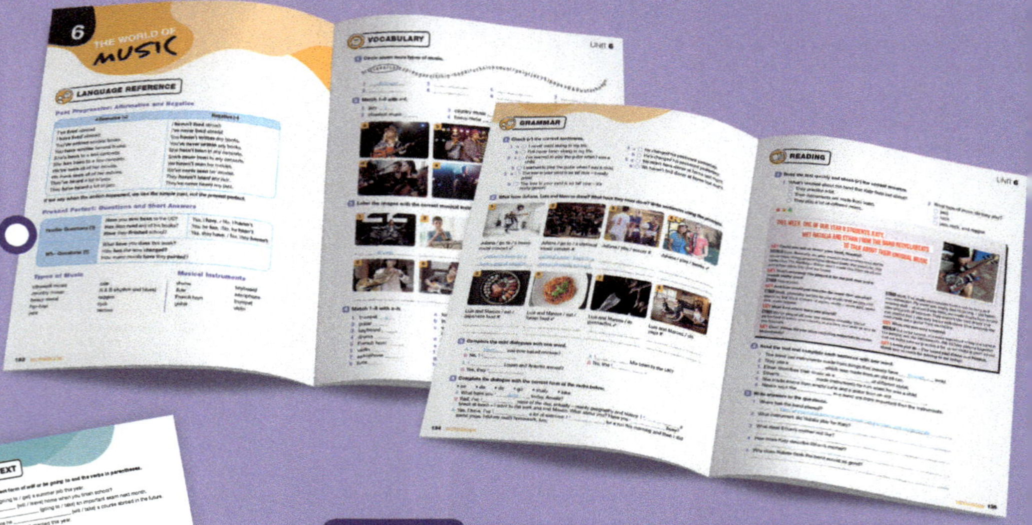

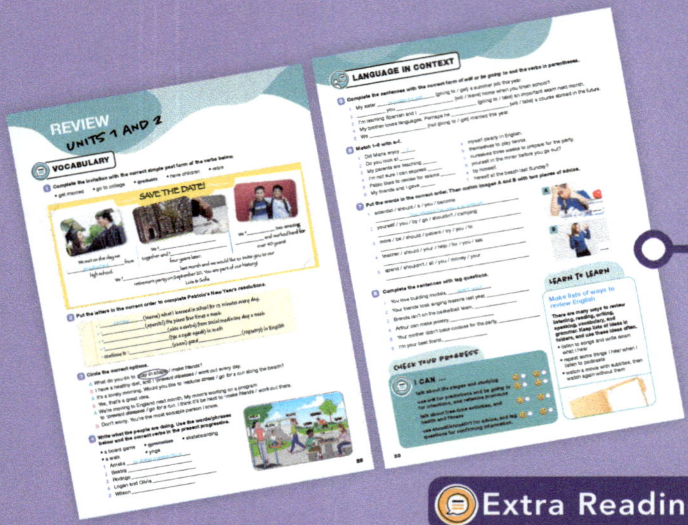

Review

The Review sections review the language from the previous two units and include a self-assessment Can-Do task, encouraging students' self-awareness.

Extra Reading

Extra *Around the World* and *Across the Curriculum* pages are provided at the end of the Student's Book, providing an attractive option for further practice of the language covered in the previous two units.

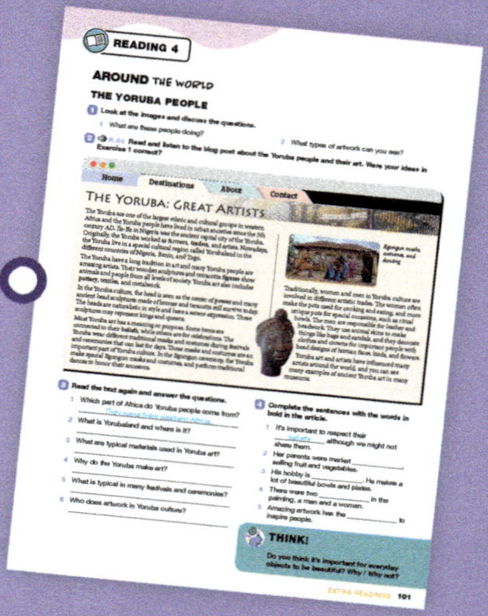

Projects

Two-page Projects provide a personalized and communicative way for students to practice the language learned in the previous semester, while developing their teamwork skills.

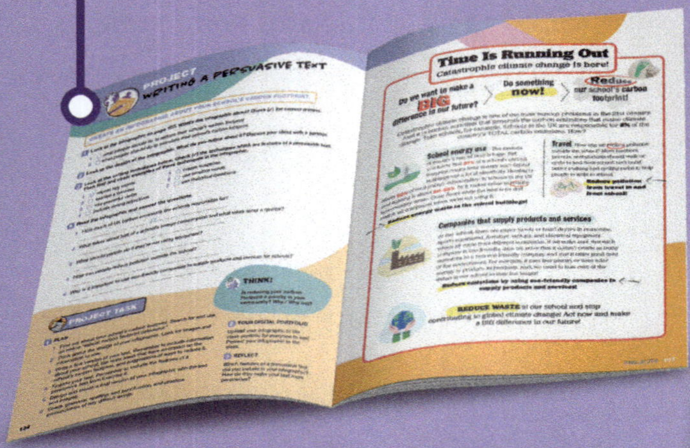

Puzzles

Puzzles for every unit provide a fun and engaging way for fast finishers to review and practice target language in class.

Global Changer Digital Resource Pack: Cambridge One

All your digital tools together in one place! With *Global Changer* everything you need is at your fingertips with classroom presentation, audio and video, additional practice, games, and an innovative digital collaboration space for students.

Presentation Plus

- Student's Book and Workbook with interactive exercises and all Answer Keys
- accessible online and offline

Teacher's Resources

- The online Teacher's Resource Bank has extra *Around the World* and *Across the Curriculum* worksheets, Grammar practice, Writing, and Speaking worksheets.
- The Test Generator includes Unit Tests, Two-unit Progress Tests, Mid-Year Tests, and End-of-Year Tests.

Collaboration Plus

- Students can collaborate digitally and upload their work online.
- Teachers can assign, track, assess and publish their students' work to the class digital portfolio.

Practice Extra

- mobile-friendly content on Cambridge One ideal for students to practice at home
- bite-sized learning activities
- grammar and vocabulary exercises
- fun and motivating games for each unit
- performance tracking

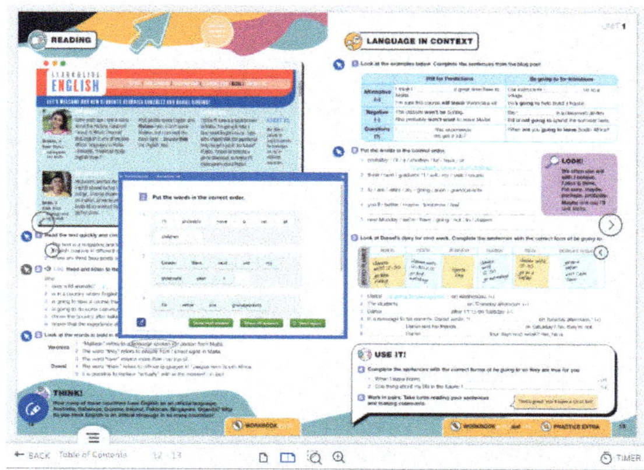

Video

- subtitles
- two videos per unit: an introduction to the unit topic and a closing video
- engaging real-world topics
- encourage cultural awareness
- reinforce language learning
- instant video lessons in Teacher's Book

eBook

- The Global Changer Student's Book and Workbook in a digital format with embedded audio and video.

For the most up-to-date information on *Global Changer*'s Digital Resource Pack, visit www.cambridge.org/globalchanger or scan the QR code to the right

CONTENTS

* This material can be downloaded from the Digital Resource Pack.

UNIT	VOCABULARY	GRAMMAR	READING	LISTENING	SPEAKING AND PRONUNCIATION	WRITING	CRITICAL THINKING
5 **My Online Self** *p.53* 5.1 Put Your Phone Down!	Strong Adjectives *p.54* The Internet *p.58*	Second Conditional *p.57* Indefinite Pronouns *p.59*	An Online Debate Site: Should Schools Allow Cell Phones in the Classroom? *p.56* Around the World: Taking a Break from Social Media *p.60* 5.2 What's up With Social Media	An Informal Talk about Digital Footprints *p.58*	Expressing Different Points of View **Pronunciation:** /ʌ/ *p.62*	A Journal*	What three words would you use to describe your online life? And your offline life? In your opinion, should schools allow students to use cell phones in the classroom?
6 **The World of Music** *p.63* 6.1 Feel the Music	Types of Music *p.64* Musical Instruments *p.68*	Present Perfect: Affirmative and Negative *p.67* Present Perfect: Questions and Short Answers *p.69*	An Online Concert Review: BTS Rocks Green Alliance Arena for a Memorable Night! *p.66* Music: The Early History of Hip-Hop *p.70* 6.2 The *Schuhplattler*	A Talk Show Interview with a Songwriter *p.68*	Showing Interest* **Pronunciation:** Rising Intonation in *Yes/No* Questions	Two Song Reviews *p.72*	How important is music to you? Why do you think a mother is worried about her son going to a big music concert? How would you reply to her? How popular are hip-hop and hip-hop artists in your country?
Review *p.73*							
7 **Africa: Past, Present, and Future** *p.75* 7.1 Amazing Africa	Achievements *p.76* Adjectives + Prepositions *p.80*	Present Perfect with *Already*, *Just*, and *Yet* *p.79* Present Perfect with *Since* and *For* *p.81*	An Online Magazine Article: Looking for Innovation? Here's Africa for You *p.78* Around the World: The Himba *p.82* 7.2 Fashion From Africa	A Podcast about a Movie from Angola *p.80*	Presenting New Information **Pronunciation:** *-ed* Verbs: /t/, /d/, and /ɪd/ *p.84*	A Biography*	What problems do you see around you and what inventions might help solve them? Think about an indigenous society. What can they teach other societies?
8 **What's Important to Me?** *p.85* 8.1 What Motivates You?	Phrases with *Do*, *Have*, and *Make* *p.86* Verbs + Prepositions *p.90*	Present Perfect vs. Simple Past *p.89* Subject and Object Questions *p.91*	A Pamphlet: Dilemma Teens *p.88* Geography: Where Do the Happiest Teenagers in the World Live? *p.92* 8.2 Mindfulness and Meditation	Street Interviews about Volunteer Work *p.90*	Describing Past Experiences* **Pronunciation:** Schwa in Unstressed Words and Syllables	A Write-up of an Interview *p.94*	How do you make decisions about things that are important in your life? How happy do you think teenagers are in your country?
Review *p.95*							

Reading: Around the World and Across the Curriculum *p.98*; **Puzzles and Games** *p.102*; **Projects** *p.106*; **Irregular Verb List** *p.110*; **Workbook** *p.111*

Lesson Aim: I can compare places, use gerunds, and talk about free-time activities.

0.01 Audioscript pT138

1 Greet students and welcome them to class. Say: *Hello, I'm* (your name). *Nice to meet you.* Encourage volunteers to introduce themselves in the same way. Talk about where you are from (city and neighborhood) and encourage students to do the same, using the comparative form. Invite students to look at the image of the city of Rio de Janeiro and ask them what they know about Rio. Have them compare Rio to their own city. Then have them complete the article using the correct comparative form.

2 Review the gerund form with students. Put students into pairs and ask them to complete the mini dialogues. Encourage peers to help each other. Check their work by eliciting the answers from volunteers.

3 **0.01** Read the verbs together with the students. Invite them to look at the images and complete the phrases below, using the correct verb. Play the audio for students to check their work and the pronunciation of the phrases.

Extension

Have students write a small paragraph about their hometown. Encourage them to talk about its highlights and compare it to any other town in Brazil. Have them use Exercise 1 as a reference.

WELCOME!

COMPARATIVES

1 Complete the article with the comparative form of the adjectives in parentheses.

Visit Rio de Janeiro

Carnival celebrations in Brazil are [1] more exciting than (exciting) in any other country, and Rio de Janeiro is Brazil's most popular destination with a lot of different neighborhoods to choose from. For example Ipanema is famous for its Carnival parties, but it's [2] more crowded than (crowded) Barra da Tijuca, and Santa Tereza is [3] more traditional than (traditional) both those neighborhoods – you'll definitely enjoy an authentic "carioca" experience there!

In Rio you'll want to have fun at the beach, too! Copacabana and Leblon are amazing, but beaches like Prainha, Reserva, and Grumari are often [4] cleaner (clean) and [5] more peaceful than (peaceful) those very popular beaches.

After enjoying the Carnival, you can visit places not too far away from Rio. Petrópolis, Itaipava, and Penedo are a lot [6] quieter than (quiet) the state capital, and are great places to relax!

GERUNDS

2 Complete the mini dialogues with the gerund form of the verbs below.

• add • avoid • ~~drink~~ • ride • take • wait

1 A Dr. Ramirez, what are some things people can do to keep healthy?
B Well, drinking enough water is very important. And avoiding sugar is a simple step. For example, adding more sugar to chocolate milk is totally unnecessary.

2 A I don't like taking the bus to school.
B Why? It's much faster than riding your bike.
A Yes, but I don't like waiting for the bus on my own at the bus stop.

FREE-TIME ACTIVITIES

3 0.01 Look at the images and complete with the words below. Then listen, check, and repeat.

• eat • go • ~~play~~ • watch

1 
play in a band

2 
eat out

3 
go to a concert

4 
watch series

4

Welcome!

Lesson Aim: : I can talk about occupations, use the simple future, and use *be going to* for intentions.

🔊0.02 Audioscript pT138

1 🔊**0.02** Review occupations with students. If you think students will be comfortable to do so, elicit their parents' occupations and write them on the board as students call them out. Check to see which occupation is the most common amongst the class. Have students look at the images in their books and unscramble the words to match them. Play the audio to check their work. Focus on pronunciation by asking students to repeat the different occupations.

2 Review with students how we use the simple future using *will*. Ask some students for personal examples. Ask students to make up a sentence using *will* and share it with a peer. Have students read the sentences and complete them with the correct simple future form. Have them check their work in pairs.

3 Remind students how to ask questions using *be going to*. Ask students simple questions, e.g.: *Are you going to soccer practice tomorrow? What time are you going to bed tonight? How long are you going to spend on vacation?* etc. Invite students to look at the prompts in their books and give them two minutes to form questions. Have them check their work in pairs.

USE IT!

4 Put students into pairs to practice asking and answering the questions from Exercise 3. Encourage them to come up with more questions to interview their partner. Monitor their work.

Extension

Have students write a small paragraph about which occupation they believe will be the most in demand in the future. Have them justify their answer. Encourage them to share their paragraphs.

OCCUPATIONS

1 🔊 0.02 **Put the letters below in the correct order and label the images. Then listen, check, and repeat.**

• ~~ahsinof snedegir~~ • camisuni • hefc • lheteta • nraced • regeenni • suern • taorc

1 
fashion designer

2 
actor

3 
musician

4 
chef

5 
athlete

6 
engineer

7 
nurse

8 
dancer

SIMPLE FUTURE

2 **Complete the sentences with the correct simple future form of the verbs in parentheses.**

1 The inventor ___will explain___ (explain) his new project in the next class.
2 We can have a picnic at the park on Sunday. I'm sure it ___won't rain___ (not rain).
3 The students ___will donate___ (donate) their old books to the local library.
4 My cell phone still works well, so I ___won't buy___ (not buy) a new one for the moment.
5 ___Will___ Julia ___live___ (live) abroad like her sister?

BE GOING TO

3 **Write questions using the prompts and the correct form of *be going to*.**

1 How long / you / stay at school today?
How long are you going to stay at school today?
2 you / do your homework immediately after class?
Are you going to do your homework immediately after class?
3 What time / you / get up tomorrow?
What time are you going to get up tomorrow?
4 What / you / do next vacation?
What are you going to do for your next vacation?

USE IT!

4 **Work in pairs. Take turns asking and answering the questions in Exercise 3.**

How long are you going to stay at school today?

I'm going to be here until 2 p.m. What about you?

5

Lesson Aim: I can talk about extreme weather, use the present progressive, and make polite offers.

0.03 Audioscript pT138

1 0.03 Have students keep their books closed. Write the word *weather* on the board. Build a mind map with your students with all the words that come to their minds when they think of the word *weather*. Have them open their books and look at the images. Ask them to check if any of the images relate to the words on their mind map. Ask volunteers to read the words in the boxes above the images. Have them match the images to the six words from the first box. In pairs, have students read sentences 1–6 and complete the sentences with the words from the box. Draw their attention to the fact that image 1 and sentence 1 are linked and so on. Play the audio to check their work. Have them pay attention to pronunciation and intonation.

2 Review the present progressive tense with students. Ask them to give you examples. Ask them to read the sentences and complete the dialogue. Encourage students to give you more examples after completing the sentences.

LOOK!

Draw attention to the *Look!* box. Read the sentence with students and ask them to give you more examples. Remind them that we use the present progressive tense for ongoing activities, and also for future arrangements and intended actions.

3 Remind students how we make polite offers to people. Write the following on the board: *the movies, a concert, a jog*. Ask volunteers to invite their peers to the different events. Have students read the sentences 1–3. Individually, have them complete the sentences using the prompts.

4 Have students complete the sentences with their own ideas.

EXTREME WEATHER

1 0.03 **Complete the sentences with a word from each box. Then listen and check.**

• ~~blizzard~~ • heatwave • flood • hurricane • forest fire • thunderstorm

• ~~cold~~ • incredible • dry • terrible • hot • wet

1 It was really *cold* here yesterday and a *blizzard* hit the city in the morning.
2 We arrived in Madrid during a *heatwave*. It was really *hot* in the afternoon.
3 A *forest fire* can start quickly in a summer with no rain, when the country is very *dry*.
4 Because of the *flood*, everything downstairs in our house got *wet*.
5 There was a big *thunderstorm* in Perth last night. Look at the *incredible* photo my cousin took!
6 The *hurricane* caused *terrible* problems for people living on the coast.

PRESENT PROGRESSIVE

2 **Complete the dialogue with the correct present progressive form of the verbs in parentheses.**

A My brother and his friend [1] *are leaving* (leave) for Australia next month.
B Wow! How long [2] *are* they *staying* (stay) there?
A For six weeks. They [3] *'re/are coming* (come) back at the end of August.
B [4] *Is* your sister *working* (work) in the mall tonight?
A No, she isn't. She [5] *'s/is studying* (study) for a test.

LOOK!
We use the present progressive for future plans, appointments, and arrangements.
Mariela **is traveling** to the UK next week. (She has her plane ticket and her hotel booking.)

POLITE OFFERS

3 **Write questions to ask a friend using the prompts and the correct object pronoun.**

1 There's a new science fiction movie at Moviemark. (see?)
Would you like to see it?
2 My dad made these chocolate cookies. (try?)
Would you like to try them?
3 We're playing video games at Isa's house tonight. (join?)
Would you like to join us?

4 **Complete the sentences with *I'd like to* or *I'd love to* and your own ideas.**

1 *Students' own answers* go tonight.
2 ______ meet ______ one day.

USE IT!

5 **Work in pairs. Take turns saying your sentences in Exercise 4 and asking questions to find out more information.**

I'd like to go to the movies tonight.

What would you like to see?

6

USE IT!

5 Put students into pairs. Have them look at the speech bubbles and model the activity with a student. Student As should read their sentences to their partners. Student Bs should react by asking for more information. Then have them change roles.

Extension

Ask students to write a small dialogue regarding their plans for the weekend. Encourage them to write three or four sentences, using the present progressive, about a plan they intend to do. However, when they hear of a change in circumstances, for example, a bad weather forecast, they have to change their plan. For example:

A *I'm going to travel to the beach next week.*
B *The weather forecast is very bad.*
A *Oh no! I will change my plans.*

Lesson Aim: I can talk about shopping; I can use countable and uncountable nouns, intensifiers, and quantifiers.

0.04 Audioscript pT138

1 **0.04** Divide students into pairs. Write the word *shopping* on the board. Give them 30 seconds to write as many words related to the topic as they can. Check to see which pair was able to write the most words. Have them read the paragraph in their books and circle the correct option. Play the audio to check their work.

2 Write the words *artist* and *money* on the board. Have them classify whether the words are countable or uncountable. Have them justify their answer. Ask students to read the words in their books and complete the chart. Have them add some of their own words.

3 Write the following intensifiers on the board: *really, extremely, quite*. Ask volunteers to come up with sentences using these intensifiers, explaining the reason for intensifiers (adverbs that make another word stronger). Ask students to read sentences 1–6 and circle the correct option. In pairs, have them check their work and justify their choices.

4 Write *how much* and *how many* on the board. Ask students to give you examples of questions with each one, and explain the reason for using them. Individually, have students read questions 1–6 and complete them with the correct option. Have them come up with other examples related to their daily activities.

SHOPPING

1 0.04 **Circle the correct options. Then listen and check.**

Olivia is at the [1]*shop* / *shopping* / *store* mall. She'd like to buy a new jacket, but she can't [2]*donate* / *earn* / *afford* it. She [3]*saved* / *spent* / *borrowed* almost all her [4]*pocket* / *customer* / *free* money last weekend, and she can't use her [5]*money* / *debit* / *bargain* card because she doesn't have enough [6]*money* / *bills* / *coins* in the bank.

COUNTABLE AND UNCOUNTABLE NOUNS

2 **Complete the chart with the words below.**

- ~~artist~~
- information
- money
- beauty
- juice
- price
- border
- message
- review
- food

Countable	Uncountable
artist	beauty
border	food
message	information
price	juice
review	money

INTENSIFIERS

3 **Circle the correct options.**

1 I put *too much* / *too many* sugar in my coffee.
2 Lucas is the most popular student I know. He has *a lot of* / *enough* friends.
3 The test was difficult. There were *too much* / *too many* questions to answer.
4 This closet is so small! There's *enough* / *not enough* space for your clothes.
5 There's *not much* / *not many* information about Carl's accident. I hope he's OK.
6 You don't need to go to the market. We have *enough* / *too many* eggs for the cake.

QUANTIFIERS

4 **Complete the sentences with *How much* or *How many*.**

1 How much homework did you do last night?
2 How much water do you drink every day?
3 How many students are there in your science class?
4 How much time do you need to get to school?
5 How many people live in your home?
6 How many subjects do you study?

LOOK!

In affirmative sentences, we use *a lot of*, not *much*.

There's **a lot of** food in the fridge.

I have **a lot of** homework to do.

USE IT!

5 **Work in pairs. Take turns asking and answering the questions in Exercise 4.**

7

LOOK!

Draw attention to the *Look!* box. Explain to students that we use *much* for uncountable nouns (singular) and *many* for countable nouns (plural). Both can be used in interrogative and negative sentences, however, *much* is never used in affirmative sentences: ~~*I have much money.*~~ *I have a lot of money.* Ask them to give you more examples by transforming the questions in Exercise 4 into affirmative sentences.

USE IT!

5 Have students ask and answer the questions in Exercise 4. Monitor the activity by walking around the classroom.

Extension

Invite students to put together a "potluck" party (a party where each guest or group contributes a different, often homemade, dish of food to be shared during the event) for the class. In pairs, have them make a list of all the food and drink they will need. Then, have them interview each other regarding how much of each item they will need, and encourage them to write the quantities beside each item. Monitor the activity by walking around the class.

Lesson Aim: I can talk about festivals and celebrations; I can use defining relative clauses and adverbs of manner.

0.05 Audioscripts pT138

1 **0.05** Invite students to look at the images and draw students' attention to the words above them. Invite students to try and match the images to the words. Invite a volunteer to read the sentences 1–6. Draw their attention to the fact that image 1 and sentence 1 are linked and so on. Individually, have students complete the sentences with the words above the images. Play the audio to check their work. Have students pay attention to pronunciation and intonation.

2 Remind students of defining and non-defining relative clauses. Explain to students that we use non-defining relative clauses to give extra information about the person or thing that is not necessarily important. Have students do the first one orally to check understanding of the task. Then have students work individually, rewriting the sentences using a non-defining relative clause. Have them check their work in pairs.

3 Read through the sentences 1–5 with the students and have them complete the sentences individually.

USE IT!

4 Have students write the list of adverbs from Exercise 3 in their notebooks. Model the activity for the students beforehand. Pair up students and have them write down three sentences (two true sentences and one false) using the listed adverbs. Have them take turns saying them to their partner and guessing the false sentence.

Extension

Individually, have students observe their classmates and what they are doing at this exact moment. Have them use the adverbs from their list in Exercise 3 and a non-defining relative clause to describe something a classmate is doing, e.g.: *Paula, who is an excellent student, is working hard on her essay*. Tell them they can also use different adverbs and make up situations, if necessary.

FESTIVALS AND CELEBRATIONS

1 0.05 **Complete the sentences with the words below. Then listen and check.**

• atmosphere • crowds • dance shows • fireworks • music events • ~~souvenirs~~

1 Many tourists like to buy *souvenirs* at street markets.
2 Everyone danced and laughed a lot at Grandma's party. The *atmosphere* was great!
3 *Crowds* of people enjoy the Carnival at Copacabana.
4 Women wear traditional dresses in *dance shows* in India.
5 *Fireworks* are a popular way to celebrate the New Year all over the world.
6 According to the reviews, PopParty Fest was one of the best *music events* of the year.

DEFINING AND NON-DEFINING RELATIVE CLAUSES

2 **Write one sentence with a non-defining relative clause using the two sentences and *who* or *which*.**

1 I watched the game with Bruna. Bruna is a big soccer fan.
I watched the game with Bruna, who is a big soccer fan.
2 The Paragon is closed this week. The Paragon is our favorite café.
The Paragon, which is our favorite café, is closed this week. / The Paragon, which is closed this week, is our favorite café.
3 Hiro lives in Portugal now. Hiro is Japanese.
Hiro, who is Japanese, lives in Portugal now. / Hiro, who lives in Portugal now, is Japanese.
4 Last month I joined the drama club. The drama club meets every Tuesday at 2 p.m.
Last month I joined the drama club, which meets every Tuesday at 2 p.m.

ADVERBS OF MANNER

3 **Complete the sentences with adverbs from the adjectives in parentheses.**

1 Sophia walked *carefully* (careful) around the gift store because she didn't want to break anything.
2 Isabela is a fantastic role model because she studies *hard* (hard).
3 Mrs. Silva was driving too *fast* (fast) in the snowy weather.
4 The teacher told us to think *creatively* (creative) to solve the math problem.
5 Santiago doesn't play volleyball very *well* (good) but he's a wonderful coach.

USE IT!

I always ride my bike very carefully.

I think that's true.

4 **Work in pairs. Think of two true sentences and one false sentence about you using the adverbs in Exercise 3. Take turns saying your sentences and guess which of your partner's sentences is false.**

8

Lesson Aim: I can talk about my different life stages and identify the importance of learning English within these phases.

Warmer

Encourage students to say a couple of sentences about why they believe learning English is important. Ask them where they use the English language nowadays and where they believe they will use it in the future.

THINK!

1 Invite students to look at the image.

Use a thinking routine from Harvard Graduate School of Education: *See, Think, Wonder* to reflect more deeply about this image. Ask: *What do you see? What do you think about it? What does it make you wonder?* Use this routine at the opening of every unit to help students observe and share their ideas regarding the image(s).

2 Invite them to share other situations in which knowing how to speak English is necessary. Have them justify their answers.

1
MY LIFE PLAN

UNIT GOALS
- Talk about life stages and studying.
- Read a blog about studying English abroad.
- Listen to a video class giving tips for studying.
- Learn about saving indigenous languages.
- Express certainty and uncertainty.

THINK!
1 What do you think is happening in the image?
2 Is learning English important for situations like the one in the image? Why / Why not?

1.1 VIDEO
1 Say three things in the video that are amazing.
2 Which invention helped us to connect the whole world?

9

1.1 Amazing People

Summary

The video is about all the amazing things that have happened in the past centuries in science, technology, literature, arts, and many other contexts.

In Class

Ask students to list, in pairs, three amazing things they believe mankind has achieved. Have them share their list before watching the video.

Exercise 1

Ask students to watch the video to answer the questions:

1 *Say three things in the video that are amazing.* Check the answer with the class.
going to the moon; building pyramids, towers, and bridges; creating paintings, music, and literature; inventing medicines, surgery, and the Internet; learning to walk or use language; being good at sports, art, and science; making people laugh or feel happy

2 *Which invention helped us to connect the whole world?* Check the answer with the class.
The Internet

Exercise 2

Play the video again and have students answer the following questions. Then, ask them to watch the video again, check their answers, and make up two more questions to ask their partners.

1 List some amazing structures built by man. Can you name one?
Pyramids, towers, and bridges. The Eiffel Tower in Paris.

2 According to the video, only scientists, inventors, and artists do amazing things.
( ) True (✗) False
Justify your answer.
We all do amazing things. We learn to walk and to use languages.

3 List some amazing things you can do.
Students' own answers.

At Home

Exercise 3

Ask students to research an amazing invention they believe changed the world. Have them write a brief description of this invention and how it changed the world. Have them post their description on a collaborative platform so all students can access it.

Resources

- Teacher's worksheets Unit 1
- Test Generator Unit 1
- Practice Extra Unit 1
- Workbook pages 112–115
- Puzzles and Games page 102

Flipped Classroom

Ask: *Is college important? Should you do volunteer work? Do we all need to get married?* Have them share their list digitally on a collaborative panel. If possible, invite them to watch the animated short movie, *A Single Life* (you can watch this film for free online). Ask them to note down the different stages in our life and the objects that represent each stage in the movie.

Unit Aims

Cambridge Life Competencies Framework

I can ...

- use simple techniques to start, maintain, and close conversations of various lengths to talk about my future plans. **(Communication)**
- present points clearly and persuasively about my life. **(Communication)**
- start and manage conversations about my life stages with confidence. **(Communication)**
- understand essential grammatical terms and concepts: Use of reflexive pronouns and future tenses. **(Learning to Learn)**
- use strategies and techniques for improving my English (e.g., mind maps to organize thoughts). **(Learning to Learn)**
- understand various aspects of society when discussing indigenous languages. **(Social Responsibility)**
- find sources of information and help (online and in school) to enhance my understanding of English. **(Learning to Learn)**

Vocabulary in Context
Lesson Aim: I can talk about my future life plans.

Warmer

Divide students into pairs and invite them to say which stage of life they believe is the happiest. Ask them to justify their answers.

Flipped Classroom Check

Invite students to share their lists of important things to do in life (have them rank them in order of importance) and the different stages of our life. Have them share the objects from the video that represent each stage. If the lists were created digitally, project them for students to see and have them discuss the items.

1.01 Audioscript pT138

Target Vocabulary

finish school	/ˈfɪn.ɪʃ.skul/
get a job	/get.ə.dʒɑb/
get married	/get.ˈmær.id/
go to college	/goʊ.tə.ˈkɑl.ɪdʒ/
graduate	/ˈgrædʒ.u.ɪt/
have children	/hæv.ˈtʃɪl.drən/
leave home	/liv.hoʊm/
retire	/rɪˈtaɪər/
take a course	/teɪk.ə.kɔrs/
take an exam	/teɪk.ən.ɪgˈzæm/

1 1.01 Have students read through the questions and ask them what sort of text they are looking at (a quiz). Ask them if they enjoy quizzes, and which question topics they like to answer. Draw students' attention to the words/phrases in bold and compare them to their list of important things they want to do in life. Then have students match the words and phrases to the images. Invite them to listen to the audio to check their answers.

VOCABULARY IN CONTEXT

LIFE STAGES

1 1.01 Read the quiz and match the words and phrases in bold with images 1–10. Then listen, check, and repeat.

What is the most important thing in your life plan?

DO THE QUIZ TO FIND OUT.

A Will you **go to college** when you **finish school**?
- No way. I'll **get a job** and earn my own money.
- Yes, of course. I want to keep studying to learn more about the world.
- I'm not sure. Maybe I'll **take a course** to get more practical skills.

B Which option best describes you?
- To be happy I need to be able to help in my community.
- I'll never **retire** – I want to work for the rest of my life.
- When I'm an adult, I want to **get married** and **have children**.

C For you, what's the most important thing about learning English?
- It helps me make new friends.
- When I **take an exam** in English, I want to get a good score.
- It connects me with other people around the world.

D What worries you the most when you think about the future?
- Not finding a job after I **graduate**.
- Being alone when I **leave home**.
- Pollution and climate change.

1 
finish school

2 
get a job

3 
leave home

4 
go to college

5 
take a course

6 
take an exam

7 
graduate

8 
get married

9 
have children

10 
retire

10

Vocabulary in Context
Lesson Aim: I can talk about my future life plans.

2 Invite students to answer the quiz. Have them check their score and ask them whether they agree with the results. Have them justify their answer.

3 Ask students to look at the chart and the headings in each column. Have them classify the words and phrases above the chart in the correct columns. Have them add any other words or phrases from their own list of important things to do in life.

4 Have a volunteer read through the sentences. Individually, ask students to complete the sentences using the words and phrases from Exercise 3.

LOOK!

Draw attention to the *Look!* box. Ask for a volunteer to read the content of the box. Have students give more examples. Some Brazilian students use the verb in the future tense in a clause with the words *when, before,* or *after*: ~~When I will get a job, I will have more money~~. *When I get a job, I will have more money.*

USE IT!

5 Have students read the example questions and replace the phrases in bold with the words and phrases from Exercise 3, or from their own list. Model the activity using the examples given and a volunteer. Monitor their work by walking around the class.

Homework

Workbook page 113, Exercises 1 and 2

Practice Extra

Unit 1

Fast Finishers

Puzzles and Games page 102, Exercises 1 and 2

2 Do the quiz and check (✓) your answers. Then look at your score below and discuss it with a partner. Do you agree with your results? Why? / Why not?

Most of your answers are ...	The most important thing in your life plan is ...	
★ (red)	WORK	You're hard-working and always busy! You'll be successful, but never forget that the people around you are very important, too.
★ (blue)	PEOPLE	You're a sociable person and you love to be around people. That's great, but remember: there's a big world out there, too!
★ (yellow)	THE WORLD	You think big and have great plans, but try to also find time for your private life. It's important to have some fun!

3 Complete the chart with the words and phrases below.

- finish school • ~~get a job~~ • get married • go to college • graduate
- have children • leave home • retire • take a course • take an exam

Work	Education	Family
get a job	finish school	get married
retire	go to college	have children
	graduate	leave home
	take a course	
	take an exam	

4 Complete the sentences so they are true for you. Use words and phrases from Exercise 3. *Students' own answers*

1 I'm going to ______ before I leave home.
2 I think I'll be busy when I ______.
3 I'm going to ______ after I ______.
4 I don't think I'll ______.
5 I'm not going to ______ before I'm 35.
6 When I ______, I'll be really happy.

LOOK!
After *when*, *before*, and *after* to talk about the future, use the simple present, not *will*.
When I **get** a job, I'll save some money.

USE IT!

5 Work in pairs. Take turns asking and answering about your future. Replace the phrases in bold with the correct form of other words and phrases from Exercise 3.

Do you think **going to college** is important?
Yes, I do.

What do you want to do after you **finish school**?
I want to take a course.

Do you want to **get married**?
I'm not sure.

WORKBOOK p.113 PRACTICE EXTRA

Extension

Ask students to interview an older family member. Have students build a timeline and then write a brief biography of their family member's life up to this moment with all the different stages they have gone through. Encourage students to ask about and take note of the most important facts of each stage. Then, ask them to identify the happiest, saddest, and most complicated stages.

Reading
Lesson Aim: I can read and understand blog posts about studying English abroad.

Warmer

Write *exchange student* on the board. Ask students whether they would like to take part in an exchange program. In pairs, have them list the places they would like to visit and the languages they would like to learn in this sort of program.

1.02 Audioscript pT138

1 Draw students' attention to the text and ask them where this kind of text can be found and encourage them to justify their answers. Have a volunteer read through sentences 1–4 to check understanding. Then have students skim the text in order to circle the sentences that are true.

2 1.02 Give students two minutes to read the text again. Individually, have them read questions 1–6 and identify the corresponding person (or *B* for both). Have them listen to the audio to check their answers.

3 Have students read the sentences individually and circle the correct option. Have them compare their answers in pairs.

THINK!

Have students sit in pairs. Give them one minute to make a list of all the English-speaking countries they can think of. Have them compare their lists. Write the places from the *Think!* box on the board and ask students if these places are on their list. Have them discuss the question in pairs. Encourage students to research on the Internet the reason why English has become a global language.

Homework

Workbook page 115, Exercises 1, 2, and 3

READING

LEARN&LIVE ENGLISH

HOME | OUR COURSES | DESTINATIONS | STUDENT LIFE | **BLOG** | CONTACT US

LET'S WELCOME OUR NEW STUDENTS VERÓNICA GONZÁLEZ AND DANIEL RIBEIRO!

Verónica, 14
From: Mexico
video games and sports

WHY MALTA?

Some years ago I saw a video about the Maltese coast and I loved it! When I learned that English is one of the two official languages in Malta, I thought, "I want to study English there." Most people speak English and **Maltese** here. I can't speak Maltese, but I can read the street signs – because **they** use English, too!

EXPECTATIONS

I think I'll have a great time here in Malta. I'm going to take a four-week English course. Later, who knows? Will this experience help me get a job in the future? Maybe. I'd love to become a game developer, so maybe I'll make games about Malta!

ABOUT US

We offer a variety of English courses for teenagers (12–17) in different countries.

Daniel, 15
From: Brazil
languages and big animals

WHY SOUTH AFRICA?

My parents wanted me to study English abroad before I go to college, and my dream is to go on a safari, so we decided that South Africa seemed like the perfect place. I found out that there are **over** ten official languages in South Africa. English is one of **them** and most people **actually** speak English as a second language here.

EXPECTATIONS

I'm very excited about this course. We're not going to sit in a classroom all day. Tomorrow our instructors are going to take us to a local village. We're going to help build a school there. How cool is that?

1 Read the text quickly and circle the sentences that are true.

1 The text is a magazine article about English courses in different countries.
2 There are three blog posts on the page.
3 The people in the images are going to start an English course.
4 This website is for teenagers who want to study English abroad.

2 1.02 Read and listen to the text. Then answer the questions. Write *V* (Verónica), *D* (Daniel), or *B* (both).

Who …
1 likes wild animals? D
2 is in a country where English is one of the official languages? B
3 is going to take a course that lasts for a month? V
4 is going to do some community work as part of the course? D
5 chose the country after talking to family members? D
6 hopes that the experience abroad will be useful in the future? V

3 Look at the words in bold in the blog post and circle the correct options in sentences 1–5.

Verónica
1 "Maltese" refers to a *language spoken in* / *person from* Malta.
2 The word "they" refers to *people from* / *street signs in* Malta.

Daniel
3 The word "over" means *more than* / *on top of*.
4 The word "them" refers to *official languages in* / *people from* South Africa.
5 It is possible to replace "actually" with *at the moment* / *in fact*.

THINK!
All of them
How many of these countries have English as an official language: Australia, Bahamas, Guyana, Ireland, Pakistan, Singapore, Uganda? Why do you think English is an official language in so many countries?

12

WORKBOOK p.115

Unit 1 My Life Plan

Language in Context
Lesson Aims: I can understand and use *will* for predictions, and *be going to* for intentions.

1 If necessary, have students look at the blog posts on page 12 again to help them complete the chart. Encourage them to notice and analyze the differences between *will* and *be going to*. Have them read the sentences in the chart and justify the use of each verb. When finished, ask them to work in pairs and give examples that are true for them. Have them write down two sentences each, using both forms.

2 Have students work individually and reorder the sentences. Have volunteers read out their answers for correction. Have students then scramble the sentences they wrote in Exercise 1 and hand them to a peer to reorder.

LOOK!

Draw student's attention to the *Look!* box. Encourage them to build sentences that are true for them using *I believe, I (don't) think, I'm sure, maybe, perhaps, probably.* Invite them to share their sentences and react to their peers' sentences, using *Yes, I agree. No, I don't think so.* etc.

3 Have students read sentences 1–6 and pay attention to the plus and minus signs at the end of sentences 1–4. Have them check Daniel's weekly planner and use *be going to* to complete the sentences. Have students check their work in pairs.

USE IT!

4 Model the activity using an example of your own. Individually, have students complete the sentences. Draw attention to the plus and minus sign at the end of each sentence.

5 Put students into pairs and have them read their sentences to each other. Encourage them to react back by making meaningful comments.

LANGUAGE IN CONTEXT

1 Look at the examples below. Complete the sentences from the blog post.

	Will for Predictions	*Be going to* for Intentions
Affirmative (+)	I think I [1] 'll have a great time here in Malta. I'm sure this course **will teach** Verónica a lot.	Our instructors [3] are going to take us to a village. He's **going to** help build a house.
Negative (–)	The classes **won't be** boring. She probably **won't want** to leave Malta!	We [4] 're not going to sit in a classroom all day. Bill **is not going to** spend the summer here.
Questions (?)	[2] Will this experience help me get a job?	When **are** you **going to leave** South Africa?

2 Put the words in the correct order.

1 probably / I'll / a / children / lot / have / of
I'll probably have a lot of children.
2 think / next / graduate / I / will / my / year / cousin
I think my cousin will graduate next year.
3 to / are / retire / my / going / soon / grandparents
My grandparents are going to retire soon.
4 you'll / better / maybe / tomorrow / feel
Maybe you'll feel better tomorrow.
5 next Monday / we're / have / going / not / to / classes
We're not going to have classes next Monday.

LOOK!
We often use *will* with *I believe, I (don't) think, I'm sure, maybe, perhaps, probably.*
Maybe one day I'**ll** visit Malta.

3 Look at Daniel's diary for next week. Complete the sentences with the correct form of *be going to.*

WEEKLY PLANNER

MONDAY	TUESDAY	WEDNESDAY	THURSDAY	FRIDAY	SATURDAY & SUNDAY
classes until 12:30 go bike riding	classes until 12:30 11:15 go bird watching	Sports Day	classes until 12:30 go swimming	classes until 12:30 go on a safari	~~go on a safari~~ visit Cape Town

1 Daniel is going to play sports on Wednesday. (+)
2 The students are going to go swimming on Thursday afternoon. ~~(+)~~ is not going to have classes
3 Daniel .... after 11:15 on Tuesday. (–) 'm going to go bird watching
4 In a message to his parents, Daniel wrote, "I .... on Tuesday afternoon." (+)
5 Are Daniel and his friends going to go on a safari on Saturday? No, they're not.
6 Is Daniel going to have classes four days next week? Yes, he is.

USE IT!

4 Complete the sentences with the correct forms of *be going to* so they are true for you.

1 When I leave home, Students' own answers .... (+)
2 One thing about my life in the future: I .... (–)

5 Work in pairs. Take turns reading your sentences and making comments.

That's great! You'll have a lot of fun!

WORKBOOK p.112 and 114 PRACTICE EXTRA

Grammar Game

In pairs, have students decide where they want to go to do an exchange program. Have them build an itinerary and make plans using *be going to*. Have them then write what they think the experiences will be like using *will*, e.g., *We're going to stay in a university dorm. I think it will be fun!* Having finished, have two pairs interview each other about their plans

A *Where are we going on our exchange program?*
B *Let's go to Granada.*
A *Wow! Where are we going to stay?*
B *Let's look for a university dorm. I think that will be fun!*
A *OK … how long are we going to stay?*
B *6 months?*
A *I will miss my family.*

Homework

Workbook page 114, Exercises 1 and 2

Practice Extra

Unit 1

Listening and Vocabulary
Lesson Aim: I can talk about study tips to make progress in a course.

Warmer

Tell students you are going to take an online Japanese course and you would like them to give you some tips. Tell them you have never taken an online course. In pairs, have them write down one tip for you. Go around the class, asking students for their tips. Write them on the board.

1.03–1.05 Audioscripts pT138

Target Vocabulary

get a good grade	/get.ə.gʊd.greɪd/
make progress	/meɪk.ˈprɑg.rəs/
practice	/ˈpræk·tɪs/
prepare	/prɪˈpeər/
review	/rɪˈvju/
take a break	/teɪk.ə.breɪk/

1 Read through the alternatives with the students. Have them look at the images and try to guess what the introduction of the video will be about. Have them check the correct option and justify their answer.

2 **1.03** Play the audio to the class. Have them check their answer to Exercise 1. Play the audio again and have them take note of some key words from the audio. Have them check the words they noted in pairs.

3 **1.04** Ask for a volunteer to read the words and phrases above the images. Play the audio. Have students complete the captions from memory. Compare the tips they gave you in the Warmer with the tips from the video class. Have them check whether there were any similar ones.

4 **1.05** Play the audio, and have students check their work. Have them repeat the word and phrases. Check for pronunciation and intonation.

5 **1.04** Ask for volunteers to read sentences 1–5. Ask students to write *T* (true) or *F* (false) from memory. Play the audio again and have students check their work.

LISTENING AND VOCABULARY

1 Look at the images. Check (✓) what you think the topic of the video class is.

1 ◯ How to do your homework quickly.
2 ◯ How to learn and make friends at the same time.
3 ☑ How to be successful when you take a course.
4 ◯ How to learn English online.

2 1.03 Listen to the teacher's introduction to the video class and check your answer to Exercise 1.

3 1.04 Listen to the video class and complete the captions with the words/phrases below.

• get a good grade • ~~make progress~~ • practice • prepare • review • take a break

1

Tips to help you make progress in this course.

2

Take a break every thirty minutes or so.

3

Use the Internet to practice your skills.

4

Use cards to review vocabulary.

5

I give myself a lot of time to prepare for an exam.

6

Do you want to get a good grade in this course?

4 1.05 Listen, check, and repeat your answers to Exercise 3.

5 1.04 Listen to the video class again and write *T* (true) or *F* (false).

1 The teacher gives five suggestions. F
2 The suggestions are only useful for learning English. F
3 One of the students thinks it's easier to learn when you often stop to rest. T
4 Three students mention technological devices in their suggestions. F
5 One of the students talks about another person's idea. T

6 Match the students in screens 2–6 with these sentences.

1 Recording yourself on your phone can help you a lot. Cataline
2 Leaving everything to the last minute is a bad idea. Alejandro
3 When you don't stop for short periods, you get too tired. Fernando
4 You can write your own bilingual dictionary. Raquel
5 Listening to podcasts and writing comments about what you hear is a good idea. Melody

14

WORKBOOK p.113

6 Have students look at the screens 2–6 in their books. Ask for a volunteer to read sentences 1–5. Ask them to match the screens with the sentences. In pairs, have them brainstorm other tips that the images could portray and write them down. Have them share their notes.

Homework

Workbook page 113, Exercises 3 and 4

1 Write on the board: *Who do you see when you look into the mirror? I see ___________.* Ask students to complete the sentence (myself). Ask students for other words ending in *self/selves*. Tell students that when the subject and object of the sentence are the same, we use reflexive pronouns. Give them examples: *I cut myself.* Have them look at the chart and the words above it. Have them complete the sentences individually. Check answers with the class.

2 Have students complete the sentences in their books and then underline the expression that means *alone*.

LOOK!

Draw student's attention to the *Look!* box. Have them read the information and then give you more examples. Some Brazilian students forget to use the preposition *by*, changing the meaning of the sentence: ~~*I do my homework myself.*~~ *I do my homework by myself.*

3 In pairs, ask students to read the sentences and identify the subject of each sentence. Then have them circle the correct alternative, justifying their answers.

4 Make sure students complete the sentences after the chosen word from the third chart. Have them write the sentences in their notebooks and then share them with the class.

USE IT!

5 Write the word *yourself* on the board. Encourage students to ask you questions using the word. Invite them to look at the verbs in chart B from Exercise 4 and use them to ask each other questions. Encourage them to use the present and past tense. Monitor the activity by walking around the class.

Homework

Workbook page 114, Exercises 3 and 4

Practice Extra

Unit 1

UNIT 1

LANGUAGE IN CONTEXT

1 Complete the sentences from the video class in the chart. Use the words below.

• herself • myself • yourself • yourselves

Reflexive Pronouns

Singular	Plural
I give [1] myself a lot of time to prepare for an exam. You need to give [2] yourself some time to rest. She recorded [3] herself reading the new words. He enjoyed **himself** in his English class. The computer will turn **itself** off soon.	**All of you**, get [4] yourselves ready for some great tips. **We** gave **ourselves** some time to rest. **The students** saw **themselves** on the screen.

2 Complete the sentences with the correct reflexive pronoun from the chart. Then underline the expression that means *alone*.

1 My friend and I enjoyed ourselves at the concert.
2 The teacher asked the students, "How much time did you give yourselves to prepare for the exam?"
3 Eve is very independent, she wants to do things by herself.
4 Use this knife but be careful, Ben cut himself with it last week.
5 My car can park itself – it's really helpful when I go downtown.
6 I'm teaching myself to play the guitar. It's more difficult than I thought.

LOOK!
***By + myself, yourself,* etc. means *alone, on one's own*.**
I usually do my homework **by myself**.

3 Circle the correct options.

1 Ben: I think George will be an artist when *he / himself* grows up.
Lottie: Yes, I agree. He knows how to express *him / himself* in his drawings.
2 Mom: You're 14, Ben! It's important to know how to take care of *you / yourself*.
Ben: Yeah, but I do. I look at *me / myself* in the mirror every day to make sure *I / myself* look fabulous.
Mom: Very funny, Ben, but I'm talking about your health. You need to take *it / itself* seriously.
3 Frank: What's the matter with Maria? She's talking to *her / herself*.
Karla: There's nothing wrong with that. People often talk to *them / themselves*.

4 Write sentences in your notebook using words and phrases from charts A, B, and C.

A	B	C	
I My best friend and I My friends from school My dad/mom/sister (etc.)	enjoy laugh at listen to talk to	myself yourself himself	herself ourselves themselves

My dad often talks to himself when he's cooking.

USE IT!

5 Work in pairs. Ask questions using *yourself* and verbs from chart B in Exercise 4.

Do you test yourself before an exam? — Yes, I do.
Did you enjoy yourself at the party? — Yes, I did.

WORKBOOK p.112 and 114 PRACTICE EXTRA 15

Grammar Game

If possible, take this game outside. Divide the class into teams of three students. Hand out a slip of paper to each team and have them write a paragraph using as many reflexive pronouns as possible. Collect the slips of paper. Each member of the team will have a specific role: reader, runner, and writer. Hand out a slip of paper to the readers. Make sure the teams do not get the paragraphs they wrote themselves. The reader must be placed at least 5 meters from the writer. The idea is for the reader to read the sentence, in small chunks, to the runner, who must then run to the writer and dictate it. The first team to finish wins. Make sure the paragraphs read by the reader are exactly the same as the paragraph written by the writer.

Extension

Have students rewrite the sentences using reflexive pronouns.

1 Mary recorded her video scene alone.
2 The problem will resolve on its own.
3 Jake plays cards alone.
4 We like to make pizza at home without help.
5 He flies an airplane on his own.

1.2 Being Bilingual

The video on page 17 and accompanying exercises below can be used as a lead-in to the topic of the Around the World text, or after the reading activities to complete the unit.

Summary

The video is about connecting the world through languages.

In Class

Tell students they are going to watch a video about how nearly half the population of the world is bilingual. Students will see that there are many different dialects and languages around the world even within the same country. Ask students if they have any idea how many languages are spoken in their own country. If they answer *one*, have them research on the Internet (this will be done during the At Home activity).

Exercise 1

Ask students to watch the video to answer the questions:

1. *Which three languages do Tomasz and Veronique's children speak?* Check the answer with the class.
   Polish, French, and German
2. *How many languages are there in Nigeria?* Check answers with the class.
   Over 500 languages.

Encourage students to watch the video again and give two reasons why they believe people become bilingual.

Exercise 2

Ask students the following questions and elicit answers.

1. How do people in tribes in Nigeria communicate if they do not speak the same language?
   They use English – which is the lingua franca.
2. Welsh is a Celtic language that is similar to English.
   ( ) True (x) False
3. Complete the sentence: *People in Wales were* ___not allowed___ *to use their own language for many years and the number of Welsh speakers* ___fell___.

Play the video again in order for students to check their answers. Invite students to make up one question for their peers to answer regarding the video.

AROUND THE WORLD

Home | **Posts** | About me

Maori Teenager Becomes Language Influencer

By ***Lawrence O'Brien***

1 **HASTINGS, NEW ZEALAND** – You look at Turei Rarere and you see a cheerful teenager like many others. When you talk to him, you understand why he is an influencer. Turei is smart, creative, and motivated.

2 "Two years ago, there was a party in my family, and I realized my younger cousins didn't speak Maori," He explains. "And worse – they didn't think that was a problem! I was really surprised. Didn't they understand that Maori is part of our cultural identity?" This question motivated Turei to create an online group for indigenous teenagers to discuss how they felt about their native languages.

3 Three years later, Turei's group has hundreds of members. It is not only a group for discussion, but also a place to learn and practice indigenous languages from around the world. "We use English to talk to a large number of people, but we use our native languages to post videos or audio with traditional stories or songs."

4 Alexandra Silva, a 15-year old Brazilian from the Terena people, says she feels more connected to her community now. "I grew up speaking Portuguese. Turei's group helped me understand why Terena is important. I can understand my grandparents' stories now."

5 Turei is certain about his plans for the future. "My aunt is a Maori teacher in our local school. I'm going to follow in her footsteps. I'm planning to go to college to study linguistics and I'll always support people who want to teach or learn indigenous languages."

KIA ORA!

"Maori is part of our cultural identity," says Turei Rarere.

A Maori graffiti

16

At Home

Exercise 3

Ask students to research on the Internet how many languages are spoken in Brazil. Have students bring a list of the different languages. Have them identify on a map of Brazil the different regions and languages spoken. Give them the choice of making a poster or a digital presentation to present to the class.

Background Information

Indigenous languages are part of our cultural identity. Many youngsters do not see the importance of learning their native language or the language spoken by their grandparents. Creating online group discussions is an amazing way to understand the importance of staying in contact with your family traditions.

1.06 Audioscripts pT138

1 Invite students to look at the text and the images. Ask them where this kind of text can be found and if they normally read or write this kind of text. Have them read the title of the text. Ask them: *What is an influencer*? Ask them to give you examples of influencers they know. Read through questions 1 and 2 with students to check understanding. Ask them to read through the text quickly with the questions in mind in order to check the correct alternatives.

2 1.06 Ask students to read the article and underline the most important words in each paragraph. Play the audio for them to check their answers for Exercise 1.

3 Ask students if they can name any indigenous languages from their country. Encourage students to talk about any different languages they might use in their households. Have a volunteer read sentences a–e. Have them match the sentences to the corresponding paragraphs in the article.

Words in Context

4 Ask for a volunteer to read sentences 1–5. Draw student's attention to the words in bold. In pairs, have them look for words with a similar meaning in the article. Encourage them to guess the meaning of the words from the context before checking in a dictionary. They can use an online dictionary, if necessary. Check their work as a class.

5 Have students read the sentence endings a–f. Give them a few minutes to reflect upon what they read. Then ask them to match the columns. Check as a class.

1 Read the article quickly and check (✓) the correct answers.

1 The topic of the article is …
a ◯ the Maori language.
b ✓ keeping languages alive.
c ◯ the importance of the Internet.

2 The article's main idea is that teenagers…
a ✓ can help make their culture stronger.
b ◯ learn languages more quickly than adults.
c ◯ are spending too much time online now.

2 1.06 Read and listen to the article. Check your answers in Exercise 1.

3 Read the article again. Match a–e with paragraphs 1–5 in the article.

a an introduction about Turei 1
b a description of Turei's online activity 3
c an example of how Turei's idea is helping people from other countries 4
d the event that gave Turei an idea 2
e what Turei wants to do when he leaves school 5

WORDS IN CONTEXT

4 Replace the words/phrases in bold with words/phrases in the article. Use a dictionary to check your answers.

1 What are the **original, native** languages in your country? indigenous
2 Turei likes to **help** people who want to learn their grandparents' language. support
3 My mother started her own business and I'm going to **do the same thing.** follow in her footsteps
4 When I talked to Turei, I **understood for the first time** he was a special teenager. realized
5 Turei is **sure** about what he wants to do in the future. certain

5 Match 1–6 with a–f.

1 Alexandra e
2 English d
3 Maori b
4 Terena c
5 Turei f
6 Turei's aunt a

a is an indigenous language teacher.
b is an official language in New Zealand, together with English.
c is an indigenous language in Brazil.
d is useful for connecting people all around the world.
e can use the native language of her community now.
f wants to teach Maori in the future.

WEBQUEST

Check (✓) the numbers you think are correct.

When the Portuguese arrived in Brazil in 1500, there were about 1,000 indigenous languages. Now there are about 150.

◯ 1,000/150 ◯ 500/50 ◯ 100/15

THINK!

Why do you think the teenagers sometimes interact in English in Turei's group?
Do you think it's important to know English to exchange ideas with people around the world?

VIDEO

1.2

1 Which three languages do Tomasz and Veronique's children speak?
2 How many languages are there in Nigeria?

17

THINK!

In pairs, have students discuss why the English language seems to be the most used in international groups. Encourage students to use the thinking routine from Harvard Graduate School of Education, *Think, Pair, Share*, for this activity. This involves posing a question to students, asking them to take a few minutes of thinking time by themselves, and then turning to a nearby student to share their thoughts.

WEBQUEST

Encourage students to reflect on what happened to some of the indigenous languages around the world. Ask: *Why do some disappear*? Ask students to guess how many indigenous languages we have now in Brazil. Ask them whether they can name at least five. Have them read the alternatives in their book and check how many they believe were around in the year 1500. Have them search the Internet for the answer.

Speaking
Lesson Aim: I can express certainty and uncertainty when talking about future courses I want to take.

1.07–1.10 Audioscripts pT139

1 1.07 Put students into pairs and ask them to cover the dialogue and discuss what is happening in the image. Play the audio for students to check their guesses. Have volunteers read the dialogue. Have students identify the course mentioned (robotics). Ask them whether they would like to take this kind of course.

Living English

2 Read the expressions 1–3 with students and have them match them to their meanings a–c. Ask them for examples of when they would use them. Have them check in pairs.

3 1.08 Play the audio as many times as necessary for students to get the correct pronunciation.

Pronunciation

4 1.09 Have students pay special attention to the pronunciation of the contraction *I'll*. Play the audio. Encourage students to practice with other sentences.

5 1.09 Play the audio again and tell students to focus on the intonation of the sentence, as well as the pronunciation of the words. Stop the audio after each sentence for students to repeat.

6 1.10 Draw students' attention to the chart and the headings. Play the audio. Stop the audio after each sentence and have students write the corresponding number in the box according to what they hear (*'ll* or *will*).

Living English

7 1.07. Play the audio for students to listen again. Encourage them to reproduce the dialogue from memory in pairs, without reading. Have them then read the dialogue, exchanging roles.

8 Read through the steps with students and model a dialogue. Divide the class into two bigger groups: Students A and Students B. Have Students A come up with ideas to replace the words in blue in Vanessa's lines (have them choose a topic they would like to study in the future: computer, theater, a musical instrument, surfing, art, cooking, biology, etc.) and Students B do the same for Martina's lines. Then, put students into pairs (Students A and B) and have them practice the dialogue. Have them present their dialogues to the class.

SPEAKING

EXPRESSING CERTAINTY AND UNCERTAINTY

1 1.07 **Read and listen to Vanessa and Martina. What course are the girls discussing?**

Vanessa: This is so cool! I think I'll study robotics when I leave school.
Martina: Oh really? Is that how you see yourself ten years from now? Making robots?
Vanessa: Definitely! I know I'm good at this, and I love it. What about you?
Martina: Well, I'm not sure. I don't really know much about robotics, but yeah, maybe I'll go for it, too.

LIVING ENGLISH

2 **Match the expressions (1–3) with their meanings (a–c).**

1 definitely b
2 I'm not sure c
3 maybe a

a I think it's possible
b I'm certain
c I'm uncertain

3 1.08 **Listen and repeat the expressions.**

PRONUNCIATION

4 1.09 **Listen and pay attention to the pronunciation of *'ll* and *will*.**

I'**ll** study robotics in college.
People **will** use robots at home.

5 1.09 **Listen again and repeat.**

6 1.10 **Do you hear *'ll* or *will*? Listen to six sentences and write 1–6 in the chart.**

'll	*will*
1, 3, 6	2, 4, 5

7 1.07 **Listen to the dialogue again. Then practice with a partner.**

8 **Role play a new dialogue. Follow the steps.**

1 Change the words in blue to write a new dialogue in your notebook.
2 Practice your dialogue with a partner.
3 Present your dialogue to the class.

YOUR DIGITAL PORTFOLIO
Record your dialogue and upload it to your class digital portfolio.

18

PRACTICE EXTRA

Your Digital Portfolio

Give students a date for uploading their work and make sure they all listen to one another's dialogues.

Practice Extra

Unit 1

Extension

As a final activity for each of the units throughout this book, invite students to look back at all the grammar and vocabulary they learned. Encourage them to build two mind maps. One related to the grammar points with the word *Grammar* as the center word, and another related to the topics and vocabulary, with the words *Topics and Vocabulary* as the center words. Have them share their work and check back to their mind maps throughout the year.

Lesson Aim: I can talk about things that make me happy.

Warmer

Write the word *happy* on the board. In pairs, have students write down five things that make them happy. Give them one minute to write the list. Elicit some of their ideas and write them on the board. Have students rank them from the most common thing mentioned to the least.

THINK!

1 Have students look at the images on the page. Ask them if any of the images relate to their daily lives. Have them analyze the images and give reasons for why these teenagers look happy.

2 Have students look at the list they wrote in the Warmer. Have them compare it to the ones listed on the board. Ask them to choose two things that make them happiest.

2.1 Happiness Around the World!

Summary

The video is about how different countries perceive happiness.

In Class

Tell students they're going to watch a video about how different countries around the world understand the concept of happiness. Some think if they work harder, they will be happier. Others think happiness comes from friends and family. Ask: *What does it mean to be happy in Brazil?*

Exercise 1

Ask students to watch the video to answer the questions:

1 *What three countries have very happy people?* Check the answer with the class.
Norway, Costa Rica, and Bhutan

2 *What makes people in Norway happy?* Check the answer with the class.
doing volunteer work and spending time outdoors

Exercise 2

Play the video again, write the following sentences on the board, and ask students to complete them. Invite them to come up with one more question to encourage question formation.

1 Norway is one of the __happiest__ countries in the world.

2 All the places below are mentioned except:
( ) Bhutan (✗) Turkey
( ) Costa Rica ( ) Norway

3 In Bhutan, children learn to be __kind__ to __people__ and the __environment__.

4 Friends, __neighbors__, and family are important for the people who live in Costa Rica.

At Home

Exercise 3

Have students find out how many hours people usually work a week around the world. Have students research at least three countries and bring in the working hours per week. Have them compare their answers. Ask: *Do you believe we should work hard in order to be happy?*

Resources

- Teacher's worksheets Unit 2
- Test Generator Unit 2
- Practice Extra Unit 2
- Workbook pages 116–119
- Puzzles and Games page 102

Flipped Classroom

Ask students to list all the extra activities their school offers them. Have them add others that they wish would be offered. Ask them to categorize the activities as active or relaxing. Give students a choice of creating this list digitally by using a collaborative panel or as a chart on a sheet of paper.

Unit Aims

Cambridge Life Competencies Framework

I can ...

- make informed choices in relation to exercising and mental health issues. **(Social Responsibility)**
- understand essential grammatical terms and concepts: *should* (advice), giving suggestions. **(Learning to Learn)**
- ask clarifying questions when necessary. **(Collaboration)**
- use strategies and techniques for improving my English (e.g., mind maps to organize thoughts). **(Learning to Learn)**
- use simple techniques to start, maintain, and close conversations of various lengths using question tags and talking about my daily routines. **(Communication)**
- take part in role plays. **(Creative Thinking)**
- make informed comparisons between my own society and other societies when discussing happiness. **(Social Responsibility)**
- give my opinion on other students' contributions respectfully. **(Collaboration)**

Vocabulary in Context
Lesson Aim: I can name fun activities and talk about ones I like and do not like to do.

Warmer

Ask students which activities they see their friends doing most on social media. Ask: *Do the people look happy? Does social media always portray reality?* Make a list on the board of the activities mentioned, and tell them they will compare this list to the activities in Exercise 1 in their books.

Flipped Classroom Check

Invite students to compare their lists of extra school activities. Ask: *Do you prefer more active activities or relaxing ones?*

2.01 Audioscript pT139

Target Vocabulary

bake cookies	/beɪk.ˈkʊk·iz/
build models	/bɪld.ˈmɑd·lz/
do gymnastics	/du.dʒɪmˈnæs·tɪks/
do yoga	/du.ˈjoʊ·gə/
go skateboarding	/goʊˈskeɪtˌbɔrdɪŋ/
make jewelry	/meɪk.ˈdʒu·əl·ri/
play board games	/pleɪ.ˈbɔrd.geɪmz/
take a walk	/teɪk.ə.wɔk/
take singing lessons	/teɪk.ˈsɪŋ.ɪŋ.ˈles·ənz/
watch the sunset	/watʃ.ðə.ˈsʌnˌset/

1 2.01 Draw students' attention to the images of the activities. Ask them what type of advertisement this is (a pamphlet) and what they believe the main reason for this advertisement is. Elicit the activities and ask students whether they would take part in any of them. Read through the words above the pamphlet and have students use them to complete it. Play the audio to check their work. Have them repeat the words/phrases while drawing their attention to pronunciation and intonation. Have them compare these activities to the ones they mentioned in the Warmer.

VOCABULARY IN CONTEXT

MORE FREE-TIME ACTIVITIES

1 2.01 **Complete the pamphlet about vacation activities for teenagers with the words and phrases below. Then listen, check, and repeat the phrases for activities.**

- board games • ~~cookies~~ • gymnastics • jewelry • models
- singing lessons • skateboarding • sunset • walk • yoga

VACATION TIME! | **What can teenagers do in OAKLAKE VIEW?**

Our city offers a lot of great activities for teenagers during school vacations. Check out some activities at our community center and at Green Park.

OAKLAKE VIEW COMMUNITY CENTER

[1] **Bake** cookies in our kitchen. Yummy!

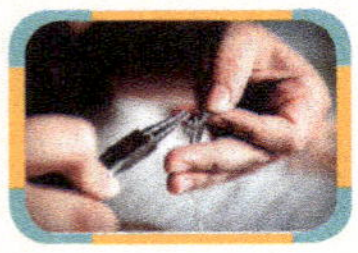

[2] **Make** jewelry in the workshop.

[3] **Take** singing lessons with our music teacher.

Try a new sport – [4] **do** gymnastics with our winning team!

Have fun with your friends! Come and [5] **play** board games or [6] **build** models.

GREEN PARK

[7] **Go** skateboarding at the best skate park in town.

Relax and enjoy nature. You can [8] **do** yoga or just [9] **take a** walk.

[10] **Watch the** sunset at the end of the day.

20

Vocabulary in Context
Lesson Aim: I can name fun activities and talk about ones I like and do not like to do.

2 Draw students' attention to the images and have them label the activities from memory. Encourage them not to look back at Exercise 1 to label the activities at first. Have them compare their work in pairs and then with the activities from Exercise 1. Have them choose their favorite. Ask them to justify their answers.

3 Divide students into pairs. Have Student A read the first part in each dialogue and Student B the second part. Have them guess which activity is being talked about. Have them justify their answer. Check as a class.

4 Draw students' attention to the chart and the headings. Write on the board: *often*, *would like to*, and *not interested in*. Elicit from students some activities to put under the headings. Have them look at the phrases from Exercise 1 and encourage students to categorize them in the chart according to their own tastes. Have them add two more for each heading if they can.

USE IT!

5 Have students work in pairs. Read the mini dialogue in the speech bubbles. Have student ask and answer questions using the vocabulary presented in the previous exercises.

Homework

Workbook page 117, Exercises 1 and 2

Practice Extra

Unit 2

Fast Finishers

Puzzles and Games page 102, Exercise 3

UNIT **2**

2 Label the images with the correct activities from Exercise 1.

1 
play a board game

2 
go skateboarding

3 
do yoga

4 
make jewelry

5 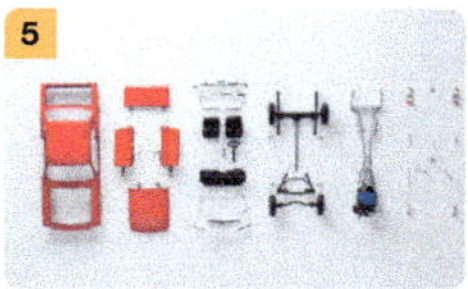
build models

6 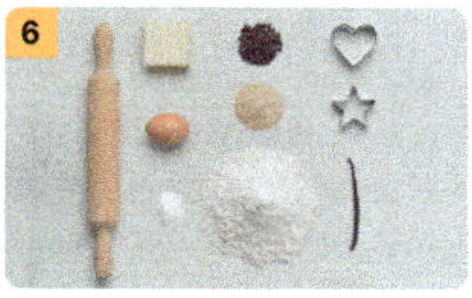
bake cookies

3 Read the mini dialogues. What activities from Exercise 1 are the teenagers doing?

1 Coach: Hands together, Jack! Keep your arms and legs straight!
Jack: Yes, coach!
He's doing gymnastics.

2 Teacher: Right, Melissa. Let's try again. The final note is higher.
Melissa: OK. La-la-la ...
She's taking singing lessons.

3 Fernanda: Look at all those colors in the sky!
Lucas: Yeah, it's beautiful!
They're watching the sunset.

4 Laura: Which way do you want to go?
Martin: Let's go down past the lake. I want to see the water birds.
They're taking a walk.

4 Complete the chart with the phrases for activities 1–10 in Exercise 1. Students' own answers

Activities I Often Do	Activities I Would Like To Do	Activities I'm Not Interested In

USE IT!

5 Work in pairs. Take turns asking and answering questions about your information and your partner's information.

Do you often take a walk?

No, I don't, but I'd like to.

WORKBOOK p.117 PRACTICE EXTRA

Extension

Ask students to draw a Venn diagram together with a friend or family member. The diagram should show the activities each individual likes, as well as the activities they both enjoy (in the intersection). Have students write corresponding sentences, e.g.: *I like to go camping. My brother likes to skateboard. We both like to read fiction books.*

Reading
Lesson Aim: I can read and understand an advice column.

Warmer

Ask students if they have ever written to an advice column on the Internet. Ask them if they know of any famous ones. Have them reflect upon why someone would write to an advice column instead of talking to friends or relatives.

2.02 Audioscript pT139

1. Have students look at the design of the article and ask them what elements help us realize it is an online forum (there is a discussion, there is a specific topic, people are interacting, there are user names). Elicit answers from volunteers. Ask them what the main goal of this online forum is. Have them skim through the reading and check the correct alternative.
2. **2.02** Have a volunteer read sentences a–c. Individually, ask students to read the forum posts and complete the missing sentences from the end of each paragraph. Play the audio to check their work. Point out that *BFF* stands for "Best Friend Forever" and is a way of referring to a person's best friend.
3. Have volunteers read questions 1–6 before reading the forum posts again. Individually, have students check the names according to what was said in the forum. Have students check their work in pairs.

THINK!

Ask students: *Do you take advice from online forums? Can we trust the advice?* Have students read the advice given to Sleepy Teen and choose the reply they believe is the best according to the situation. Have them first discuss in pairs and then open the discussion to the class.

Homework

Workbook page 119, Exercises 1, 2, and 3

READING

The Teen Oracle

The place for no-nonsense advice from teens to teens

Home | Lifestyle | School work

Sleepy Teen
Level: Apprentice II
Questions: 6
Replies: 12

I'm sooooo tired – I feel sleepy every day, all the time. I have a lot of responsibilities – besides school from Mon to Fri, I bake cookies to raise money for our class trip at the end of the school year and I help at an animal shelter on Sat and Sun. I hardly ever see my friends and never have time to go skateboarding, the only physical activity I really enjoy. I love studying, baking, and helping animals, and I don't want to disappoint others. What should I do? [1] *c*

REPLY

Delphi
Level: Teen Oracle III
Questions: 24
Replies: 112

IMO, you're doing too much. If you're feeling tired and your health is OK, it's clear you should reduce the number of activities in your routine. How about asking for help? Your classmates should bake all of the cookies for a change. And maybe you should go to the animal shelter only on Saturday or Sunday. [2] *b*

LIKE

MelindaT
Level: Teen Oracle I
Questions: 18
Replies: 76

When I feel I have too much on my plate, making a list of activities helps me decide on priorities. Maybe a relative or your BFF can help you with that. One important thing: you shouldn't stop exercising, even if you just take a quick walk. Should you go skateboarding? Yes, you should! [3] *a*

LIKE

1 Look at the online forum. Check (✓) its purpose.

1. ✓ to give advice to teenagers who have problems
2. ○ to give suggestions for free-time activities for teenagers

2 2.02 Read the forum posts and complete them with the missing sentences (a–c). Then read, listen, and check.

a. Being active will definitely make you feel better.
b. That way you'll have some time for yourself.
c. The thing is, I simply don't have time to relax anymore.

3 Read the forum posts again. Check (✓) the names in the chart.

Who ...	Sleepy Teen	Delphi	MelindaT
1 wants to sleep all the time?	✓		
2 believes physical activity is important?			✓
3 gives advice about asking for help?		✓	✓
4 is afraid of making people sad?	✓		
5 thinks writing a list is a good idea?			✓
6 gives advice about reducing responsibilities?		✓	

THINK!
Delphi and MelindaT gave advice to Sleepy Teen.
Which piece of advice do you think is better? Why?

22

WORKBOOK p.119

Language in Context
Lesson Aim: I can use the modal verb *should (not)* to give advice to someone.

1 If necessary, have students look at the online forum on page 22 to help them complete the chart. Encourage them to notice and analyze the affirmative, negative, and question forms of the modal verb.

2 Read through the sentences 1–5 with the students and draw attention to the context of each sentence in order to choose whether they should use the affirmative or negative form of *should*. Have them complete the sentences individually and then compare their work in pairs. Have them choose the one they agree with the most.

LOOK!

Draw attention to the *Look!* box. Have a volunteer read the sentence and then give an example with the correct form and the incorrect form. Brazilian students tend to use *to* in front of many verbs, even modal verbs: ~~*He should to go home.*~~ *He should go home.*

3 Have students look at the images. Without looking at the phrases, ask them to come up with a sentence using *should* or *shouldn't* for each image. In pairs, have them then look at the phrases and make sentences accordingly.

USE IT!

4 Model the activity using the examples in the speech bubbles with a volunteer. Read over the prompts with the class. Put them into pairs and have them use the prompts to ask for advice. Have their partner give some advice. Have students take turns giving and asking for advice.

Homework

Workbook page 118, Exercises 1 and 2

UNIT 2

LANGUAGE IN CONTEXT

1 **Look at the examples below. Complete the sentences from the forum posts.**

***Should/Shouldn't* for Advice**

Affirmative (+)	Negative (–)	Questions (?) and Short Answers
You [1] should reduce the number of activities in your routine. Sleepy Teen **should** go skateboarding. Your classmates [2] should bake all of the cookies.	You [3] shouldn't stop exercising! She **shouldn't** go to the shelter on Sunday. Her parents **shouldn't** allow her to have so many activities.	[4] Should you go skateboarding? Yes, you [5] should. / No, you **shouldn't**. **Should** she stop baking cookies? Yes, she **should**. / No, she **shouldn't**. What [6] should I do? Who **should** she ask for help?

2 **Complete the sentences with *should* or *shouldn't*.**

1 If you have trouble concentrating at school, you should try to do yoga every morning.
2 Your dog behaves badly because he's bored. You should take him to the park every day.
3 Dante's grades are low. He should spend more time on his school work.
4 People shouldn't drive fast on the roads when it's foggy.
5 Isabella is checking her cell phone for messages. She shouldn't do that in class.

LOOK!
Don't use *to* with the verb after *should*.
I think you **should do** yoga every morning.

3 **Look at the images. Write sentences with *should* and *shouldn't* using the words below.**

- eat so much junk food
- listen to loud music on the train
- go to bed early
- ~~study late at night~~
- have some fruit
- turn the volume down

1 Ava shouldn't study late at night. She should go to bed early.
2 Matias shouldn't eat so much junk food. He should have some fruit.
3 Hiro shouldn't listen to loud music on the train. He should turn the volume down.

USE IT!

4 **Work in pairs. Imagine you have one of the problems below. Ask your partner for advice.**

- You feel anxious before school tests.
- You feel tired all the time.
- You're late for school every morning.
- You're having problems with homework.

I feel anxious before school tests. What should I do?

I think you should …

WORKBOOK p.116 and 118 PRACTICE EXTRA

Practice Extra

Unit 2

Grammar Game

Individually, have students write out five things they would ask for advice about, e.g., *I can't concentrate when I study. I play too many video games.* etc. Have them exchange their lists with a partner. Encourage students to write a thread in an online forum, using the five things their partner wrote as ideas. Have students post their online forum, pretending to run an online advice column. Have students read the advice column and see if they agree with the advice given.

Listening and Vocabulary
Lesson Aim: I can listen to and understand a podcast about the benefits of exercising for mental health.

Warmer

Ask students if they enjoy listening to podcasts. If yes, ask them when they listen to podcasts. Ask them to share ideas of good podcasts to listen to.

2.03–2.04 Audioscripts pT139

Target Vocabulary

go for a run	/goʊ.fɔr.ə.rʌn/
make friends	/meɪk.frendz/
prevent diseases	/prɪ'vent.dɪ'zizɪz/
reduce stress	/rɪ'dus.stres/
stay fit/stay in shape	/steɪ.fɪt/ /steɪ.ɪn.ʃeɪp/
work out	/wɜrk.aʊt/

1 Ask for volunteers to read definitions 1–6. Individually, have students read the podcast information, paying attention to the underlined expressions in order to match them to their corresponding definitions. Ask students if they agree that exercising reduces mental health issues. Ask them if they exercise and if so, how often, what kind of exercise, and how they feel after exercising.

2 2.03 Play the audio in order for students to check their work. Have them repeat the expressions, drawing attention to pronunciation and intonation.

3 Have students look at the images and elicit from them the places they can see. Have them read the podcast information again and check the places where they believe the interview could have happened. Have students justify their answers.

4 2.04 Play the audio and check students' answers in Exercise 3. Have students also give different alternatives of places where the interview could have been conducted to those given in Exercise 3.

5 2.04 Have students read through the expressions in Exercise 1 again. Play the audio again. Have students write down the action which is not mentioned in the video. Have students think about other positive benefits of exercising which were not mentioned.

6 Invite a volunteer to read sentences 1–5. Individually, have students write *T* (true) or *F* (false) according to the podcast. Have them correct the false answers. If necessary, play the audio again.

LISTENING AND VOCABULARY

1 Read this podcast. Match the underlined expressions with the definitions (1–6).

HEALTHY TEENS PODCAST
Episode #33
May 7
13 min

Mental Health Benefits of Exercising for Teens 0:00:00

For this episode, we asked the question "**Why do you work out?**" Here are some answers from followers:

"Yoga helps me reduce stress. I have a busy life, but I sleep better on the days I do yoga." – Sophia, 14

"When we do physical activities, our brain produces chemicals that make us happy. I feel great every time I go for a run." – Syed, 15

"I play soccer to stay fit and have fun! And playing any team sport is a great way to make friends – you meet people that like the same things as you." – Mika, 13

"I know working out is good to prevent diseases. I have asthma, and swimming is very good for my health." – Jiro, 14

0:13:00

1 do an activity where you move fast ....go for a run....
2 keep your body strong and healthy ....stay fit....
3 do physical exercise ....work out....
4 feel less anxious ....reduce stress....
5 stop medical problems from happening ....prevent diseases....
6 start friendships with other people ....make friends....

2 2.03 Listen, check, and repeat your answers to Exercise 1.

3 Check (✓) the places you think the podcast host visited to talk to teenagers.

1 
○ a mall

2 
✓ a park

3 
✓ a school gym

4 
○ a café

4 2.04 Listen to the podcast and check your answers to Exercise 3.

5 2.04 Listen again. Which of the actions 1–6 in Exercise 1 is not mentioned in the podcast?
prevent diseases

6 Read the sentences and write *T* (true) or *F* (false).

1 Emma talks to two teenagers who are doing team sports. ..F..
2 The girl says running helps her do well on exams. ..F..
3 Emma and the girl agree that running reduces stress. ..T..
4 Emma talks to the PE teacher during a game. ..F..
5 The boy had more friends after he joined the basketball team. ..T..

24

WORKBOOK p.117

Homework

Workbook page 117, Exercises 3 and 4

Unit 2
What Makes Us Happy?

Language in Context
Lesson Aim: I can understand and use tag questions.

1 Remind students of the podcast on page 24. Have them read through the chart and the words above the chart in order to complete the sentences. If necessary, play the podcast again for them to complete it. Ask them to come up with a rule for how and why we use questions tags by analyzing the sentences.

2 Do the example sentence together with the class, on the board. Draw students' attention to the subject and the verb, then have them find the corresponding question tag. Have students do the rest of the exercises in pairs. Check their work and have them justify their answers.

LOOK!

Draw attention to the *Look!* box. Have a volunteer read the sentence. Then have students write a sentence using the question tag *aren't I?* Have them share their sentences.

3 Have students read the dialogue individually and complete it with the correct question tags. Have them refer to the chart from Exercise 1 and the sentences in Exercise 2 if they need help. Have them check their work in pairs and justify their answers.

USE IT!

4 Put students into pairs. Draw their attention to the chart and ask them to complete it according to the instructions at the top of the chart. Give some examples of your own and write them on the board to support them. Encourage them to notice that they will be writing sentences in the past, present, and future.

5 Read the questions and answers in the speech bubbles with them. Model an example of your own with a volunteer. In pairs, have students take turns asking questions with question tags, and using the guesses about their partners from Exercise 4 as prompts. Monitor the activity by walking around the class, listening to the students.

Homework

Workbook page 118, Exercises 3 and 4

UNIT 2

LANGUAGE IN CONTEXT

1 **Complete the sentences from the podcast in the chart. Use the phrases below.**

• can we? • didn't it? • don't you? • isn't it?

Tag Questions

Affirmative (+) Sentence	Negative (–) Tag	Negative (–) Sentence	Affirmative (+) Tag
It's a nice way to reduce stress,	1 *isn't it?*	**Emma isn't** very fit,	**is she?**
Emma was talking with a runner,	**wasn't she?**	**We weren't playing** volleyball,	**were we?**
You also **feel** good after exercising,	2 *don't you?*	**The two teenagers don't know** Emma,	**do they?**
Basketball helped you make friends,	3 *didn't it?*	**The girl didn't stop** to talk to Emma,	**did she?**
People can download the podcast,	**can't they?**	**We can't** escape PE,	4 *can we?*

2 **Match 1–6 with a–f.**

1 You like to exercise, *b*
2 Mike and Samuel aren't fit, *d*
3 The students didn't have PE yesterday, *c*
4 Hassan is going to take a walk in the park, *f*
5 Exercising helps people feel better, *e*
6 You can ride a skateboard, *a*

a can't you?
b don't you?
c did they?
d are they?
e doesn't it?
f isn't he?

LOOK!
The negative tag for *I am (I'm)* is *aren't I?*.
I'm a good friend, aren't I?

3 **Kelly and Nori are talking about the podcast. Complete with the correct tag questions.**

Kelly Emma Madison is the host of the podcast, 1 *isn't she?*
Nori Yes, she is. And she does a great job.
Kelly Yeah, I like her, too. She talked to two teenagers in the last podcast, 2 *didn't she?*
Nori No, to six. When I called you yesterday, you were listening to the episode, 3 *weren't you?*
Kelly Yes, I was, but I only heard the first five minutes. I need to write a report about it for my science class. According to Emma, people feel good after exercising, 4 *don't they?*
Nori Yes, but I'm not here to answer your questions, 5 *am I?* Why don't you download the episode?
Kelly I don't have time! You don't have classes right now, 6 *do you?*
Nori No, but soccer practice starts in five minutes and I really need to go. Bye!

USE IT!

4 **Work in pairs. Complete the chart with guesses about your partner.** *Students' own answers*

Two Things You Think He/She Did Last Week	Two Facts About His/Her Life	Two Things You Think He/She's Going To Do

5 **Take turns asking your partner tag questions to find out if your guesses were correct.**

You went to the movies yesterday, didn't you?
No, I didn't. My sister went to the movies. I stayed home.

WORKBOOK p.116 and 118 PRACTICE EXTRA

Practice Extra
Unit 2

Fast Finishers
Puzzles and Games page 102, Exercise 4

Extension
In pairs, encourage students to choose a short video, movie, or book they have both read. Have them talk about it and ask questions using question tags to confirm something they remember about the movie, book, or short video, e.g.: *The soundtrack was really good, wasn't it? I loved the ending, didn't you?*

Grammar Game
Put students into pairs, preferably with a person they are not too close to. Have students write ten questions to ask a partner about their life such as their favorite movies, family members, things they did last week, future plans, etc. Give them some examples of your own. Have them interview their partner, taking turns as the interviewer. Do not allow students to write down any answers.

After they finish their interviews, the first student must return to their questions and check how many answers they can remember by asking tag questions to their partner, e.g.: *Your favorite film is Star Wars, isn't it? You have three brothers, don't you?*

Across the Curriculum
Lesson Aim: I can read and understand an article about how art can benefit my mental health.

2.2 Dealing with Emotions

The video on page 27 and accompanying exercises below can be used as a lead-in to the topic of the Across the Curriculum text, or after the reading activities to complete the unit.

Summary
The video is about different ways people deal with emotions.

In Class
Tell students they are going to watch a video about different ways people deal with emotions. It talks about positive and negative emotions, and the different activities that can help us deal with them. Ask: *What do you do to deal with your emotions?* Discuss with the class.

Exercise 1
Ask students to watch the video to answer the questions:

1 *Say three emotions in the video.* Check answers with the class.
stress, anger, sadness, happiness, excitement, pride

2 *What is the name of the chemical that makes us feel good?* Check answers with the class.
endorphins

Exercise 2
Write the following questions on the board and encourage students to answer them from memory. Ask: *Do you think you are stressed? Why/ Why not?* Have students watch the video again and make up two more questions to ask their partners.

1 Which of these things stress people out?
(✗) traffic, exams, and relationships
(   ) work, art, and meditation
(   ) relationships, music, and coloring

2 According to the video, which of the following activities do people do to deal with their emotions?
(✗) exercise and coloring
(   ) eating a lot and painting
(   ) writing music and working

3 Why is exercise good to destress?
Exercise releases chemicals called endorphins – they make us feel good.

ACROSS THE CURRICULUM

ART

CAN MAKING ART MAKE YOU HAPPY?

By David Hurley
March 12

Art classes are usually fun, aren't they? Well, experts tell us that there are good reasons for that.

- Making art increases activity at the front of the brain, which makes us feel positive. And just looking at works of art can release the "feel-good" chemical called dopamine in the brain.
- Making art is a way to express emotions. When you create any piece of art, you have an opportunity to understand your feelings and deal with emotions.
- Working with art also helps you to focus on the moment. Some people mention that when they are creating art, they don't feel tired or hungry – they lose sense of time.

We talked to two teenagers about how art helped them in difficult times.

"Last year I moved away from my hometown. The art teacher in my new school noticed how sad I was and invited me to her art workshops with other students after school. Creating art definitely helped me feel better. I especially love to model clay and make sculptures. Every time I work on a piece, I feel relaxed and peaceful."
Chloe, 15

"When I was going through a hard time last year, my mom bought a coloring book and pencils for me. At first, I found the idea ridiculous – she didn't think I was a little kid again, did she? But she persuaded me to give it a try. When I started coloring, I found that I could 'turn off' the outside world and only focus on filling the forms with color. And my problems didn't seem that bad when I got to the end. Coloring calms my mind when I'm anxious."
Lucas, 14

26

At Home
Exercise 3
Have students track their eating habits, the amount of time they exercise and sleep, their stress levels, etc. for a week. Based on their results, invite them to create a weekly wellness plan and encourage them to follow it for a week. Have them bring the planners into class and present them.

Background Information

Crafts and art can alleviate symptoms such as anxiety, depression, and loneliness. Expressing emotions and focusing on the moment are all strategies to calm the mind. There is a great deal of research showing the benefits and healing power of crafts and manual activities.

2.05 Audioscript pT139

1 Have students read the title and look at the images on page 26. Ask: *Can art make you happy?* Listen to what they have to say and ask if any of them do any sort of art as a hobby. Read topics 1–3 in Exercise 1. Have students skim through the article on page 26 and check the correct alternative.

2 2.05 Have students look at the images, identify the materials used, and what sort of art it is (1 sculpture, 2 photography, 3 coloring). Play the audio and have students check which pieces of art belong to which student. Have them check their work in pairs. Ask them which one they like best and why.

3 Put students into pairs. Have them first read through the words and check pronunciation. Have them read the sentences before completing them with the correct words. Have them compare their answers in pairs. Check their work as a class.

Words in Context

4 Have students find the expressions 1–4 in the article. In pairs, have students match the expressions to the definitions a–d. Have them try to understand the expressions in context before looking them up in the dictionary. They can use an online dictionary, if necessary.

THINK!

Encourage students to visit some art museums virtually. These can easily be found by just writing "virtual art museums" in a search engine. As students are navigating through the online galleries, have them make a list of adjectives that could describe some of the artworks. Encourage students to write at least five different adjectives. Have them share their words. Invite them to look at the art on pages 26 and 27 and describe it.

WEBQUEST

Ask students if they believe coloring is a relaxing activity and if they are familiar with any famous coloring books. Have them research Johanna Basford on the Internet and find out more about her books. Have them check the correct alternative. Tell students to always crosscheck the information they find on two or three websites.

---

1 Look at the article. Check (✓) its main topic.

1 ◯ Tips for people who want to make art as a hobby
2 ✓ Mental health benefits of making art
3 ◯ How teen artists started to create works of art

2 2.05 Read and listen to the article. Which two works of art do you think Chloe and Lucas created? Write *C* (Chloe) and *L* (Lucas).

1  C

2 

3  L

3 Read the article again. Complete the statements with the words below. There are three extra words.

- anxious
- ~~brain~~
- emotions
- difficult
- mother
- pencils
- problems
- sculptures
- teacher
- understand

1 Creating and looking at art have a positive effect on the brain.
2 Art can help people understand their feelings.
3 Chloe's art teacher helped her when she was having a difficult time.
4 Chloe's favorite activity at the art workshops is making sculptures.
5 Lucas didn't like it when his mother bought him a coloring book.
6 He feels better about his problems when he finishes coloring.

WORDS IN CONTEXT

4 Match the expressions from the article with their definitions.

1 focus on c
2 move away a
3 go through d
4 give something a try b

a go to live in a new place
b attempt to do something new
c give a lot of attention to one particular person, subject, or thing
d experience something, especially something difficult

THINK!

Choose one of the artworks on page 26 and this page. Think of four adjectives to describe it.

WEBQUEST

Learn more! Check (✓) *True* or *False*.
Johanna Basford, the author of *Secret Garden*, and other coloring books, sold over 21 million copies of her books in the 2010s.

✓ True ◯ False

VIDEO

2.2

1 Say three emotions in the video.
2 What is the name of the chemical that makes us feel good?

27

2.06 Audioscript pT139

1 Have students look at the post and remind them about online forums. Have them skim the posts and identify who is asking for advice and who is giving advice.

2 2.06 Ask for a volunteer to read questions 1–3. Individually, ask students to look for the answers in the forum posts. Then, have students check their answers in pairs and play the audio to check their work.

LOOK!

Draw attention to the *Look!* box. Point out the use of the expressions *I (don't) think* and *maybe* before *should* to soften the tone of a statement. Have students write two sentences using both alternatives for them to realize the difference of tone. Have them read out both alternatives to the class.

3 Tell students they are now going to take part in an online forum, giving advice to Worried_Sis. Have a volunteer read the instructions 1–4 to the class. Have a student explain the steps again in their own words. Encourage them to look back at the vocabulary learned during this unit to write their advice. Tell students to make sure they give a piece of advice to each problem that Worried_Sis states in her post.

4 Have students switch their posts in order to assess a peer's work. Have a volunteer read through the checklist and make sure students understand each item in order to assess their classmate's work. If time allows, have them read each other's advice and ask students to choose the best advice.

Your Digital Portfolio

Give students a date for uploading their work and make sure they all look at one another's posts.

Practice Extra

Unit 2

WRITING

1 **Look at the posts. Who is asking The Teen Oracle for advice?** *sister / Jake's sister / Worried_Sis*

The Teen Oracle The place for no-nonsense advice from teens to teens

Home | Lifestyle | School work

Worried_Sis
Level: Apprentice I
Questions: 1
Replies: 1

Hi, everyone! I'm here because I need help. My brother Jake feels sleepy all the time. He doesn't play any sports and eats junk food. I want to help him, but I work long hours and I don't see him much. What should I do?

REPLY

Delphi
Level: Teen Oracle III
Questions: 24
Replies: 112

Well, I don't think you should worry too much if Jake often wants to sleep. We need a lot of sleep when we're teenagers – it's part of growing up, I guess.
But I know that physical exercise helps me feel more energetic, even during boring classes at school. 😉 Maybe you should invite him to take walks with you – that way he can be more active and you two can spend time together.
My older brother works long hours too and, believe me, I miss him!
Jake's eating habits are bad. He should include fruit and vegetables in his diet. Why don't you cook some healthy meals or snacks together? Eating well will help him have more energy and you will have another moment to talk and be together.

LIKE

2 2.06 **Read and listen to the posts and answer the questions.**

1 What three things is Worried_Sis anxious about?
Her brother feels sleepy all the time. He doesn't play any sports. He eats junk food.

2 What three pieces of advice does Delphi give to Worried_Sis?
She shouldn't worry too much if her brother often wants to sleep. She should invite her brother to take walks with her. They should cook some healthy meals together.

3 Does Delphi give reasons and examples to support his advice?
Yes, he does.

LOOK!
When we give advice, we often make our point less direct by using ***I (don't) think*** and ***maybe*** before using ***should***.
I think you should suggest a different type of exercise.
Maybe he should join a gym.

3 **Write a post with different advice from Delphi for Worried_Sis.**

1 Think of a piece of advice for each problem.
2 Support your advice with reasons and examples.
3 Find or draw an image for your avatar and choose a username.
4 Write the first version of your post. Use the words/phrases in the Look! box and the vocabulary from Unit 2.

4 **Switch your forum post with a classmate and check his/her work. Use the checklist below.**

- ◯ avatar and username
- ◯ advice for the three problems
- ◯ reasons and examples for the advice
- ◯ *should/shouldn't*
- ◯ *I (don't) think* and *maybe*

YOUR DIGITAL PORTFOLIO
Edit your forum post and upload it to the class portfolio for everyone to see!

28

Extension

Encourage students to build a mind map related to what they have learned throughout this unit. Remind them to do this at the end of each of the subsequent units.

Lesson Aim: I can review what I have learned and reflect on my progress.

Tell students that the exercises on these pages review the vocabulary and language they have learned in Units 1 and 2. Point out that they can also check their progress and reflect on what they can do.

Vocabulary

1 Have students look at the invitation and guess what it is for. Have them look at the images and try to identify the events happening in each of them. Have them share their guesses. Ask for a volunteer to read the verb phrases above the invitation. Have them complete the invitation using the verb phrases in the simple past. Have them check their work in pairs.

2 Ask students if they make New Year's resolutions every year. Then ask them if they stick to them. Have them share their New Year's resolution for the current year. Invite them to read through Patricio's list of resolutions and unscramble the words. Have them compare their list to Patricio's. Ask: *Are any similar?* Check their work in pairs.

3 Have students read the dialogue individually. Remind them to circle the correct option, taking the context of the dialogue into consideration. Check their work with the class. Have students summarize the main idea of the dialogue.

4 Remind students of the activities they listed during the unit that make them feel happy. Have them look at the image and identify the ones they like. Have them read the activities listed and complete the sentences using the present progressive, describing what each person is doing in the image.

REVIEW
UNITS 1 AND 2

VOCABULARY

1 Complete the invitation with the correct simple past form of the verbs below.

• get married • go to college • ~~graduate~~ • have children • retire

SAVE THE DATE!

We met on the day we [1] graduated from high school.

We [2] went to college together and [3] got married four years later.

We [4] had two amazing children and worked hard for over 40 years!

We [5] retired last month and we would like to invite you to our retirement party on September 20. You are part of our history!

Luis & Sofia

2 Put the letters in the correct order to complete Patricio's New Year's resolutions.

- [1] review (iwerve) what I learned in school for 15 minutes every day.
- [2] practice (aperctci) the piano four times a week.
- [3] take a break (akte a ekrba) from social media one day a week.
- [4] get a good grade (tge a ogdo agedr) in math.
- continue to [5] make (ekam) good progress (rogsesrp) in English.

3 Circle the correct options.

A What do you do to [1] stay in shape / make friends?
B I have a healthy diet, and I [2] prevent diseases / work out every day.
A It's a lovely morning. Would you like to [3] reduce stress / go for a run along the beach?
B Yes, that's a great idea.
A We're moving to England next month. My mom's working on a program to [4] prevent diseases / go for a run. I think it'll be hard to [5] make friends / work out there.
B Don't worry. You're the most sociable person I know.

4 Write what the people are doing. Use the words/phrases below and the correct verbs in the present progressive.

• a board game • ~~gymnastics~~ • skateboarding
• a walk • yoga

1 Amelia is doing gymnastics.
2 Beatriz is going for a walk.
3 Rodrigo is skateboarding.
4 Logan and Olivia are playing a board game.
5 Wilson is doing yoga.

29

Lesson Aim: I can review what I have learned and reflect on my progress.

Language in Context

5 Remind students of *will* and *be going to*, and the main difference between their uses. Ask them to give you an example of each. Individually, have students read through the sentences and complete them with the correct form of the verb. Have them check their work in pairs, justifying their answers.

6 Write the reflexive pronouns on the board. Have students come up to the board and write sentences exemplifying each one of them. Have them explain the use of the reflexive pronoun in their sentences. Individually, ask student to match the columns in the exercise. Have them compare their work in pairs.

7 In pairs, have students unscramble the sentences and then choose two sentences to match to each image. Have them come up with two more pieces of advice using a softer tone. Remind them of the expressions they should use in order to do this (*I [don't] think* and *maybe …*)

8 Have students read through the sentences. Draw their attention to the verb tenses used in each sentence. Have them complete the task individually and then compare their work in pairs. Ask them to make up two more sentences using question tags.

Check Your Progress

This section gives students an opportunity to reflect on what they have learned. Read each statement with the class. Elicit examples and/or information students remember. Alternatively, students could go through the statements in pairs or groups. If necessary, have them go back to the relevant unit to review each topic. Students then do the task in the Check Your Progress box individually. When they finish, ask: *What can you practice more? What is easy/difficult/interesting?* Invite students to give feedback.

LANGUAGE IN CONTEXT

5 Complete the sentences with the correct form of *will* or *be going to* and the verbs in parentheses.

1 My sister _is going to get_ (going to / get) a summer job this year.
2 _Will_ you _leave_ (will / leave) home when you finish school?
3 I'm learning Spanish and I _'m/am going to take_ (going to / take) an important exam next month.
4 My brother loves languages. Perhaps he _'ll/will take_ (will / take) a course abroad in the future.
5 We _'re not going to get_ (not going to / get) married this year.

6 Match 1–6 with a–f.

1 Did Maria enjoy _f_
2 Do you look at _d_
3 My parents are teaching _b_
4 I'm not sure I can express _a_
5 Pablo likes to review for exams _e_
6 My friends and I gave _c_

a myself clearly in English.
b themselves to play tennis.
c ourselves three weeks to prepare for the party.
d yourself in the mirror before you go out?
e by himself.
f herself at the beach last Sunday?

7 Put the words in the correct order. Then match images A and B with two pieces of advice.

1 scientist / should / a / you / become
You should become a scientist.
2 yourself / you / by / go / shouldn't / camping
You shouldn't go camping by yourself.
3 more / be / should / patient / try / you / to
You should try to be more patient.
4 teacher / should / your / help / for / you / ask
You should ask your teacher for help.
5 spend / shouldn't / all / you / money / your
You shouldn't spend all your money.

A

_4_

B

_3_

8 Complete the sentences with tag questions.

1 You love building models, _don't you?_
2 Your friends took singing lessons last year, _didn't they?_
3 Brenda isn't on the basketball team, _is she?_
4 Arthur can make jewelry, _can't he?_
5 Your mother didn't bake cookies for the party, _did she?_
6 I'm your best friend, _aren't I?_

CHECK YOUR PROGRESS

I CAN …

- talk about life stages and studying
- use *will* for predictions and *be going to* for intentions, and reflexive pronouns
- talk about free-time activities, and health and fitness
- use *should/shouldn't* for advice, and tag questions for confirming information.

LEARN TO LEARN

Make lists of ways to review English

There are many ways to review listening, reading, writing, speaking, vocabulary, and grammar. Keep lists of ideas in folders, and use these ideas often.

- listen to songs and write down what I hear
- repeat some things I hear when I listen to podcasts
- watch a movie with subtitles, then watch again without them

30

Learn to Learn

Throughout the course, students do a variety of *learn to learn* activities, which offer them techniques for retaining vocabulary. In this case, we give ideas of how students can review the different skills by making lists of words and expressions they hear while listening to podcasts, movies, and songs. Making lists and keeping them in places where students can easily find them helps them learn to learn. Have them read through the list of ideas and share with the class if they already use any of them. Encourage them to think of other ideas to add to the list.

Lesson Aim: I can talk about my buying behavior.

Warmer

Invite students to think about all the items they have bought over the past two weeks. Have them make a list of the products, leaving nothing out. Have them compare their lists and rank the items in the whole class from most to least common.

THINK!

1. Invite them to list the positive and negative aspects of shopping in this kind of store. Ask them to make a chart in their books and work in pairs. Have them share their work.
2. Ask students what they take into consideration when buying items. Give them two minutes to do this, then invite them to share their ideas with the class.

3.1 How We Sell

Summary

The video discusses how advertisements are intended to make us buy things.

In Class

Put students into pairs and have them tell each other about an occasion they bought a product because of an ad. Ask: *What aspects of the ad made you buy the product? Are there too many ads on TV and the Internet? Are ads a normal part of life?*

Exercise 1

Ask students to watch the video to answer the questions.

1. *Say two places where you can find adverts.* Check answers with the class.
   Two of the following: on TV, online, in movie theatres, while you work out, or on billboards.
2. *What helps you to remember a product in an advertisement?* Check answers with the class.
   humor

Exercise 2

Play the video again and ask students to answer the following questions. Then, ask them to make up two more questions to ask their partners.

1. What aspects of ads mentioned in the video catch people's attention?
   bright colors and designs, music, and humor
2. Why are the colors blue and green better to advertise soap?
   These colors make us think of cleanliness and water.
3. In pairs, talk about other colors you believe are good for advertising other products.

At Home

Exercise 3

Ask students to research an advertisement at home and take a photo of it or bring it in to class. Have students analyze the colors and the product, and define the characteristics of the final consumer (age, gender, etc.). If possible, use a collaborative panel for students to share the images. Prepare the panel before the class and share the link with your students.

Resources

- Teacher's worksheets Unit 3
- Test Generator Unit 3
- Practice Extra Unit 3
- Workbook pages 120–123
- Puzzles and Games page 103

Flipped Classroom

Ask students: *Can you remember an advertising campaign that caught your attention?* Describe an ad and the products involved. Encourage students to list different methods of advertising nowadays. If possible, use a digital collaborative platform so that students can share their work.

Unit Aims

Cambridge Life Competencies Framework

I can ...

- use simple techniques to start, maintain, and close conversations of various lengths when talking about products and advertisements. **(Communication)**
- understand essential grammatical terms and concepts using the modal verbs *have to* and *must*. **(Learning to Learn)**
- act parts in role plays talking about buying presents for friends. **(Creative Thinking)**
- create questions about a video and discuss its content. **(Creative Thinking)**
- assess strengths and weaknesses of a product or advertisement. **(Critical Thinking)**
- make informed choices about buying products with a lot of packaging. **(Social Responsibility)**

Vocabulary in Context
Lesson Aim: I can talk about how advertisements persuade consumers to buy products.

Warmer

Encourage students to use a dictionary to find as many words as possible related to advertising. Apart from synonyms, have students also list words that are commonly used to talk about advertising, such as *persuade*, *influence*, etc. If necessary, they can use a dictionary to get more ideas: https://dictionary.cambridge.org/pt/dicionario/learner-english/. Give them 5 minutes for this task. Have students share their work as a class.

Flipped Classroom Check

Put students into pairs and have them share their favorite advertisements. Have them justify why they chose them and the products involved. If a digital tool was used to collate their ideas, project it for the class.

3.01 Audioscript pT140

Target Vocabulary

advertise	/ˈæd·vərˌtɑɪz/
advertisement	/ˌæd·vərˈtɑɪz·mənt/
attract	/əˈtrækt/
headline	/ˈhedˌlɑɪn/
influence	/ˈɪn.flu·əns/
logo	/ˈloʊ·ɡoʊ/
persuade	/pərˈsweɪd/
product	/ˈprɑd·əkt/
promise	/ˈprɑm·ɪs/
value	/ˈvæl·ju/

1 3.01 Ask students if they often take part in surveys on the Internet and what kind of survey mostly comes up on their social media. Have students look at the images and ask them what kind of product they believe is being advertised in this survey. Ask students to read through the sentences in the survey individually and circle the best alternatives. Do not ask them to answer the survey at this moment, just circle the words. Play the audio to check their work. Encourage them to repeat the words, paying attention to intonation and pronunciation.

VOCABULARY IN CONTEXT

ADVERTISING

1 3.01 **Circle the correct words in the survey. Then listen, check, and repeat.**

HOME SURVEY ABOUT US MY ACCOUNT

1 Think of an [1]*advertise* / *advertisement* that persuaded you to buy something in the past. What product did it [2]*advertise* / *advertisement*? ______

2 How did the ad present the [3]*product* / *influence* to [4]*value* / *persuade* you to buy it?
☐ modern ☐ good [5]*promise* / *value* ☐ necessary ☐ fun ☐ other ______

3 Do ads often [6]*influence* / *headline* your decisions about what to buy? ☐ Yes ☐ No

4 Which of these two pop-up ads works better to [7]*attract* / *logo* your attention? ☐ A ☐ B

A

B

5 Which [8]*headline* / *product* do you prefer?
☐ Feel alive! ☐ OFFER ENDS TODAY!

6 Which [9]*value* / *logo* do you prefer?
☐ OUTPACE ☐ OUTPACE

7 What benefits does each ad [10]*attract* / *promise* to give you? Write *A* or *B*.
☐ staying fit ☐ feeling good ☐ saving money ☐ enjoying the taste

Thanks for taking the time to complete this survey!

32

Vocabulary in Context
Lesson Aim: I can talk about how advertisements persuade consumers to buy products.

2 Remind students that what they heard was a survey. Invite them to answer the survey, and then discuss their answers with a partner. Encourage them to justify their choices.

3 Invite a student to read the sentences to the class. Then, individually, have students write *T* (true) or *F* (false). Have them check their answers in pairs.

4 Read the words in the charts with the students. Draw their attention to the headings. Write the headings on the board. Allow them to refer to Exercises 1 and 3 to complete the charts. Have them do the task individually and then compare their work in pairs. Have a student come up to the board and write the answers. Then, ask them to match the charts to the sentences a–b.

5 Have students work in pairs. Ask each pair to choose two words in bold from Exercise 3 and make up two sentences using the words. Have them share their sentences with the class. Then ask them to read sentences 1–6 and complete them with words from Exercise 3. Check their work as a class. Then, have them check the sentences that are true for them and justify their answers.

USE IT!

6 Write the following sentence on the board: *I don't think ads influence me, but I like to watch them.* Draw their attention to the speech bubbles in the chart and model the activity by asking them, using one of the prompts: *Do you think ads influence you?* Tell them they should use the prompts to make questions about the sentences in Exercise 5. Write the following example answer on the board: *I don't think ads influence me, but I like to watch them.* Pair students up for the activity. Monitor the activity by walking around the class.

Homework

Workbook page 121, Exercises 1 and 2

Practice Extra

Unit 3

UNIT 3

2 **Complete the survey in Exercise 1. Then share your answers with a partner.**

3 **Write *T* (true) or *F* (false).**

1 The **product** in ads A and B is an energy drink. T
2 The **logo** in ad A shows a person running. T
3 Both advertisements are trying to **persuade** people to save money. F
4 The **headline** appears at the bottom of a pop-up ad. F
5 Ads often **promise** to improve our lives. T
6 Every **advertisement** has an **influence** on people's decisions about what to buy. T
7 Some ads **attract** us to the product by showing that it's not good **value**. F
8 Companies **advertise** their products on the Internet, on TV, and on the radio. T

4 **Complete charts 1–3 with the words in bold in Exercise 1. Then match the charts with a or b below.**

1 b

Verb	Noun
persuade	persuasion
attract	attraction

2 a

Verb	Noun
influence	influence
promise	promise

3 b

Verb	Noun
advertise	advertisement

a The verb has the same form as the noun.
b The verb and the noun forms are different.

5 **Complete the sentences using the words in bold in Exercise 3. Then check (✓) the sentences that are true for you.**

1 ◯ I don't think ads influence me but I like to watch them.
2 ◯ I never believe ads that promise to change my life.
3 ◯ It's always easy to persuade my grandparents to buy what I want.
4 ◯ I like to wear clothes that have a famous logo.
5 ◯ Headlines in pop-up ads usually attract my attention.
6 ◯ Before buying a product, I often compare prices to make sure I get a good value.

USE IT!

6 **Work in pairs. Take turns asking and answering questions about the ideas in Exercise 5.**

Do you think ads …?

Do you believe ads that …?

WORKBOOK p.121 PRACTICE EXTRA 33

Fast Finishers

Puzzles and Games page 103, Exercise 1

Extension

Have students choose one of their favorite advertisements from social media. Ask them to write a short paragraph using the vocabulary learned in this unit so far, describing the ad and its main objective. Have them share their work on a collaborative platform. If possible, have them post the ad as well.

Reading
Lesson Aim: I can read and understand a blog about advertisements.

Warmer

Ask students to think silently for one minute about a time when they believe they were influenced by an advertisement. Ask them to list the product that was being sold and why the ad influenced them. Write the word *Emotions* on the board. In pairs, encourage them to think of different advertisements that made them feel different emotions: *sad, happy, angry, surprised*, etc. Ask them if the ad they chose influenced them emotionally, and in what way.

3.02 Audioscript pT140

1 Draw student's attention to the images and title of the blog. Ask students where this kind of article could be found (social media posts and forums). Have them read the sentences in bold at the start of the four paragraphs 1–4 in the blog. Individually, ask them to read the sentences in Exercise 1 and circle the correct words.

2 **3.02** Ask students why they think this blog post was written. Ask students: *What is the writer trying to point out*? Have a volunteer read the questions and options in Exercise 2. Then have students read the blog to check the correct options. Play the audio to check their work. Encourage students to write Mason's reply to Blogger Boy.

3 Have a student read sentences a–d. In pairs, have students match the sentences to the sentences in bold in the blog. Check with the class, asking volunteers to read out the sentences. Ask: *Can you think of an ad that uses famous people to influence the viewers?*

THINK!

In pairs, ask students to list different ads that use the strategies mentioned in the blog post. Encourage them to list the strategies used and add any other techniques they notice in each ad (uses award systems, repeats the brand's name, appeals emotionally, uses famous people's names, etc.). Have them choose their favorite two and share them with the class, mentioning all the techniques applied. Use a collaborative platform, if possible.

READING

SMART TEEN A BLOG FOR SMART TEENAGE CONSUMERS
HOME | ABOUT | PAST POSTS | WRITE FOR US

4 THINGS WE MUST NOT FORGET ABOUT ADS
by Mason Carlson

Do you sometimes decide to buy a product just because of an advertisement? Well, we all do. But here are some things to remember when we read or watch ads.

1 People produce ads to influence you
Behind all ads there are professionals who know what techniques will persuade us to buy. Even the funniest and most creative ads have one basic aim: to sell us something.

2 Ads want you to think you have to buy something – now!
Ads make you think you must act urgently: there's something fantastic out there and everyone else is enjoying it. And they also say it's easy to get it. Look! This burger is the "best" and "only" costs $3.99!

3 Ads use your emotions to get what they want
Are you worried about your friends thinking you're not attractive and cool? Ads show you beautiful, successful people having fun. Their idea? You buy what they advertise and you'll feel great, like the people in the ads.

4 Ads use famous people to attract you
Advertising companies pay a lot of money to celebrities. They know that fans will buy the product, not because they need it, but just because they love the star.

Comments

mei
I sometimes feel I have to buy something after I watch an ad. I buy it, I'm happy for a while, and then I want to buy something else.
reply

Blogger Boy
Ads don't influence me. You don't have to buy what they advertise.
reply

1 Look at the blog page and circle the correct options.

1 The blog Smart Teen is about *ads* / *money*.
2 The people who write are *adults* / *teenagers*.
3 The readers are usually *adults* / *teenagers*.
4 Mason's post is about *advertising* / *allowances*.
5 Successful people *earn* / *save* a lot of money from advertising.

2 3.02 Read and listen to the blog post and comments. Check (✓) the correct answers.

1 What opinion does Mason have about ads?
a ✓ They influence us.
b ○ They don't influence us.
c ○ He's not sure about their influence.

2 Who disagree(s) with Mason in the comments?
a ○ mei
b ✓ Blogger Boy
c ○ mei and Blogger Boy

3 Read these people's comments during a meeting for an ad. Match them with 1–4 in the blog post.

a This will be a big hit with teens if we can persuade Taylor Swift to appear. 4
b We can start by asking, "Do you sometimes feel sad when you look at yourself in the mirror?" 3
c Let's go with the cartoon dog. If we can make people laugh, they'll feel good about the product. 1
d Let's end with "Hurry! This offer ends Saturday!" 2

THINK!
Think of two ads you like. Do they use any of the techniques listed in the blog? If so, how? What other techniques do they use?

34

WORKBOOK p.123

Homework

Workbook page 123, Exercises 1, 2, and 3

Language in Context
Lesson Aim: I can use the modal verbs *have to* and *must* in different contexts.

1 If necessary, students look at the blog post on page 34 again to help them complete the chart. Draw students' attention to the difference between the negative and affirmative statements for each modal. When they finish, encourage students to make sentences about their own buying behaviors, using the modal verbs in the affirmative and negative forms. Have them use the chart as reference.

2 Have volunteers read through the sentences 1–5 and a–e. Encourage students to look at Exercise 1 to help them match the sentences. Have them check their work in pairs, before rewriting sentences a–e with the other modal verb in each case. Ask volunteers to read their rewritten sentences to check answers. (***a** must get; **b** has to study; **d** has to take; **e** must read*).

3 Have students refer to the blog post and the chart in Exercise 1 again. Draw attention to the fact that they will now be using the negative form of the modal verbs to complete the sentences. Have them do the exercise individually and then check in pairs. Point out that *must* is not very common in American English, but it is common in British English.

LOOK!

Draw attention to the *Look!* box. Have a volunteer read the sentence. Ask students to come up with more examples that are true for them, using *must not*. Brazilian students tend to use *don't have to* or *can't* instead of *mustn't*: ~~*You can't forget to bring some sun lotion and a camera to take some photographs.*~~ *You mustn't forget to bring some sun lotion.* ~~*You don't have to (mustn't) be shy!*~~ *You mustn't be shy!*

USE IT!

4 Tell students to work individually and complete the sentences so that they are true for them. Give them one minute to do this.

5 Model the activity with a student using the examples from the speech bubbles. Then put students into groups. Invite them to read their sentences to the

UNIT 3

LANGUAGE IN CONTEXT

1 Look at the examples below. Complete the sentences from the blog post.

Have to		
Affirmative: Obligation		
I/You/We/They	[1] have to	buy something.
He/She	has to	
Negative: No Obligation		
I/You/We/They	[2] don't have to	buy what they advertise.
He/She	doesn't have to	

Must		
Affirmative: Obligation		
I/You/He/She/We/They	[3] must	act urgently.
Negative: Prohibition		
I/You/He/She/We/They	[4] must not	forget four things about ads.

2 Match 1–5 with a–e. Then write the other form for obligation for the words in bold in a–e.

1 The students have an exam next week. c
2 Fernando is going to fly to Tokyo. a
3 You started reading two hours ago. d
4 Caroline wants to be a doctor. b
5 This is a fantastic book. e

a He **has to get** a passport. must get
b She **must study** hard. has to study
c They **have to review** their lessons. must review
d You **must take** a break. have to take
e You **have to read** it. must read

3 Complete the sentences with *don't/doesn't have to* or *must not*.

1 You don't have to go now. You can stay here if you want.
2 She has a lot of clothes. She doesn't have to buy a new skirt.
3 You must not tell Ren about the party. It's going to be surprise.
4 The teacher said, "Put your phones in your bags. You must not use them in class."
5 You don't have to buy something just because it's a bargain.
6 He likes his job. He doesn't have to look for a new one.

LOOK!
We use *must not* to say something is the wrong thing to do.
You **must not forget** to do your homework.

USE IT!

4 Complete the sentences so they are true for you. Students' own answers

1 When I'm in the library, I must not ____________.
2 To get to school on time, I have to ____________.
3 When I'm at home, I don't have to ____________.
4 When I'm at school, I must ____________.

5 Work in groups. Take turns reading your sentences in Exercise 4 to your group. Then tell the class one thing you have in common and one thing you don't have in common.

When we're in the library, we must not talk on our cell phones.

To get to school on time, Fernando has to get up at 6 a.m. The rest of the group don't have to get up so early.

WORKBOOK p.120 and 122 PRACTICE EXTRA

group. Each group should then choose a reporter to tell the class one thing they had in common as a group and one thing which was different.

Grammar Game

Divide students into smaller groups. Have them create a poster using the modal verbs of obligation and prohibition regarding their school rules. If possible, use a collaborative platform. Have students share their work. Have them build a final one, using everyone's examples. Draw their attention to the context in order to use the correct modal verbs for each situation. (Possible answers: High school students don't have to wear uniforms. You must sanitize your hands. You must not run in the corridors. You must take good care of school property. You don't have to join a sports team. You have to hand in your homework on time.) Have them share their poster with the school and if possible, hang it on a wall.

Homework

Workbook page 122, Exercises 1 and 2

Practice Extra

Unit 3

Listening and Vocabulary
Lesson Aim: I can understand a dialogue about ideas for making extra money.

Warmer

Ask students if they help at home in any way. Divide students into groups of three. Have them list some ideas of small jobs they could do to earn some extra money at home or around their neighborhood. Have them share their ideas. Write the most common suggestions on the board.

3.03–3.05 Audioscripts pT140

Target Vocabulary

cost	/kɔst/
invest	/ɪn'vest/
label	/'leɪ·bəl/
on sale	/ɔn.seɪl/
own	/oʊn/
sell	/sel/

1 Ask students to look at the image and say the first word that comes to their minds without looking at the word box. Have them tell you where they think the boys are and what they are doing. Read through the words with students to check understanding. Individually, have students check the words they think they will hear in the dialogue.

2 3.03 Play the audio for students to check whether the words they checked in Exercise 1 are correct. Have them summarize the first part of the dialogue in their own words. Ask: *What does "big label" mean? Do you think he should buy it?*

3 3.04 Have students look at the images and describe what is happening in each one. Have students compare their list of small jobs from the Warmer with the images. Ask: *Are any the same?* Play the audio and have students match each image with the teenagers. Ask them to check in pairs.

4 3.04 Have a volunteer read the sentences without giving the answers. Ask students to circle the correct words from memory. Then play the audio again and check answers with the class.

LISTENING AND VOCABULARY

1 **Look at the image. Check (✓) the words you think you will hear in the first part of the dialogue between Wilson and Diego.**

1 ◯ afford
2 ◯ buy
3 ◯ expensive
4 ◯ money
5 ◯ price
6 ◯ spend

2 3.03 **Listen to the first part of the dialogue and check your answers to Exercise 1.**
buy, money, spend

3 3.04 **Diego and Wilson discuss how teenagers can make money. Look at these images. Whose ideas are they? Listen to the whole dialogue and write *D* (Diego), *W* (Wilson), or *N* (neither).**

1  W

2  N

3  D

4 3.04 **Listen again and circle the correct options.**

1 At the beginning of the dialogue, Wilson (*wants*) / *doesn't want* to buy new shoes.
2 Wilson (*can*) / *can't* afford the sneakers.
3 Wilson's parents think that we *must* / (*don't have to*) buy things because they are a good price.
4 Diego (*agrees*) / *doesn't agree* with Wilson's parents.
5 Diego gives Wilson some ideas about *donating* / (*saving*) money.
6 At the end of the dialogue, Wilson is *bored* / (*excited*) by Diego's suggestion.

5 3.05 **Match the words below with the definitions 1–6. Then listen, check, and repeat.**

• cost • invest • label • on sale • own • ~~sell~~

1 opposite of *buy* ... sell
2 have, possess ... own
3 company ... label
4 with a reduced price ... on sale
5 need payment of an amount of money ... cost
6 put your money into something that will produce more money ... invest

6 **Complete the sentences with the words in Exercise 5.**

1 Diego tells Wilson that the things we ... own ... don't have to be from a big ... label ... .
2 Wilson's parents don't think it's always a good idea to buy things ... on sale ... .
3 Diego thinks Wilson should save or ... invest ... his money.
4 Wilson wants to make models and ... sell ... them.
5 Cleaning materials don't ... cost ... much.

36

WORKBOOK p.121

5 3.05 Have a volunteer read the words. Individually, ask students to match the words to the definitions 1–6. Play the audio for them to check their work. Have students come up with two sentences which are true for them using two of the words.

6 Have students complete the sentences individually. Have students volunteer one at a time to read their answers.

Homework

Workbook page 121, Exercises 3 and 4

Language in Context
Lesson Aim: I can ask questions and give short answers using *have to*.

1 Draw students' attention to how we form questions using *have to*. Write the first question from the chart on the board. Ask for a volunteer to ask the same question using the second-person *you*. Elicit the short answers from the class. Ask students to complete the rest of the questions in the chart and draw attention to the changes that occur. Have them check answers with the class.

2 Put students into pairs and invite them to complete the questions using the correct form of *have to*. Check as a class and encourage students to ask two more questions.

3 Draw students' attention to the weekend to-do list of Juliana and Mateo. Have students read through what each of them has to do. Invite students to write questions and short answers according to the to-do list. Allow students to refer to the initial chart for reference. Have students check in pairs.

USE IT!

4 Have a volunteer read through the phrases 1–5. Model the activity with a student using the speech bubbles under the chart. Have students stand up and walk around the class to find someone who has to do the activities in the chart. When they find a person, have them ask for more information regarding the activity with *what time*, *who*, *where*, etc. Monitor the activity by walking around the class.

Homework

Workbook page 122, Exercises 3 and 4

Practice Extra

Unit 3

Fast Finishers

Puzzles and Games page 103, Exercise 2

LANGUAGE IN CONTEXT

1 Complete the sentences from the dialogue in the chart. Use the words and phrases below.

• does ... have to (x 2) • do ... have to • don't

Have to: Questions and Short Answers	
Do I **have to** use this product?	Yes, you **do**. / No, you **don't**.
1 Do you have to get them now?	Yes, I **do**. / No, I **don't**.
2 Does everything have to be from a big label?	Yes, it **does**. / No, it **doesn't**.
3 Do we have to buy everything that's on sale?	Yes, we **do**. / No, we 4 don't.
How much **does** Diego **have to** spend on cleaning materials?	
When **do** they **have to** pay for the products?	

2 Complete the questions with the correct form of *have to*.

1 Do you have to go to bed early on Friday?
2 Do we have to add salt to the food?
3 Does the owner of the store have to invest money in big labels?
4 When does Ana have to take her exams?
5 How many books do I have to buy for this course?

3 Look at the chart. Then write questions using *have to* and short answers.

Weekend To-do List	Juliana	Mateo
1 prepare for English exam	✓	×
2 go to the ATM	✓	×
3 finish school project	×	×
4 bake cookies	✓	✓

1 Juliana / exam?
Does Juliana have to prepare for her English exam? Yes, she does.

2 Mateo / ATM?
Does Mateo have to go to an ATM? No, he doesn't.

3 Juliana and Mateo / school project?
Do Juliana and Mateo have to finish their school project? No, they don't.

4 Juliana and Mateo / cookies?
Do Juliana and Mateo have to bake cookies? Yes, they do.

USE IT!

4 Ask your classmates questions to find names for 1–5. Then ask *Wh–* questions (*what*, *where*, *why*, etc.) to get extra information and complete the chart. Students' own answers

Find Someone Who Has To ...	Name	Extra Information
1 get up early on Saturdays.		
2 help at home.		
3 buy something soon.		
4 save some money for something.		
5 take a bus home after school.		

Do you have to get up early on Saturdays? Why do you have to do that?

Yes, I do. Because I have soccer practice at 8 a.m.

WORKBOOK p.120 and 122 PRACTICE EXTRA

Extension

Encourage students to think of a job they could do during their break to make some extra money. Have them write a brief description of this job. In pairs, have students interview each other in order to discover what job their partner is thinking about. Students should ask as many questions as possible such as: *Do you have to wake up early? Do you have to wash a car? Do you have to work in an office? Do you have to work in a shop?* etc.

Grammar Game

Write the following activities/places on the board: *shopping mall*, *school*, *movie theater*, *restaurant*, *sailing club*, *driving*, and *vacationing*. Divide students into pairs. Each pair should choose two activities/events and write as many sentences and questions using *have to*, *has to*, *must*, and *must not* related to the activity/place as they can think of. Give students three minutes to do this. The pairs with the most sentences/questions wins.

Lesson Aim: I can read and talk about activities and ideas to reduce waste in the world.

3.2 The Problem with Plastic

The video on page 39 and accompanying exercises below can be used as a lead-in to the topic of the Around the World text, or after the reading activities to complete the unit.

Summary

The video is about our excessive use of plastic in our daily lives.

In Class

Tell students they are going to watch a video about how plastic is destroying our environment. The video gives students an idea of how much plastic we use on a daily basis and how we can decrease its use. Have students look around them and count how many things made out of plastic they can see. In pairs, have them make a list. Give them two minutes to write the list and share it with the class before watching the video.

Exercise 1

Ask students to watch the video to answer the questions:

1 *When did people start to use plastic?* Check answers with the class.
In the 1950s.

2 *How much plastic waste gets recycled?* Check answers with the class.
Less than 10%.

Exercise 2

Write the following questions on the board and have students answer them from memory. Have them watch the video again to check their answers. Then, ask them to make up two more questions about how to reduce waste to ask their partners.

1 The video mentions the main reason why we should stop using plastic. What is it?
Plastic doesn't decompose like other materials. It only breaks into smaller pieces.

2 Mention two positive aspects of plastic.
Thanks to plastic packaging, food can stay fresh for much longer, and medicine can stay safe and effective.

3 Write two ideas the video mentions that can help us reduce our use of plastic.
Buy food and drink in glass bottles or metal cans, rather than plastic containers; stop buying bottled water today; use a reusable bottle and fill it up at home; stop using plastic bags.

At Home

Exercise 3

Ask students to research more about how plastic waste is destroying our environment. Divide students into four smaller groups and have each group focus on one of the following topics and consider how plastic waste is affecting it:

- oceans
- forests
- rivers
- cities

AROUND THE WORLD

HOME | ABOUT | PAST POSTS | WRITE FOR US

Rethinking Waste: Lessons From Japan

Some years ago, people in a Japanese village called Kamikatsu had the idea to go "zero waste." For this to happen, all residents would need to collaborate in important ways. A central idea in the project was the creation of a waste center where the residents had to take all their trash.

At first not everyone welcomed the idea because it involves a lot of work. Before going to the center, residents have to wash their non-organic trash, including plastic bags and bottles. At the center they have to put their waste in separate containers for different materials. There are 45 different categories of waste: for example, different places for different kinds of metal like aluminium and steel, and seven containers for paper, including newspapers, cardboard, and paper tubes. There are special places for toothbrushes, pillows, and furniture.

Nowadays, however, most people agree that the waste center is a great idea. Recycling makes money for the village. The fact that all waste is separated and cleaned adds value to it because it's easier to recycle. People also enjoy going to the *kuru-kuru* store in the center (*kuru-kuru* means "circular" in Japanese), where they can leave clothes, plates, or other useful items they don't want anymore. And a person who wants something from the store can take it away for free.

The village now recycles more than 80% of its waste but the project isn't only about recycling. As one of the organizers explained, "People have to avoid buying things that will go to waste. We must also avoid unnecessary packaging and try to use our own containers when possible." In other words, we must think about waste not only after we use something. We have to do it before use as well.

38

Background Information

A small village in Japan decided to go zero waste. The city of Kamikatsu, at first, did not think it would succeed, but now, apart from successfully recycling their waste, zero waste also brings in money for the city. Recycling is not only about waste, but also about your buying behavior. When we buy things, we must avoid unnecessary packaging. Zero waste makes us aware of how we buy things and how we throw things away.

3.06 Audioscript pT140

1 Write the word *waste* on the board. Encourage students to come up with as many related words as possible. Ask them if they recycle things at home and what their thoughts are about recycling. Have students look at the text on page 38 and guess what it is about. Have them look at the images and the title. Have a volunteer read sentences 1–3. Individually, have students circle the correct alternatives.

2 3.06 Have students read the article and take notes of the main things that happened in each paragraph in their notebooks. Have them check their work in pairs. Have a volunteer read sentences 1–6. Individually, have students write *T* (true) or *F* (false). Play the audio for them to check their work in pairs. Then, ask them to underline the sentences that justify their answers in the article.

Words in Context

3 Ask students to find the words in bold in sentences 1–4 in the article to figure out their meaning from the context. Then, invite students to match the words to the definitions a–d. Ask them to use a dictionary, if necessary. They should then choose another four words from the article and write them and their definitions on separate strips of paper. Put students into pairs, and have them swap their strips of papers and match the words to the definitions. Have them make up sentences using the words.

4 Invite students to look at the images and describe what they see. Ask them whether any of the images relate to their daily lives, encouraging them to justify their answer. Have a volunteer read the question. Have them match the sentence to the corresponding image. Ask them how we could encourage people to use less packaging.

5 Individually, ask students to read the last paragraph of the text. Have a volunteer read sentences 1–4. Have students check the sentence that best summarizes the last paragraph of the text. Have them justify their answer.

1 **Look at the article: the title, image, and the first paragraph. Circle the correct options.**

1 The words "waste" and "trash" (have) / *don't have* the same meaning.
2 A possible caption for the image is (*Kamikatsu*) / *Zero waste*.
3 The article is about a project to *spend less money* / (*produce less waste*) in a village.

2 3.06 **Read and listen to the article. Write *T* (true) or *F* (false). Underline the parts of the article that justify your answers.**

1 There is a trash collection at all residents' homes in Kamikatsu. F
2 At the beginning of the project not everyone liked the "zero waste" idea. T
3 People have to put newspapers and cardboard tubes in the same place. F
4 The village gets more money when it can sell clean waste. T
5 It is possible to donate things at the center. T
6 People can also buy recycled objects from the center. F

WORDS IN CONTEXT

3 **Match the words in bold in 1–4 with their definitions a–d.**

1 Residents must separate **steel** from other types of metal. d
2 They must avoid unnecessary **packaging**. b
3 They mustn't put **cardboard** together with paper tubes. a
4 They have to choose the correct **container** for all their waste. c

a thick, hard paper, for example to make boxes
b materials used to cover products you buy
c object used for holding something
d very strong metal

4 **Which image illustrates "We must also avoid unnecessary packaging and try to use our own containers when possible"?** 2

1

2

5 **Check (✓) the sentence that summarizes the main idea of the last paragraph.**

1 ◯ When you have new ideas, it's important to advertise them.
2 ◯ When a city wants to do something, all residents must agree.
3 ◯ It's possible to invent creative ways to use old materials again.
4 ✓ Consumers must think about waste before they decide to buy something.

WEBQUEST

Learn more! Check (✓) the correct answer.
Some stores use the letters BYOC to show they don't have any packaging for some products. What do these letters mean?

◯ **Borrow your own container**
✓ **Bring your own container**
◯ **Buy your own container**

THINK!

Think about something you bought recently. Did it have a lot of packaging? Did it create a lot of waste? Next time you buy something similar, what can you do to avoid unnecessary waste?

VIDEO 3.2

1 When did people start to use plastic?
2 How much plastic waste gets recycled?

THINK!

If possible, bring in a product that can normally be bought in a supermarket and that has excessive packaging or find images on the Internet of such products. Encourage students to think about how this waste can be reduced and why companies use excessive packaging. Have them give you examples of things they recently bought that also had excessive packaging. In pairs, encourage students to make a list of ideas for how we can reduce our packaging on a daily basis. Have them share their lists.

WEBQUEST

Ask for a student to read the sentence. Have them check the alternative they believe is correct and then check it on the Internet. Remind students to check two or three websites to confirm their answers. Have them also look up the meaning for BYOD (Bring Your Own Device). Ask them if they know any other general acronyms to share.

Speaking
Lesson Aim: I can keep a conversation going, and talk about why I am going to different stores.

3.07–3.10 Audioscripts pT140

1 **3.07** Ask students to look at the images and, as a class, discuss what they think the friends might be talking about. Encourage them to think about the topic of the unit to make their guesses. Play the audio for them to check whether they were right. Ask: *What are they planning to do? Does Emilio sound surprised? Why?* Have them read the dialogue silently and then play the audio again to notice intonation and pronunciation.

Living English

2 Check understanding of the expressions 1–3. Ask students to find them in the dialogue in Exercise 1 and see how the speakers use them. Ask: *Which expression shows the speaker agrees 100%?* (Ah, OK, so) *Which expression sounds less sure about the fact?* (Yeah, OK, I guess) *Which expression shows that the speaker does not fully agree?* (Well, you know) Encourage students to think of similar expressions in their own language. Have students match the expressions to their meanings a–c. To check answers, ask volunteers to read the sentences.

3 **3.08** When students repeat the expressions, have them mimic the intonation they hear.

Pronunciation

4 **3.09** Look back at the dialogue in Exercise 1 and ask students to underline the modal verb *have to*. Ask: *How do we pronounce this?* Invite students to repeat it to themselves many times before answering. Have them check the correct alternative and ask them to come up with other examples.

5 **3.09** Have students listen to the audio and repeat after it.

SPEAKING

KEEPING A CONVERSATION GOING

1 3.07 **Read and listen to Helen and Emilio. Where are they planning to go? Why?**
to the secondhand store downtown, to buy a present for Cristian.

Helen: Hey **Emilio**. It's **Cristian's** birthday **tomorrow**. We have to buy **him** a present.
Emilio: Ah, OK, so let's go to **the mall**!
Helen: Well, you know, I was thinking we could go to **the secondhand store downtown**.
Emilio: What?
Helen: Yeah, why not? We don't have to **get an expensive present**. I bet we'll **find something special there**.
Emilio: Yeah, OK, I guess ... Maybe **sports clothes** or stuff like that ...
Helen: Great. Let's go.

LIVING ENGLISH

2 **Match the expressions (1–3) with their meanings (a–c).**

1 Ah, OK, so — a I agree
2 Well, you know — b Yes, maybe, but I'm not sure
3 Yeah, OK, I guess — c I don't agree

3 3.08 **Listen and repeat the expressions.**

PRONUNCIATION

4 3.09 **Listen and pay attention to the pronunciation of the *v* in *have to*. Check (✓) the sound you hear.**

have to
We **have to** buy him a present.
☑ /f/ ◯ /v/

5 3.09 **Listen again and repeat.**

6 3.10 **Listen and circle the sound you hear: /f/ or /v/.**

1 I always **have** time for my friends. /f/ (/v/)
2 The students **have to** review for the exam. (/f/) /v/
3 Liz doesn't **have** a lot of furniture. /f/ (/v/)
4 We **have** a lot of cousins – what about you? /f/ (/v/)
5 This is awful! We **have to** do something about it. (/f/) /v/

7 3.07 **Listen to the dialogue again. Then practice with a partner.**

8 **Role play a new dialogue. Follow the steps.**

1 Change the words in **blue** to write a new dialogue in your notebook.
2 Practice your dialogue with a partner.
3 Present your dialogue to the class.

YOUR DIGITAL PORTFOLIO
Record your dialogue and upload it to your class digital portfolio.

40

PRACTICE EXTRA

6 **3.10** Have students read through sentences 1–5 individually. Then put students in pairs and encourage them to read the sentences to one another in order to practice the correct pronunciation. Play the audio to check their work.

7 **3.07** Have the class read the dialogue along with the audio. Then play the audio again, pausing after each speaker for the class to repeat what they say. Finally, have students practice the dialogue in pairs.

8 Read through the steps with the students and check understanding. Encourage them to use the vocabulary learned throughout this unit. Monitor as they practice and provide feedback on intonation and linking. If time allows, have them present their dialogue to the class.

Your Digital Portfolio

Give students a date for uploading their work and make sure they all listen to one another's dialogues.

Practice Extra

Unit 3

 Lesson Aim: I can talk about environmental problems.

Warmer

Write the phrase *Protecting the environment* on the board in a center circle. In pairs, encourage students to talk and come up with words related to ways to help our planet. Then, have students come up to the board and add their words to the mind map.

THINK!

1 Have students look at the image and describe what they see. Ask them if they believe our planet is suffering and elicit their ideas. Ask: *Do you believe we can save the planet? Do you believe we are part of the problem?* Have them interpret the image and explain their interpretation.

2 Encourage students to reflect upon some of the environmental problems they face on a daily basis. Have them share their ideas as a class

4.1 Take Action Now!

Summary
The video is about how global warming is affecting our lives and what we can do about it.

In Class
Tell students they're going to watch a video about global warming, its causes, its consequences, and how we can fight it. Before playing the video, draw three columns on the board and write in the following headings: *Causes, Consequences,* and *Action*. In pairs, have students complete it. Have them watch the video to add other ideas and check their own. Ask: *What are people in your area doing to fight global warming?*

Exercise 1
Ask students to watch the video to answer the questions:

1 *Say two effects of global warming.* Check the answer with the class.
The ice at the north and south poles is melting; the oceans are getting warmer; some sea life is dying; there is more extreme weather (floods or drought)

2 *What gas do plants breathe in?* Check the answer with the class.
carbon dioxide

Exercise 2
Write the sentences below on the board. Play the video again. Students watch and write *T* (true) or *F* (false) for each sentence. Check answers with the class. Ask them to correct the false sentences.

1 Global warming is a natural fact and human activity does not interfere. True or false? Justify your answer.
False. Global warming may be happening naturally. But human activity makes it happen more quickly.

2 In the future, many cities may be underwater.
True. The ice at the north and south poles is melting, and sea levels are rising.

3 The Amazon rainforest alone cleans up 10% of the world's carbon dioxide.
False. The Amazon rainforest alone cleans up 5% of the world's carbon dioxide.

At Home
Exercise 3
Have students list actions they can take at home on a daily basis to prevent global warming. Have students share their work on a collaborative platform.

Resources
- Teacher's worksheets Unit 4
- Test Generator Unit 4
- Practice Extra Unit 4
- Workbook pages 124–127
- Puzzles and Games page 103

Flipped Classroom
Present the 3–2–1 strategy to your students. Ask them to write three facts they know about environmental issues, two opinions, and one question. If possible, have them post them on a collaborative panel.

Unit Aims
Cambridge Life Competencies Framework
I can …
- use simple techniques to start, maintain, and close conversations of various lengths. **(Communication)**
- understand essential grammatical terms and concepts using *if* clauses and modal verbs to talk about possibilities. **(Learning to Learn)**
- use notes to construct original output. **(Learning to Learn)**
- state opposing opinions in a respectful way when discussing actions to protect the environment. **(Emotional Development)**
- understand various aspects of society and my role to protect it. **(Social Responsibility)**
- give my opinion on other students' contributions respectfully. **(Collaboration)**
- Engages with and responds to creative works from art, music or literature. **(Creative Thinking)**
- Identifies the basic structure of an argument. **(Critical Thinking)**
- Identifies ways in which personal habits and behaviour have the capacity to affect the environment. **(Social Responsibilities)**

Vocabulary in Context
Lesson Aim: I can talk about ways of protecting the environment.

Warmer

Ask students to list which main environmental issues we are facing nowadays around the world. Encourage each student to write down at least four issues and describe them briefly to a partner. Ask them to reflect on how society is dealing with environmental issues.

Flipped Classroom Check

Have students sit in smaller groups and share their facts, opinions, and questions. Allow them some time for this discussion and encourage them to try to answer each other's questions.

4.01 Audioscript pT140

Target Vocabulary

cut down	/kʌt.daʊn/
destroy	/dɪ'strɔɪ/
pollute	/pə'lut/
protect	/prə'tekt/
recycle	/ri'saɪ·kəl/
reduce	/rɪ'dus/
reuse	/ri'juz/
throw away	/θroʊ.ə'weɪ/
turn off	/tɜrn.ɔf/
waste	/weɪst/

1 4.01 Have students look at the images. Elicit what they think each image portrays. Have volunteers call out words for each image (ask them not to look at the words above the images, yet). Read the words together with the students. Individually, have them complete the posters with the words. Play the audio to check their work. Have students repeat the words, paying attention to pronunciation and intonation. Have them look at the images again and ask which they believe is the most endangering for our future. Have them justify their answers.

VOCABULARY IN CONTEXT

THE ENVIRONMENT

1 4.01 **Complete the posters with the words/phrases below. Then listen, check, and repeat the words/phrases.**

• cut down • destroy • pollute • protect • ~~recycle~~
• reduce • reuse • throw away • turn off • waste

[1] Recycle your trash. Everybody's doing it.

Think of our future. Don't [2] cut down the trees!

[3] Turn off the lights. Don't [4] waste energy.

Be part of the solution, not part of the pollution! Bike more, [5] pollute less.

Don't feed the fish on plastic. [6] Protect our rivers and oceans!

Free our planet! [7] Reduce the use of plastic.

There's no Planet B. Don't [8] destroy the environment!

Don't [9] throw away things you can [10] reuse another day!

42

Vocabulary in Context
Lesson Aim: I can talk about ways of protecting the environment.

2 Have volunteers read sentences 1–6. Individually, ask students to circle the correct word in each sentence. Check their work in pairs.

3 Put students into pairs for this activity. Read through the words and the headlines with the students. Have students choose the best alternative for each headline. Have them check in pairs. Then ask: *What are the headlines referring to?* Have students make up a headline using the words/phrases they did not use in the activity.

4 Draw students' attention to the chart. Read the headings with them. In pairs, have students complete the chart with the actions. Have them add any other actions they believe necessary. Have them share their ideas.

USE IT!

5 Ask students to work in groups of three. Have them review the vocabulary used in the videos, the Warmer, and Exercises 1–4. Have them observe the images and encourage them to come up with a motivating slogan for each image. Have them share their work.

Homework

Workbook page 125, Exercises 1 and 2

Practice Extra

Unit 4

Fast Finishers

Puzzles and Games page 103, Exercise 3

2 Circle the correct options.

1. We *pollute* / *(recycle)* most of the trash in our house.
2. My sisters never *waste* / *(turn off)* the light when they leave their bedroom.
3. Mr. Kim wanted to *(cut down)* / *reduce* a tree in his yard, but he changed his mind.
4. People can *reduce* / *(reuse)* plastic bottles in different ways.
5. Hey, don't *pollute* / *(throw away)* that box! I can use it for an art project.
6. The school started a campaign to *destroy* / *(protect)* the life in the local river.

3 Complete the newspaper headlines with the correct form of the words/phrases below. There are two extra words/phrases.

• cut down • destroy • pollute • protect • recycle • reduce

1 TESTS CONFIRM: CHEMICAL COMPANY pollutes GREENVILLE RIVER

2 Mayor Robbins: "Factories must not destroy the life in our river!"

3 Company president promises to reduce Greenville River pollution to zero

4 "Protect our river!" is the slogan of Greenville Middle School eco movement

4 Complete the chart with the actions below.

• ~~cut down forests~~ • destroy the environment • pollute the air • protect wild animals
• recycle trash • reduce CO_2 in the atmosphere • reuse paper • throw away batteries
• turn off electronic devices • waste energy

Good For The Environment	Bad For The Environment
protect wild animals	cut down forests
recycle trash	destroy the environment
reduce CO_2 in the atmosphere	pollute the air
reuse paper	throw away batteries
turn off electronic devices	waste energy

USE IT!

5 Work in groups of three. Write slogans for the posters.

Students' own answers

WORKBOOK p.125 PRACTICE EXTRA

Extension

Have students stay in the same groups of three as in Exercise 5. Encourage students to review the content and the vocabulary learned in Unit 4 so far. Tell students they will create pamphlets to spread around the school, encouraging other students to take care of the planet. Tell them they should make students aware of the small actions they can take that will make all the difference for the future of our planet. Encourage students to use images, slogans, and captivating sentences.

Reading
Lesson Aim: I can read and interpret an infographic about a "green" house.

Warmer

Encourage students to think about their houses. Ask: *Do you believe your house is environmentally friendly?* In pairs, ask students to list each of the different rooms in their houses and think of ideas that could be done in each room to make it more environmentally friendly. Have them build a mind map portraying their ideas. Ask them to share their work. Have them reflect more deeply and ask: *What is an eco-friendly house?*

4.02 Audioscript pT141

1 Have students look at the infographic. Elicit from students if they think an infographic is the best way to represent something. Have them justify their answer. Ask: *When and why do we use infographics? What are their main elements?* Have them focus on the design and images. Invite them to read the alternatives in Exercise 1 and check the best option. Ask: *Have you ever been inside an eco-friendly house?*

2 **4.02** Ask students to read the sentences 1–8. Play the audio and have them listen and read the infographic at the same time. Have them match the sentences to the sections in the infographic. Check answers with the class.

3 Have volunteers read the sentences out loud while the rest of the class thinks whether they believe these actions can really happen in the near future. Have them call *true* or *false* out loud. Then have them read the infographic again and write *T* (true) or *F* (false) according to the information they read. Have them compare their answers in pairs.

THINK!

Draw two columns on the board and write down *Pros* in the first and *Cons* in the second. In pairs, have students write down the pros and cons of living in an eco-friendly house. Then, have them look at the infographic again and list what they like best about the house shown. Have them share their pros and cons list and their favorite features of the house.

READING

We all know we need to take action now so that we still have a planet in the future. And we can start at home! According to experts, houses in the next decades will be greener and more efficient. Check out some features:

A Houses will have a **"living wall"** – a wall covered with plants. If a living wall is 20 m², it converts 46 kg of carbon dioxide into oxygen per year! If you have a living wall in your house, you will help to clean the air.

B A living wall will also work as a **vegetable garden** to supply fresh, healthy food for the kitchen.

C Houses will have a **water tank** to **collect rainwater for the garden and the toilets**. If people use less water from the public water system, they will save money and help the local ecosystem.

D **Garages** will **provide electricity for the family car** – in fact, experts predict that 57% of cars will be electric in 2040. If this really happens, we will have much less air pollution.

H All the **energy** will come from **solar panels on the roof** of the house.

G People will use **recycled wood and glass** to build their houses.

F People will **control the whole house from their smartphones or tablets**. And if you forget to turn off a light, sensors will do it for you!

E We will use more electricity than today because **many people will work from home**. This new lifestyle will demand **office spaces** at home with **the latest technology**.

1 Look at the infographic. Check (✓) the best title.

1 ○ Advantages and Disadvantages of Electric Cars
2 ○ How to Grow Plants in Your Garden
3 ✓ This is How Your "Green" House Will Look in 2040!

2 4.02 Read and listen to the infographic. Match 1–8 with sections A–H.

People living in houses in 2040 will …

1 produce their own electricity. H
2 store water from the rain. C
3 grow things to eat. B
4 have a computer system to control the house. F
5 have office spaces to work in. E
6 reuse materials for building. G
7 probably use electricity for driving. D
8 have plants on the walls. A

3 Read the infographic again. Write *T* (true) or *F* (false).

1 We can change our habits to save resources. T
2 We'll use new materials to build greener houses. F
3 Houses will help save water and money. T
4 In the future, people will not work at home. F
5 People will be able to turn off their lights from anywhere in the world. T

THINK!

What feature of the house in the infographic do you like best? Can you think of any disadvantages of living in this house?

44

WORKBOOK p.127

Homework

Workbook page 127, Exercises 1, 2, and 3

1 Read through the charts with students. Encourage them to look back at the infographic on page 44 to help them complete the charts. Check answers with the class by having a volunteer read out the sentences. Draw students' attention to the difference in sentence structure between the zero and first conditionals.

2 Encourage students to use the first grammar chart in Exercise 1 to help them. Individually, have students read the prompts and build sentences using the zero conditional. Draw their attention to the verb tenses they are using.

3 Encourage students to use the second grammar chart in Exercise 1 to help them. Read through the verbs with them and have a volunteer read the sentences 1–6. Individually, have them complete the sentences using the correct verb tense. Have them check their answers in pairs. Have them compare the sentences in Exercise 2 with the ones in Exercise 3.

USE IT!

4 Read through the sentence starters with the students. Have them refer to the second chart in Exercise 1 to remind themselves how to write sentences using the first conditional. Encourage them to complete the sentences individually so they are true for them.

5 Model the activity using the examples in the speech bubbles. Put students into pairs to take turns sharing their sentences. Have some students share their sentences with the whole class.

Grammar Game

Hand out a sheet of blank paper to each student. Have each student write a sentence starter using the first conditional at the top of the page. Have students pass the sheet of paper to the students on their right (or in front of them). This student must complete the sentence using the correct verb tense and write another sentence starter following the same topic as the sentence they received. It is sort of like a chain story but using conditionals. Repeat the procedure until the sheet of paper has been passed to at least six students. Then have students read the "story" out loud.

UNIT 4

LANGUAGE IN CONTEXT

1 Look at the examples below. Complete the sentences from the infographic.

Zero Conditional	
***If* Clause (*If* + Simple Present)**	**Result Clause (Simple Present)**
If a living wall [1] is 20 m²,	it [2] converts 46 kg of carbon dioxide into oxygen.
If the air **becomes** polluted,	it **has** serious effects on people's health.

First Conditional	
***If* Clause (*If* + Simple Present)**	**Result Clause (*will/won't* + Infinitive)**
If you [3] forget to turn off a light,	sensors [4] will do that for you!
If people [5] use less water,	they [6] will save money.
If people **drive** electric cars,	we **won't need** so much oil.

2 Write zero conditional sentences using the verbs in parentheses.

1 plants (not have) water – they (die)
If plants don't have water, they die.
2 I (go) shopping – I (not use) plastic bags
If I go shopping, I don't use plastic bags.
3 my grandpa (visit) us on Sundays – he (not use) his car
If my grandpa visits us on Sundays, he doesn't use his car.
4 it (rain) a lot – our water tank (collect) 50 liters of water
If it rains a lot, our water tank collects 50 liters of water.
5 a house (have) solar panels – it (produce) its own energy
If a house has solar panels, it produces its own energy.
6 we (buy) water bottles – we always (recycle) them
If we buy water bottles, we always recycle them.

3 Complete the first conditional sentences with the correct form of the verbs below.

• be • ~~buy~~ • cut down • not be • ride • work

1 If my aunt buys an electric car, she will need electricity in her garage.
2 There will be less traffic on the roads if more people work from home in the future.
3 If Lucas leaves home early, he won't be late for school.
4 If people ride bikes to school and work, they will reduce transportation costs.
5 Cities will be cleaner if everyone recycles their trash.
6 If our neighbor cuts down that big tree on our street, my mother will plant a new one.

USE IT!

4 Complete the first conditional sentences with your own ideas.

1 If I live in a "green" house in 2040, Students' own answers
2 I'll be happy in 2040 if ....
3 If I don't have much homework tomorrow, ...
4 I'll .... if it doesn't rain on the weekend.

5 Work in pairs. Take turns sharing your ideas from Exercise 4.

If I live in a "green" house in 2040, I'll grow my own vegetables What about you?

I'll have a water tank to collect rainwater.

WORKBOOK p.124 and 126 PRACTICE EXTRA 45

Homework

Workbook page 126, Exercises 1 and 2

Practice Extra

Unit 4

Lesson Aim: I can listen and understand an interview about vegetarian diets.

Warmer

Write the phrase *Vegetarian Diet* in the central circle of a mind map on the board. Ask students to call out words related to vegetarian diets and add them to the mind map. Have them copy the final mind map onto a sheet of paper or in their exercise books. Ask them if they believe vegetarian diets are healthy, and if they could become vegetarian. Ask if there are any vegetarians in the class.

4.03–4.04 Audioscripts pT141

Target Vocabulary

agree with	/əˈgri. wɪθ/
depend on	/dɪˈpend.ɔn/
pay attention to	/peɪ. əˈten·ʃən.tə/
succeed in	/səkˈsid.ɪn/
take care of	/teɪk.keər.ʌv/
worry about	/ˈwɜr·i.əˈbɑʊt/

1 Draw students' attention to the image and elicit what they see. Read the questions orally with the students. Give them a couple of minutes to read the information in the pamphlet and have them answer the questions. Ask: *Would you go to this talk?* Have them justify their answers.

2 Have students refer to the mind map they built at the beginning of the class. In pairs, have them add more things they know about being vegetarian. Encourage them to write their feelings about it and why they believe people become vegetarians. Have them share their thoughts with the class.

3 **4.03** Play the audio. Have students compare Mariana's talk to what they wrote in Exercise 2. Play the audio again and have them add what is missing to their mind maps.

4 **4.03** Have a volunteer read sentences 1–6. Have them check the sentences mentioned in Mariana's talk from memory. Play the audio again to check their work.

LISTENING AND VOCABULARY

1 Read the pamphlet about a talk at a school. Answer the questions.

1 What is the talk about?
a vegetarian diet

2 Who will give the talk?
Mariana Lopez

3 Who will probably go to the talk?
students at Lakeview Middle School

2 Work in pairs. What do you know about being vegetarian? Write notes.

Students' own answers

3 4.03 Listen to Mariana's talk. Does she mention any of your ideas from Exercise 2?

4 4.03 Listen again. Check (✓) the ideas you hear in Mariana's talk.

1 ○ Mariana became a vegetarian to protect the environment.
2 ✓ Keeping cows, pigs, and chickens uses a lot of resources.
3 ✓ Vegetarians sometimes need extra vitamins in their diet.
4 ○ Vegetarian meals are cheap and simple to make.
5 ✓ People who become vegetarians will probably enjoy their new diet.
6 ○ Mariana's parents didn't want her to become a vegetarian.

5 4.04 Complete the sentences from the talk with the words below. Then listen, check, and repeat the phrases in bold.

• about • in • of • ~~on~~ • to • with

1 The environment and the future of our planet **depend** on reducing the use of animal products.
2 I **worry** about climate change.
3 You should **pay attention** to what you eat.
4 If you **succeed** in making this change, I think you'll soon enjoy your vegetarian diet.
5 We need to **take care** of our planet.
6 At first, your meat-loving friends and parents might not **agree** with you.

46

WORKBOOK p.125

5 **4.04** Read the prepositions with the students. Have a volunteer read sentences 1–6. Individually, have students complete the sentences with the correct prepositions. Play the audio to check their work. Write the verb plus prepositions on the board and have students make up more sentences using them.

Homework

Workbook page 125, Exercises 3 and 4

Language in Context
Lesson Aim: I can use *may* and *might* to talk about possibility.

1 If necessary, play Track 4.03 again to help students to complete the chart. Then play the track again for them to check their answers. Draw their attention to the use of the modal verbs *might* and *may*. Have students infer their meanings (possibility).

2 Ask students to read the dialogues individually to understand their context. Have them think about when they will use the negative form or the affirmative form of the modal verb. Have students complete the dialogues and compare their answers with their peers. Draw their attention to the affirmative and negative form of the verb and ask them: *When do we use the question form?* Listen to your student's comments. Have them read the *Look!* box for the answer.

LOOK!

Draw attention to the *Look!* box. Have a volunteer read the sentences in the box. Have students look back at Exercises 1 and 2 and have them form sentences using the prompts in the *Look!* box.

3 Draw students' attention to the words in parentheses. Ask for a volunteer to rewrite the first sentence and say it out loud. Have students do the rest individually. Have students compare their work.

USE IT!

4 Go through the examples with the class, drawing students' attention to the positive and negative forms. Ask students to work individually to write affirmative and negative sentences which are true for them. They should use Exercises 1–3 as reference.

5 Put students into pairs and have them share their sentences. Have them use the speech bubbles as examples. Encourage students to react to their partner's statements in order to continue the conversation.

Homework

Workbook page 126, Exercises 3 and 4

UNIT 4

LANGUAGE IN CONTEXT

1 Complete the sentences from Mariana's talk in the chart. Use the words below.

• may find • might need • might not agree

	May and *Might* for Possibility
Affirmative (+)	You [1] may find it hard to stop eating animal products. You [2] might need extra vitamins. Mariana **might discuss** vegetarian recipes in another talk.
Negative (–)	The restaurant **may not offer** vegetarian dishes on its menu. Your meat-loving friends and parents [3] might not agree with you.

2 Complete dialogues with *may (not)*, *might (not)*, and the verbs.

1 Liz: In the future, students will have classes online at home.
Hank: I'm not sure about that. They may/might not want (want) to be away from their classmates.

2 Yuki: I'm going to the park this afternoon. Do you want to come?
Sara: Hmm … I may/might need (need) to help my grandpa after school. I'll send you a message, OK?

3 Nick: Vegetarians may/might not get (get) enough vitamins in their food.
Ava: Yeah, they have to pay attention to what they eat.

LOOK!

We don't usually use *may* and *might* in questions. We can form questions using *Is it possible that …?* or *Do you think …?*.

Is it possible that people will stop eating meat in the future?

3 Rewrite the sentences using the words in parentheses (*may* or *might*).

1 There's a chance Mariana will cancel her talk today. (may)
Mariana may cancel her talk today.

2 Perhaps my parents will buy electric bikes. (might)
My parents might buy electric bikes.

3 Maybe this store doesn't open on Sundays. (might)
This store might not open on Sundays.

4 It's possible that people won't eat so much meat in the future. (may)
People may not eat so much meat in the future.

USE IT!

4 Complete the sentences with your own ideas.

1 I might (not) Students' own answers
2 Our school may (not) ……
3 My friends might (not) ……
4 The world may (not) ……

5 Work in pairs. Share your ideas from Exercise 4 and ask your partner questions.

I might study in another country next year.

Really? Where?

WORKBOOK p. 124 and 126 PRACTICE EXTRA

Practice Extra

Unit 4

Fast Finishers

Puzzles and Games page 103, Exercise 4

Extension

Ask students to write a short story about what will happen if we do not take care of the environment. The story should contain the first conditional and use the modal verbs *may* and *might*. As a suggestion, students could write it in a comic format, with images and captions. Students can refer to digital storytelling websites for help and inspiration.

Grammar Game

Divide students into five groups (A, B, C, D, and E). Tell students they are going to prepare questions on the possible changes that might take place in the next 30 years in the following topics:
A: technology, B: fashion, C: housing, D: government and laws, E: schools. Have them refer to the example from the *Look!* box for their questions and use *might* and *may* for their answers. When they have finished, have them make up a group of five with one member from groups A–E. Students will take turns to ask and answer the questions. When they have finished, they will go back to their original groups to collect all the answers.

4.2 Inspired by Nature

The video on page 49 and accompanying exercises below can be used as a lead-in to the topic of the Across the Curriculum text, or after the reading activities to complete the unit.

Summary

The video is about how nature inspires artists.

In Class

Tell students they are going to watch a video and learn how nature inspires artists around the world. Not only painters, but architects too are inspired by nature and use their creative work to remind us how nature is important. Ask: *Can you think of a creative piece that reminds you of nature? Why do you think nature inspires artists?*

Exercise 1

Ask students to watch the video to answer the questions:

1 *What animals did the artists paint in caves in France?* Check the answer with the class.
deer, horses, and bulls

2 *What is the sculpture in the video made of?* Check the answer with the class.
plastic

Exercise 2

Play the video again, write the following questions on the board and ask students to answer them.

1 Cave paintings in France portrayed
( ) beautiful rivers and cathedrals.
(✗) deer, horses, and bulls.
( ) the land or plants around them.

2 Which of the following is false?
( ) Llamas were important to the people who lived in the Atacama Desert.
(✗) Landscapes are not an inspiration for artists.
( ) Artists are trying to teach people about environmental problems through art.

3 How much does the whale sculpture in London weigh?
250kg

Ask students to watch the video again and make up two more questions to ask their partners.

ACROSS THE CURRICULUM

LITERATURE

Poetry and the Environment: HAIKUS

Invented by the Japanese, haikus became popular in the western world in the 20th century. Nowadays people all over the world read, write, and love these short but powerful poems.

Haikus have three lines, but their organization is not so simple. Traditional haikus must have exactly 17 syllables, like this:

- line 1 – five syllables
- line 2 – seven syllables
- line 3 – five syllables

They are usually about nature and combine powerful images in a few words, to connect to one of our five senses: sight, sound, smell, taste, and touch. Haikus often have a *kigo* – a word or phrase that has a connection with a period of the year. Look at the English translation of two classic haikus by Matsuo Basho:

MEET BASHO, THE HAIKU MASTER

Matsuo Basho (1644–1694) was a samurai in his early days, but spent most of his life traveling around Japan, writing and teaching poetry. His haikus gained popularity all over Japan during his lifetime. He wrote about nature and the environment and expressed strong feelings through beautifully clear, simple images.

An old silent pond ...
A frog jumps into the pond,
Splash! Silence again.

None is traveling
Here along this way but I,
This autumn evening.

Modern haikus, however, don't always have such rigid structure, but are still organized into three lines. If you want to write a haiku, you don't need to worry about the number of syllables, but you may like to stick to nature themes.

Haikus for the environment

We asked our readers to send their haikus about the environment. Look at two poems we selected for this article (you can read all the haikus in our online magazine).

We cut down the trees
They sadly fell to the ground
Birds are silent now.
Julia, 15 – Brazil

Men burn ancient trees
Melt glaciers, raise oceans
There's no Planet B.
Santiago, 14 – Colombia

48

At Home

Exercise 3

Ask students to look around their neighborhoods and places around them that use nature to create art. Ask them to pay attention to the parks, look at buildings, look at street art, etc. Have them share their findings during the next class.

Background Information

Haiku is a form of Japanese poetry made of short, unrhymed lines that evoke natural imagery. *Haikus* can come in a variety of different formats of short verses, though the most common is a three-line poem with a 5–7–5 syllable pattern.

🔊4.05 Audioscript pT141

1 Ask students if they like poems. Ask them what their initial thoughts about poems are and if they know of any famous poets. Have students read the title and look at the text on page 48. Ask: *Have you ever heard of* haikus? Listen to their comments. Have a volunteer read 1 and 2 in Exercise 1 and have them answer together as a class.

2 🔊4.05 Have volunteers read the first three paragraphs of the text in order to answer the question in Exercise 2. Draw their attention to the word: *powerful*. Have them infer the meaning. Having answered the question, play the audio for the students. As they listen, ask them to take notes about the following: *What are* haikus *normally about? Write down two more interesting facts about* haikus. Check their answers as a group.

3 Read the word/phrases with the students. Have a volunteer read sentences 1–6. Individually, have students complete the sentences with the correct words/phrases. Have students share their answers in pairs. Have students make a summary of what a *haiku* is in their own words. Encourage some students to share their summaries.

4 Ask students: *Who is the haiku master?* Listen to their answers. Have them look up the meaning of *samurai* and ask them how old the master was when he died. Individually, have students read sentences 1–3. Then have them read the small extract about the *haiku* master and check the incorrect sentence. Check their work as a class.

5 Encourage students to count the syllables in the teenagers' *haikus* at the end of the article and debate whether they are traditional *haikus*. Have them justify their answers. If time allows, have them write a *haiku* themselves. Have them read "*Haikus* for the environment" by Julia and Santiago again to stimulate creative ideas and help students to come up with their own *haiku*.

1 **Look at the magazine article. Check (✓) the people who might read it.**

1 ✓ people who like poems
2 ◯ people interested in international news

2 🔊 4.05 **Read and listen to the article. What is a haiku? Check (✓) the correct answer.**

1 ✓ a short poem 2 ◯ a poem about Japan 3 ◯ a Japanese poet

3 **Read the first part of the article again. Complete the sentences with the words/phrases below. There is one extra word/phrase.**

• ~~after 1901~~ • complicated • Japanese • modern • season • theme • three lines

1 Haikus became popular in western countries after 1901.
2 Traditionally haikus are short, but that doesn't mean they're not complicated.
3 Haikus only have three lines, but their message is powerful.
4 Traditional haikus may have a word or phrase connected to a season.
5 Modern haikus might have more than 17 syllables.
6 Nature is an important theme in most haikus.

4 **Read the information about Matsuo Basho again. Check (✓) the sentence that is not correct.**

1 ◯ When he was young, Matsuo Basho was a samurai.
2 ✓ Basho's poems became famous after his death.
3 ◯ Basho taught and wrote poems while he was traveling around Japan.

5 **Read the last part of the article again. Do the teenagers' haikus have the same structure as traditional haikus? Work with a partner to count the syllables.**

The teenagers' haikus have the same structure as traditional haikus.

WORDS IN CONTEXT

6 **Match the words with the images.**

1 pond b
2 splash a
3 melt d
4 glacier c

a
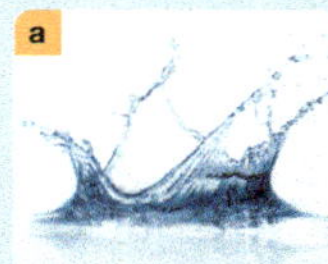
b

c

d
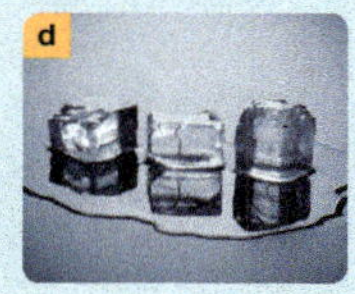

THINK!

Which of the four haikus in the article do you like best? What other poems do you like?

WEBQUEST

Learn more! Check (✓) *True* or *False*.
The theme of the World Children's Haiku Contest in 2019–2020 was animals.

◯ True ✓ False

VIDEO

4.2

1 **What animals did the artists paint in caves in France?**
2 **What is the sculpture in the video made of?**

Words in Context

6 Ask students to find the four words in the text and reread the sentences where the words appear. This should help them work out their meaning. Have them match the words to the images and check their answers with the class.

THINK!

Put students into groups to discuss the questions. Have them justify their answers. Have them share poems from other poets, both English and Brazilian. Encourage them to find poems on the Internet and share them with the class. If possible, have them share them on a collaborative platform.

WEBQUEST

Ask students to raise their hands if they have ever entered any kind on contest. Listen to student's response and have them elaborate on their answers. Invite them to research the World Children's Haiku Contest and find the correct answer. Encourage them to search on more than one website. Have them take note of previous themes as well as the latest one. Have them share their answers.

Writing

Lesson Aim: I can express my opinion in writing for an online forum.

4.06–4.07 Audioscript pT141

1 4.06 Have students look at the design of the text and ask them what kind of text they think it is and where it can be found. Have them justify their answer. Have them read the paragraph and ask: *Is it a negative opinion? Is it a positive opinion?* Have them listen to the audio to confirm their answers. Have them pay attention to the intonation used by SkepticalTeen. Ask students if they agree with him. Have them justify their answers again.

2 4.07 Draw students' attention to how GreenGirl responded to the comment. Play the audio and, again, have them pay attention to the intonation and reasons she gives for agreeing or disagreeing. Have students make a list of her main reasons for disagreeing. Have them read the comment again to check their answers.

3 Read through the words and phrases a–e with students. Individually, have students read the reply again and put the words/phrases in the correct order. Have them compare their answers in pairs.

4 Have a volunteer read the instructions 1–4. Stop after each sentence to check understanding. Put students who have a similar opinion in pairs. Ask them to make notes of their ideas and start to structure their answer. Encourage them to look back at the language learned in this unit and try to use it in their answer. Have them use modal verbs to express possibility, and the first conditional. Have them discuss actions people can take to protect the environment and encourage them to come up with an avatar and username. Have them write the first draft of their reply.

LOOK!

Draw attention to the *Look!* box and the different phrases used to express opinions. Have students look back at their first draft and see if they can make any changes using the phrases from the box.

WRITING

1 4.06 **Read and listen to an online comment about the infographic on page 44. Does it express a positive or negative opinion about it?** negative

SkepticalTeen

I think that this house of the future is a joke! In my opinion, there's nothing we can do, as individuals, to stop climate change. I strongly believe that governments and politicians should take action, not teenagers like us.

15 comments | Premium Member LIKE REPLY

2 4.07 **Now read and listen to a reply to the comment. Does the writer agree with the comment?** No, she doesn't.

GreenGirl

I don't agree with SkepticalTeen at all! I loved the infographic about the house of the future, and many of the ideas presented in it are already available – they're just too expensive for our houses at the moment! I'd say that most people might not live in that type of house in 2040, but there's so much more we can do now! I'm certain that we can all find the time and energy to do some of the things below:

- Recycle plastic bottles.
- Turn off lights and save energy.
- Reuse things instead of throwing them away.

It's our responsibility to take action to help save our planet. If we don't act, we won't have a planet to save.

27 comments | Premium Member LIKE REPLY

3 **Read the reply again and put a–e in the correct order 1–5.**

a conclusion 5
b opinion about the infographic 2
c examples of suggested actions 4
d opinion about the comment 1
e suggested actions 3

4 **Write a reply to SkepticalTeen's comment.**

1 Consider your opinion about SkepticalTeen's comment and the house in the infographic.
2 Think about possible actions governments, politicians, and teenagers can take to protect the environment.
3 Find or draw an image for your avatar and choose a username.
4 Write the first version of your reply. Use vocabulary from Unit 4.

LOOK!

When we express opinions, we can use different phrases to make it clear how we feel about the topic.

- Strong opinion → *I strongly believe that … / I'm certain that …*
- Less strong opinion → *I think that … I'd say (that) …*

5 **Switch your reply with a classmate and check his/her work. Use the checklist below.**

- ○ avatar and username
- ○ opinions about the comment and the infographic
- ○ actions people can take to protect the environment
- ○ conclusion
- ○ *may/might*
- ○ zero/first conditional

YOUR DIGITAL PORTFOLIO

Edit your reply, then publish it. Upload it to the class portfolio for everyone to see!

50

5 When students peer correct, ensure students focus on the items in the checklist. Monitor and help as necessary. Remind students to be clear and respectful in their feedback. Encourage students to listen to their peer's feedback and adjust their comment as necessary.

Your Digital Portfolio

Give students a date for uploading their work and make sure they all look at one another's work.

Practice Extra

Unit 4

Lesson Aim: I can review what I have learned and reflect on my progress.

Tell students that the exercises on these pages review the vocabulary and language they have learned in Units 3 and 4. Point out that they can also check their progress and reflect on what they can do.

Vocabulary

1 Remind students of the vocabulary related to advertisements learned in Unit 3. If necessary, have them refer to pages 32–33. In pairs, have them read the descriptions in the boxes before trying to complete them by guessing the words from context. Encourage them to cross out the letters once used. Check answers with the class. Have them discuss what the ad is trying to sell.

2 Have a volunteer read the sentences 1–5 and the words to check understanding. If necessary, have students use a dictionary. Individually, have them complete the sentences. Check their work in pairs. Encourage them to write more sentences using the words and share their work.

3 Read through the words to check understanding. Have students complete the opposite words individually, then ask volunteers to read out their words to check answers. Have them choose four words and write sentences with them.

4 Have students read through the sentences 1–5. Draw their attention to the words in the boxes and have them match them to make expressions. Individually, have them replace the words in bold in the sentences with the correct expressions. Have them make up more sentences using the expressions.

REVIEW
UNITS 3 AND 4

VOCABULARY

1 Complete the descriptions in the boxes with advertising words. Use the letters below.

E T R O R T I M H M R E D C P E O E U R T U V N C B I T R G E D S T A L O P D S A E R E A E R A E N T S P L O

A an [1] advertisement to [2] persuade consumers to buy something

B a creative [3] headline to [4] attract consumers' attention

C a description of the [5] product

D something that the company [6] promises to do

E a stylish [7] logo

Ding-dong! Who's at the door?

Organic fruit and vegetables from local farmers. You choose what you want and when you want it. We'll bring it directly to your door.

HealthInABox4U (312) 679-5678
www.healthinaboxforyou.com

2 Complete the sentences with the words/phrases below.

• ~~cost~~ • invest • label • on sale • own • sell

1 These secondhand clothes are good value: they cost less than new ones from a famous label.
2 I own a few gadgets, but my favorite ones are my headphones.
3 This T-shirt is too expensive. I'll wait until it's on sale.
4 They sell their jewelry in the local markets.
5 I'm going to invest some money in my friend's company.

3 Write the opposites of verbs 1–5.

1 clean p o l l u t e
2 plant c u t d o w n
3 protect d e s t r o y
4 recycle t h r o w a w a y
5 save w a s t e

4 Make expressions with a word from each box. Then replace the words/phrases in bold in sentences 1–5 with the expressions.

• ~~agree~~ • depend • pay attention • take care • worry

• about • of • on • to • ~~with~~

1 I **have the same opinion as** Francisco. agree with
2 All of us should **protect** the environment. take care of
3 Do you **think about the problems of** the planet? worry about
4 **Listen carefully to** the speaker and you'll understand. Pay attention to
5 I **need the support of** my parents for money. depend on

51

Lesson Aim: I can review what I have learned and reflect on my progress.

Language in Context

5 Remind students of the modal verbs *have to* and *must* (affirmative and negative forms). Have a volunteer read through sentences 1–4. Ask them to infer from context whether the verb would be affirmative or negative. Have students refer to the charts on page 35, if necessary. Individually, have them complete the sentences with the correct option. Check answers as a class.

6 Review zero and first conditionals with students. Have them refer to the charts on page 45, if necessary. Ask students to observe the instruction in parentheses. Individually, have them complete the sentences. To check answers, invite volunteers to read out the sentences.

7 Draw students' attention to the modal verbs in the first box. Remind them of the meanings of *may* and *might*. Have them give you examples of sentences using the modal verbs. Invite them to look at the images and the verbs in the second box. Have them complete affirmative or negative statements, using the modal verbs, according to the images. Check their work as a class. Encourage students to write affirmative and negative statements using modal verbs about their school.

Check Your Progress

This section gives students an opportunity to reflect on what they have learned. Read each statement with the class. Elicit examples and/or information students remember related to it. Alternatively, students could go through the statements in pairs or groups. If necessary, have them go back to the relevant unit to review each topic. Students then do the task in the Check Your Progress box individually. When they finish, ask: *What can you practice more? What is easy/difficult/interesting?* Invite students to give feedback.

LANGUAGE IN CONTEXT

5 **Complete the sentences with the words below.**

• doesn't have to • ~~has to~~ • have to • must • must not

1 My father has to fly to the US tomorrow for an interview.
2 Gisela's parents insist on some rules in their house. For example, Gisela must turn off the lights when she leaves her bedroom. And she must not be on the Internet for more than two hours a day.
3 Philip doesn't have to wake up early tomorrow, so he's going to watch the late movie before going to bed.
4 Do you have to get a visa to travel to Brazil?

6 **Write zero and first conditional sentences with the correct form of the prompts and *if*.**

1 fish / die – they / not have / enough oxygen / in their water (zero)
Fish die if they don't have enough oxygen in their water.
2 we / turn off / the lights – we / save / electricity (zero)
If we turn off the lights, we save electricity.
3 you / read / this book – you / know / how to make a cake (first)
If you read this book, you will know how to make a cake.
4 people / not buy / this product – the company / not reduce / the price (first)
People won't buy this product if the company doesn't reduce the price.

7 **Complete the sentences using words/phrases from both boxes below.**

• don't have to • have to • may • might • ~~must not~~

• be • drive • see • stop • ~~use~~

1 You must not use cell phones.
2 You have to stop here.
3 You may/might see cows on the road.
4 You don't have to drive so slowly now.
5 The road may/might be dangerous on a rainy day.

CHECK YOUR PROGRESS

I CAN…

- talk about ads and money
- use *have to, don't have to, must,* and *must not*
- talk about the environment
- use the zero and first conditionals, and *may* and *might*.

LEARN TO LEARN

Make a sticky note dictionary

Write new vocabulary on sticky notes. On the other side, write translations of the words.
Read the note, say its translation, and check.

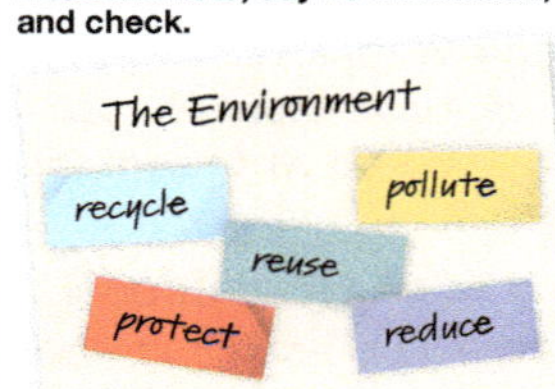

52

Learn to Learn

Throughout the course, students do a variety of *learn to learn* activities, which offer them techniques for retaining vocabulary. Point to the images of the sticky notes. Ask them: *How can we remember new words from Units 3 and 4 using sticky notes?* Have them read the idea in the box and encourage them to think of different ideas of how to use sticky notes. Elicit ideas.

You could also start a word wall in class using sticky notes. Have students add words to the word wall at any time and encourage them to look at them at the beginning of each lesson. Have them also write the words in their vocabulary notebooks. Encourage them to look them up in a dictionary, write a translation, use them in context, and/or draw a picture. You can also suggest students keep a word wall at home using sticky notes.

Lesson Aim: I can talk about my internet behavior.

Warmer

Ask students to imagine their life without the Internet. In pairs, have them list three facts in their lives that would definitely be different. Have them share their ideas.

THINK!

1 Ask students to look at the image and ask: *What do you see?* (girl, thoughts, busy mind). Then ask: *How does the photo make you feel?* Ask students if their online life is very different from their offline life.

2 Encourage students to use an interactive survey platform to do this activity. Have them share their words.

Put Your Phone Down!

5.1

Summary

The video is about the consequences of being online all the time.

In Class

Draw a mind map on the board with the word *Cell Phone* as the middle bubble. Have students think of positive and negative aspects and share their ideas with the class. Ask: *Do you spend too much time online?*

Exercise 1

Ask students to watch the video to answer the following questions:

1 *What is the most important effect of being online all the time?* Check the answer with the class.
Nobody wants to be around you.

2 *Where can you find sidewalks with "smartphone lanes"?* Check the answer with the class.
China

Exercise 2

Play the video again and write the following true or false sentences on the board for students to answer. Then, ask them to make up two more questions to ask their partners.

1 People don't only show you the good times on the Internet, they show the really bad times, too.
False. "People only show you the good stuff, and you think everyone's having a fantastic time … except you!"

2 Wearing headphones can be dangerous, because you can't hear cars.
True.

3 People have accidents and get hurt a lot while using their phones.
True.

Have students share moments when they believe they should not use their cell phones, but they do.

At Home

Exercise 3

Have students monitor their use of their cell phone for one week. Have them share their times and rank them for the most to the least time.

Resources

- Teacher's worksheets Unit 5
- Test Generator Unit 5
- Practice Extra Unit 5
- Workbook pages 128–131
- Puzzles and Games page 104

Flipped Classroom

Ask students to search the Internet for three amazing headlines that catch their attention. Tell students the headlines must be about different topics (sports, politics, science, etc).

Unit Aims

Cambridge Life Competencies Framework

I can …

- use simple techniques to start, maintain, and close conversations of various lengths to talk about my online behaviors. **(Communication)**
- understand essential grammatical terms and concepts: using the second conditional and indefinite pronouns to talk about my online self. **(Learning to Learn)**
- use strategies and techniques for improving my English (e.g., mind maps to organize my thoughts). **(Learning to Learn)**
- analyze causes and effects of problems related to my digital footprint. **(Critical Thinking)**
- state opposing opinions in a respectful way when talking about online behavior. **(Emotional Development)**
- make informed choices about my digital footprint. **(Social Responsibility)**
- understand how personal habits and behavior have the capacity to affect others and the environment. **(Social Responsibility)**

Warmer

Divide the class into two or more teams. Write a noun on the board. Give each team a minute to write down as many adjectives as they can to describe this noun. Encourage students to be creative. Teams get one point for every adjective that is appropriate, and two points if they are the only team to come up with it.

Flipped Classroom Check

Put students into smaller groups and have them share their headlines. Ask them to classify the headlines into topics. Have groups read out the most interesting headlines and ask them to notice whether the headlines have strong adjectives or not.

5.01 Audioscript pT141

Target Vocabulary

brilliant	/ˈbrɪl.jənt/
crazy	/ˈkreɪ.zi/
freezing	/ˈfri.zɪŋ/
huge	/hjudʒ/
shocking	/ˈʃɑk.ɪŋ/
silly	/ˈsɪl.i/
spectacular	/spekˈtæk.jə.lər/
ugly	/ˈʌg.li/
useless	/ˈjus.ləs/
weird	/wɪərd/

1 **5.01** Invite students to look at the images and headlines and infer what they will be about. Read through the words with them to check understanding. Individually, have students read the headlines and complete them with the missing words. Play the audio for them to check their work. Have them repeat the words to check pronunciation and intonation.

VOCABULARY IN CONTEXT

STRONG ADJECTIVES

1 5.01 **Complete the headlines with the words below. Then listen, repeat, and check the words.**

- brilliant
- ~~crazy~~
- freezing
- huge
- shocking
- silly
- spectacular
- ugly
- useless
- weird

LinkSocial your social media 34,657 followers

Man breaks his own record
You'd have to be [1] crazy to do this!

Brr! It's [2] freezing out there!
◀ Emergency services have to work in difficult conditions

Talking toothbrushes!
A [3] brilliant invention or a [4] useless product?

Nature
10 [5] weird things that science can't explain

1 Mystery in European forests: no one understands what causes these lights to appear every year.

Fruit&Veg4allofus
@Fruit&Veg4allofus
[6] Ugly vegetables shouldn't go to waste
Fruit & veggies don't have to be perfect. #stopwaste #uglyfruitishealthyfruit
2 days ago

Bad acting and a [7] silly story
Don't waste your time watching this movie

NEWS

[8] Huge hurricane hits US coast!

[9] Shocking scenes! Volcano destroys thousands of homes

[10] spectacular journeys in South America
Discover the continent's amazing natural beauty

54

Vocabulary in Context
Lesson Aim: I can use adjectives to express my opinions about something.

2 Draw students' attention to the words written in the charts and the headings. Check understanding. Read through the words from Exercise 1 with the students. In pairs, have them complete the chart with the corresponding words. Check answers with the class.

LOOK!

Draw attention to the *Look!* box. Have a volunteer read the sentence. Ask students to write two sentences using words with the same meaning, but intensifying their opinion in the second version of the sentence. Encourage them to use the words from Exercise 2 and also check the dictionary for others.

3 Go through the headings in the chart. Individually, have students classify the words from Exercise 1. Check answers with the class. In pairs, have them add one more adjective to each column.

USE IT!

4 Look at the images 1–3 with students and have them describe what they see. Have them write an opinion about the use of technology in each of the images. Have them use the words from Exercise 3.

5 Have student sit in groups of three. Model the activity with students using the examples in the speech bubbles. Have them follow the same procedure, using their opinions from Exercise 4. When students have finished, ask them to report their opinions to the class.

Homework

Workbook page 129, Exercises 1 and 2

Practice Extra

Unit 5

Fast Finishers

Puzzles and Games page 104, Exercise 1

2 Complete the charts with the words in Exercise 1.

	Same Meaning
1 very strange	weird
2 very large	huge
3 insane	crazy
4 of no use	useless
5 very surprising	shocking
6 very intelligent	brilliant
7 very cold	freezing

	Opposite Meaning
8 pretty	ugly
9 smart	silly
10 dull	spectacular

LOOK!
Large means *big*.
I have a **large** dog, but my cousin has a small one.

3 Complete the chart with the words in Exercise 1. Add one more adjective in each column. Use a dictionary if necessary.

Positive Opinion	Negative Opinion	No Opinion
brilliant	crazy, freezing, shocking,	huge
spectacular	silly, useless, ugly, weird	traditional, unusual
great, wonderful	terrible, awful	

USE IT!

4 Write three different adjectives from Exercise 3 to describe the use of technology in images 1–3.

1

Students' own answers

2

3

5 Work in small groups. Discuss your opinion of the use of technology in the images in Exercise 4.

I think using a laptop underwater a brilliant idea.

Me too.

Really? I think it's silly.

WORKBOOK p.129 PRACTICE EXTRA

Extension

Divide students into smaller groups. Encourage students to write a short paragraph using as many adjectives as possible to describe one of the following situations or things:

- your day so far
- a game you played yesterday
- a new gadget you learned about
- a new series you are watching

Guide students into giving descriptive opinions. Afterwards, ask: *What adjectives did the group use to describe (the new gadget)?*

Reading
Lesson Aim: I can read, understand, and give my opinion about the use of cell phones in the classroom.

Warmer

In pairs, ask students to list the main things they do with their cell phones. Have them list at least five things. Have them name the places they normally use their cell phone. Make a quick survey of the most popular things they use their phones for, and the top location. If possible, use a digital tool for this survey.

5.02 Audioscript pT141

1 Focus students' attention on the text's title, subheadings, image, and design. Ask: *How would you answer the title's question?* Have them justify their answers. Read through the questions 1–2 and the options. Ask students to skim the text without reading in detail to complete the exercise. Check answers with the class.

2 5.02 Have a volunteer read through the sentences 1–4 to check understanding. Then have them read the text in detail to find the answers. Have them check the sentences individually. Play the audio for them to check their answers. When you check answers, you can pause the audio after each point is mentioned.

3 Have a volunteer read the instructions 1–2 so students know what they are supposed to do while reading. Have them read Eduardo's comment and underline and circle the points mentioned. Check the answers first in pairs and then as a class. Have students write their own reply to the post.

THINK!

Divide students into smaller groups. Ask students to brainstorm and make a list of all the pros and cons of allowing students to use cell phones in the classroom. Have students share their ideas. Have them also come up with problems and solutions.

Homework

Workbook page 131, Exercises 1, 2, and 3

READING

WHAT DO YOU THINK?
Join the debate

ARTS&CULTURE | **EDUCATION** | SCIENCE&TECH | SPORTS | OTHER

SHOULD SCHOOLS ALLOW CELL PHONES IN THE CLASSROOM?

Around the world, more and more teenagers have cell phones and use them often. Cell phones can bring excellent learning opportunities, but they can also cause problems. Some countries (for example, France, Israel, and parts of China) don't allow any use of phones while students are at school, but this debate is very much alive.
Posted by: **Marion Smith**

Eduardo Morales, 2 days ago
I'm a high school teacher. Students wouldn't be able to concentrate if they had phones in the classroom: they would check their social media all the time. Some people say that cell phones can make it easier for students to share information and ideas in class, but I think that's ridiculous. Teenagers already spend too much time on their phones: if we allowed cell phones in class, students would spend even less time in face-to-face interactions. It's important to learn to work with people, not with electronic screens. Allowing cell phones in class is a crazy idea. If it was a good idea, most schools would allow them.

Sophie Graham, 1 day ago
I'm a principal. But before that I'm a teacher. I know a cell phone can bring huge benefits for students: they can use their phones as calculators and cameras, they can go on the Internet to look for information, read news stories, or use a dictionary. However, studies show that most students use cell phones in class to do other things not related to schoolwork. That's why we don't allow them in our school. If students didn't spend time texting and playing games, I wouldn't be against cell phones in class.

1 Look at the text. Check (✓) the correct answers.

1 Where is the text published?
a in a high school blog
b in a magazine about technology
c on a website for discussing ideas ✓

2 What is the text about?
a opinions about using cell phones in class ✓
b advantages of having cell phones in schools
c about how students use cell phones at school

2 5.02 Read and listen to the text. Check (✓) the correct answers.

1 Marion thinks that using cell phones in class …
a is a good idea. b is a bad idea. c can be both good and bad. ✓
2 French schools … the use of cell phones in class.
a prohibit ✓ b support c don't have rules about
3 In …, students must not use cell phones.
a Eduardo's school b Sophie's school c Eduardo and Sophie's schools ✓
4 … doesn't see anything positive in allowing students to use phones in class.
a Marion b Eduardo ✓ c Sophie

3 Read Eduardo's comment again and answer the questions.

1 Underline the argument Eduardo disagrees with. 2 Circle Eduardo's opinion of the argument.

THINK!
In your opinion, should schools allow students to use cell phones in the classroom? Why / Why not?

56

WORKBOOK p.131

Language in Context
Lesson Aim: I can use the second conditional to express my opinion.

1 Ask students to look back at the website on page 56 to complete the sentences in the chart. Have them read through the "*If clause*" column and observe the verb tense used. Have them do the same for the "Result Clause" column. Have them answer the last two questions in the chart. Explain to students the use of *were* rather than *was* for *I* and *he/she/it*. *If I were* is appropriate in the subjunctive mood, e.g.: *If I were you, I would not go to the movies tonight. If it were lighter, I would see better. If I was* is only acceptable in conditional past-tense sentences: *I apologize if I was rude. I will let you know if I was accepted.* (both situations could have happened)

2 Point out to students that the "*If clause*" always has a verb in the simple past and the second part of the sentence, the result clause, has *would* (affirmative or negative) + infinitive. Have students read through the sentence halves 1–6 and a–f. Ask them to underline the verb in the simple past and circle *would/wouldn't* + infinitive before matching the sentence halves. Have them check in pairs.

3 Go through the example with students. Draw their attention to the verb in the simple past and *would* + infinitive. Have them look at the verbs in parentheses and complete the sentences using the correct verb tense. Check their work in pairs.

LANGUAGE IN CONTEXT

1 Look at the examples below. Complete the sentences from the opinion website.

Second Conditional

If Clause (*If* + Simple Past)	Result Clause (*would/wouldn't* + Infinitive)
If it [1] was a good idea,	most schools [2] would allow cell phones.
If we [3] allowed cell phones in class,	students [4] would spend less time in face-to-face interactions.
If students [5] didn't spend time texting and playing games,	I [6] wouldn't be against cell phones in class.

Questions (?)

If you **had** the money, **would** you **buy** a new cell phone every year?
How **would** you **feel** if your friend **stopped** speaking to you?

2 Underline the simple past verbs and circle *would/wouldn't* + infinitive in 1–6 and a–f. Then match the two parts of the sentences.

1 If I had a camera, c
2 If you wrote blog posts, f
3 Your friends would be happier a
4 What would you do d
5 If the students didn't have a break between lessons, b
6 If you were a parent, e

a if they spent less time watching videos.
b they wouldn't be able to concentrate in class.
c I would become a vlogger.
d if people wrote bad comments about you online?
e would you allow your teenage child to have a debit card?
f I'm sure they would be brilliant.

3 Complete the sentences with the correct form of the verbs in parentheses.

1 If I had (have) more time, I would take singing lessons.
2 If I knew (know) how to cook, I would make healthy snacks and sell them.
3 If we didn't throw away (not throw away) so much stuff, there would be less pollution.
4 Would you live (live) abroad if you had a chance?
5 Your collage would look (look) nicer if you added (add) some black and white images.
6 I don't have a smartphone, but if I had (have) one, I wouldn't use (not use) it to buy things.

LOOK!
To talk about unreal conditions, we use *would/wouldn't* (not *will/won't*).
If I had more time, I **would learn** to play the piano.

USE IT!

4 Work in pairs. Take turns asking and answering questions using the second conditional. Use the ideas below or your own ideas.

• be/fashion designer • have/airplane • live/abroad • own/skatepark • speak/five languages

Where would you work if you were a fashion designer?
I'd have my own business and work for myself.

WORKBOOK p.128 and 130 PRACTICE EXTRA

LOOK!

Draw attention to the *Look!* box. Ask: *When do we use the second conditional?* Encourage them to look back at the zero and first conditionals and compare the situations in which they are used with the second conditional. Listen to their answers and ask them to confirm their ideas by reading the sentences and examples in the chart in Exercise 1. Remind them that in the second conditional we use the verb *would* and not *will*, e.g.: ~~*It will be better if you could wear sports clothes.*~~ *It would be better if you could wear sports clothes.*

USE IT!

4 Draw attention to the examples in the speech bubbles. Have students read through the prompts. Model the activity with a student. Put students into pairs and tell them to ask and answer their questions using the second conditional. When they finish, ask students to report back to the class about what their partner told them.

Grammar Game

In pairs, invite students to play the *Consequences* game. Have Students A say or write a sentence in the second conditional about themselves. If necessary, provide a list of possible sentence stems for them such as: *If I were not in this class now, (I'd still be in bed).* Then Students B should continue and say or write a consequence to that action like: *If you were still in bed now, you wouldn't have time to study.* Then Students A continue: *If I had no time to study, I would fail my exams.* Have them continue until they reach a certain number of steps (usually eight to ten is a good number) or come to a natural conclusion.

Homework

Workbook page 130, Exercises 1 and 2

Practice Extra

Unit 5

Listening and Vocabulary
Lesson Aim: I can understand a chat about digital footprint.

Warmer

Begin the class with a KWL chart. Draw a KWL chart on the board consisting of three columns with headings: 1) *What I Know*, 2) *What I Want to Know*, and 3) *What I Learned*. Write the phrase *digital footprint* on the board. In pairs, have students draw the chart in their notebooks and complete the first two columns regarding the phrase. Make sure you refer to the chart during this unit to update the information and ensure students' questions have been answered. Invite students to complete the last column at the end of the unit.

5.03–5.04 Audioscripts pT142

Target Vocabulary

download	/ˈdaʊnˌloʊd/
file	/faɪl/
password	/ˈpæsˌwɜrd/
post	/poʊst/
screenshot	/ˈskriːn.ʃɑːt/
search	/sɜrtʃ/
tweet	/twiːt/
upload	/ʌpˈloʊd/

1 5.03 Have students look at the icons and have a volunteer read the words. Have students write the corresponding word next to each number. After they finish, play the audio for them to check and repeat. Encourage them to make up sentences that are true for them using the words.

2 Ask students to analyze the image and predict what is happening in the photograph. Ask a volunteer to read the three questions to check understanding and have students answer them. Have students compare their predictions in pairs.

3 5.04 Play the audio and have students check their answers in Exercise 2. Ask: *Did anyone predict correctly?* Have them add two more things they heard on the audio which they believe are important.

4 5.04 Read through the diagram with the students. Have them complete it by memory. Then play the audio for them to add any other necessary information. Have them compare the diagram to the KWL chart they did in the Warmer. Have them add any other information or questions to their KLW chart. Have them compare their charts and diagrams with a partner.

5 Have a volunteer read sentences 1–6 to check understanding. Individually, have students write *T* (true) or *F* (false) and ask them to compare their answers in pairs. Have students read the questions they wrote in the second column of the KLW chart to see whether all their questions were answered. If not, have them ask their friends or research on the Internet. Have them complete the last column with all they learned about digital footprints.

Homework

Workbook page 129, Exercises 3 and 4

LISTENING AND VOCABULARY

1 5.03 **Label the icons with the words below. Then listen, check, and repeat.**

• download • file • ~~password~~ • post • search • screenshot • tweet • upload

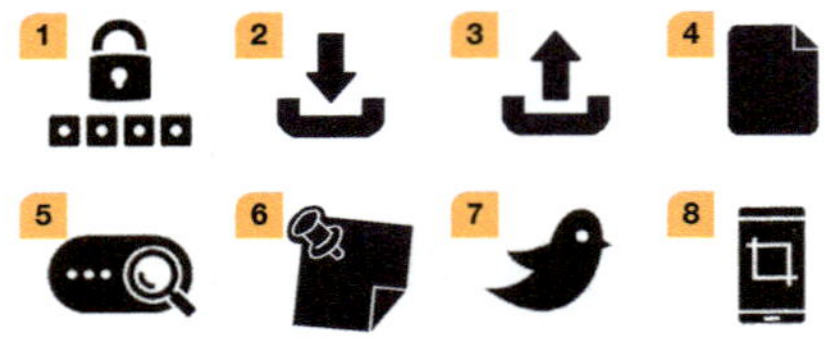

1 password 5 search
2 download 6 post
3 upload 7 tweet
4 file 8 screenshot

2 **Look at the image and answer the questions with your predictions.**

1 Who is the young woman wearing glasses?
She's an ex-student / a girl who was in this class three years ago.
2 Where is she?
She's in a school classroom.
3 Why is she there?
She's there to give a talk to the class.

3 5.04 **Listen, check, and correct your answers to Exercise 2.**

4 5.04 **Listen again and complete the diagram with notes about the main ideas. Compare your notes with a partner.**

DIGITAL FOOTPRINT

1 What is it? information we leave online about what we do and where we go

2 How do we produce it? when we text, tweet, download or upload a file, search for something, like something.

3 Do we all have one? ☑ Yes ○ No

5 **Write *T* (true) or *F* (false).**

1 We always leave a digital footprint when we "like" something online. T
2 Strong passwords avoid digital footprints. F
3 People can take images of chats that stay online for only seconds and post them in different places. T
4 Hannah didn't get a job because of her digital footprint. T
5 None of the students are surprised by Hannah's talk. F
6 It is possible to change our digital footprint. F

58

WORKBOOK p.129

Language in Context
Lesson Aim: I can understand and use indefinite pronouns in affirmative, negative, and interrogative sentences.

1 If necessary, play Track 5.04 again to help students complete the chart. Read the words with the students. Draw their attention to the use of indefinite pronouns in the affirmative, negative, and interrogative sentences. After checking answers, have students write sentences and questions using the pronouns. Have them share their sentences.

2 Read the instructions with the class to check comprehension. Draw students' attention to the fact that they have two tasks in this activity. They must first circle the correct option and then classify the option circled. Do the first dialogue with the students. Have them do the rest individually and then check in pairs.

3 Draw students' attention to the poster. Read the sentences with them. In pairs, have them complete them using the correct indefinite pronoun. Check as a class. Have a volunteer read the sentences and ask students if they follow these instructions when using the Internet. Have them add any other advice they believe is important.

USE IT!

4 Have students read the advice from the poster and make questions to ask their partners regarding the advice given. Have them read the example in the speech bubble.

Homework
Workbook page 130, Exercises 3 and 4

Practice Extra
Unit 5

Fast Finishers
Puzzles and Games page 104, Exercise 2

Grammar Game
You will need a ball that is soft and a list of sentences written by the students using indefinite pronouns (affirmative, negative, and interrogative). Begin the game by first asking students to write two sentences each on a slip of paper. Have them hand in their sentences. Then start by tossing the ball to a student. Before you toss the ball, choose a sentence, and say it out loud. The student should catch the ball and name the indefinite pronoun. Before he/she tosses it again, he/she should repeat the sentence but substitute a pronoun that could potentially make sense. The next student should follow the same procedure and substitute a different pronoun before tossing the ball again. Students keep playing through at least five substitutions and tosses. Then, start again with a different sentence.

Teacher: *Someone in my company searched for my name online.*

Student: Someone *is the indefinite pronoun. No one in my company searched for my name online.*

Extension
Invite students to write a short paragraph (about a vacation they have been on, a movie they've watched, or a book they've read) using as many indefinite pronouns as they can. Have them refer to the chart in Exercise 1 to get ideas. The ideas in the paragraph must connect and make sense. Have students read out their paragraphs and have them choose the most creative one.

UNIT 5

LANGUAGE IN CONTEXT

1 Complete the sentences from Hannah's talk in the chart. Use the words below.

• anyone • anything • nothing • ~~someone~~ • something • somewhere

Indefinite Pronouns

Affirmative (+)	Negative (–)	Questions (?)
1 *Someone* in the company searched for my name online.	There isn't **anyone** here who has a vlog. **No one** can have total privacy on the Internet.	Does 5 *anyone* know what "digital footprint" means?
When you search for 2 *something*, you always leave a trace.	You can't keep **anything** private when you go online. 4 *Nothing* gives you complete protection.	Is there 6 *anything* we can do to avoid problems?
They can post the screenshot 3 *somewhere* else.	I can't find my file **anywhere**. My file is **nowhere** on this computer.	Did you go **anywhere** interesting last weekend?

2 Circle the correct options. What do the circled words describe? Write *T* (thing), *PE* (person), or *PL* (places).

1 Logan: Look! There's *anyone* / *someone* (circled) behind the tree. *PE*
Patricio: Where? I can't see *anyone* (circled) / *someone*. *PE*
2 Mariana: How about going to the mall? I need to buy *something* (circled) / *anything* for Helen. *T*
Kathy: OK. I don't need to buy *something* / *anything* (circled), but I'll go with you. *T*
Mariana: Great. Let's go by bike then.
Kathy: Hmm … I'm not sure. There's *somewhere* / *nowhere* (circled) to leave our bikes at the mall. *PL*
3 Jorge: Is there *anything* (circled) / *nothing* new on this channel? *T*
Karla: Yes. There's *something* (circled) / *nothing* about the history of social media. Do you want to watch it? *T*
Jorge: OK. Where's the remote control? I don't see it.
Karla: It's *anywhere* / *somewhere* (circled) near that chair. *PL*

3 Complete the poster using words with *some–* or *any–*.

THINGS TO REMEMBER ABOUT ONLINE ACTIVITY
✓ Don't share your passwords with 1 *anyone*.
✓ If you see 2 *something* online that makes you uncomfortable, tell an adult.
✓ Use different passwords, change them often, and store them 3 *somewhere* safe.
✓ If 4 *someone* makes a comment you don't like about you, ask them to delete it.
✓ Don't write your address or phone number 5 *anywhere* on social media.
✓ Don't share 6 *anything* private that you receive from your friends without their permission.

USE IT!

4 Work in small groups. Ask and answer questions about the advice in the poster in Exercise 3.

Do you share your passwords with anyone?

WORKBOOK p.128 and 130 PRACTICE EXTRA

59

5.2

What's Up with Social Media?

The video on page 61 and accompanying exercises below can be used as a lead-in to the topic of the Around the World text, or after the reading activities to complete the unit.

Summary

The video is about the causes and consequences of talking about our personal lives on social media.

In Class

Tell students they are going to watch a video about the benefits and disadvantages of social media. This topic has been discussed ever since social media began but still seems to have no solution. Ask: *How dangerous can social media be? What are the advantages and disadvantages of social media?* In small groups, have students share their ideas.

Exercise 1

Ask students to watch the video to answer the questions:

1 *How many internet users were there in July 2020?* Check the answer with the class.
59% of the world's population: 4.5 billion people

2 *What are trolls?* Check the answer with the class.
People who enjoy saying mean things online.

Invite students to answer the last question on the video: *What can we do to solve the problems with social media?*

Exercise 2

Play the video again, write the following questions on the board and ask students to find the answers. Then, have them make up two more questions to ask their partners.

1 What are the benefits of social media mentioned in the video? Check all that apply.
( ) We show our true self.
(X) We post our thoughts.
(X) We can easily get information.
( ) We keep our life private.

2 Social media makes us open-minded. True or false? Justify your answer.
False.

AROUND THE WORLD

about me posts contact me

Taking a Break from Social Media

Fernando Alves, Brazil

Until last month, I never paid too much attention to comments like "Teenagers are always on social media!" or "Too much time on social media can make you depressed." But then we had a school project: to find some facts about how Brazilian teens use the Internet and to compare the results to our habits. Here's a summary of what I discovered.

Facts	Comparison
82% of 9–17-year-olds are on social media.	My class: 100%
Brazilian teens check their social media 63 times a day on average.	Me: 71 times
Over half of teenagers in a study in Brazil said they almost always had a smartphone or tablet with them during meals.	My class: 80%

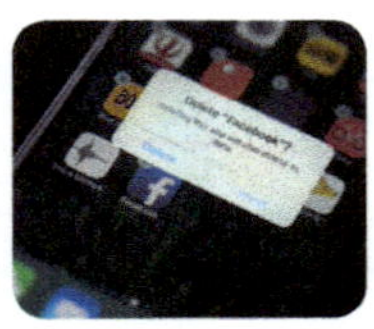

The project made me think: did I use social media too much? Did I feel anxious if no one liked my posts immediately? And I wondered: how would I feel if I didn't use social media for five days? So that's exactly what I did.

Day 1 I woke up and went straight to my phone. It was weird: no social media! __b__
Day 2 I'm still anxious: did my friends like the photos I posted the day before yesterday? But I'm trying to keep busy with other things. __e__
Day 3 Stress levels are lower. I texted some friends and enjoyed the one-to-one conversations. __c__
Day 4 I spent my free time exercising and hanging out with my friends at the park. I left my phone at home. __d__
Day 5 I decided to close some social media accounts and keep just two. I'll try to open them just two or three times a day in the future. __a__

60

3 Read the sentences about using social media. Write *T* (True) or *F* (False).
(T) We feel more connected to friends and family.
(F) Social media is very safe.
(T) Social media can make us more divided.
(T) In July 2020, 59% of the world's population were internet users.

At Home

Exercise 3

Ask students to find out where social media is used most in the world. Have them research what countries use it the most, and what the most used platforms are. Have them build an infographic to share their findings.

Background Information

Over the years, we have heard more and more about teen depression and teen addiction to social media. The number of hours Brazilian students tend to stay on social media is increasing as we speak.

5.05 Audioscript pT142

1 Put students into small groups. Ask them to look at the design and title of the text. Ask: *What sort of text is it?* (a blog post) Invite them to look at the images and discuss what they think the text will be about. Ask: *What does "taking a break" mean?* Ask students to skim the blog post individually and check the correct options. Check their answers as a class.

2 **5.05** Have a volunteer read sentences a–e. Individually, have students complete the blog post with the sentences. Have students compare their answers in pairs before playing the audio to check their work. Ask: *Have you ever taken a break from social media? Do you want to?*

Words in Context

3 Read the words with the students to check understanding. Ask students to find the words in the blog post. This should help them work out their meaning. Have students complete the sentences individually. After checking answers, you can ask personalized questions, e.g.: *How many days on average do you spend on social media a week? Do you wonder whether social media damages your mental health? How many social media accounts do you have?*

4 Read through questions 1–3 to check understanding. Have students work in pairs to answer the questions. Have them discuss their answers. Invite each pair to make up another question related to social media to ask their friends.

1 **Look at the blog post. Check (✓) the options that describe what's in the post.**

1 ✓ an introduction explaining why Fernando became interested in the topic
2 ✓ a diary describing Fernando's actions and feelings
3 ◯ advice that Fernando gives to other teenagers
4 ✓ the results of research Fernando did
5 ◯ recommendations about the best social media sites for teens

2 **5.05 Read the blog post. Write a–e in the post to complete Fernando's diary entries. Then read, listen, and check.**

a I think I'll feel happier that way.
b ~~During the day, I felt disconnected.~~
c It felt personal.
d I realized I don't depend on it to keep me happy.
e In fact, this evening I learned how to make sushi!

WORDS IN CONTEXT

3 **Complete the sentences with the words below. Check your answers in the blog post.**

• account • average • summary • wonder

1 This is not the full text: it's just a *summary* with the main ideas.
2 I spend 15–25 hours a week on homework – that's 20 hours on *average*.
3 It's getting dark. I *wonder* what time it is. Do you know?
4 I can't persuade my cousin in the US to open an *account* on social media. He hates the idea.

4 **Read the facts in the chart in the blog post and answer the questions. Then discuss your answers in pairs.**

1 Did you know about these facts before reading the blog post?
Students' own answers
2 Which is the most surprising fact in your opinion?
3 Do you have your phone with you during meals?

THINK!

Why do you think there may be a link between social media and depression? What can you do to avoid negative effects from social media?

WEBQUEST

Learn more! Check (✓) the correct answer.
The logo of a famous social media site is a blue (or white) bird. What's the bird's name?

◯ Tweet ✓ Larry ◯ Jack

VIDEO 5.2

1 How many internet users were there in July 2020?
2 What are trolls?

61

THINK!

Discuss with students the impact of social media on mental health. In pairs, have them discuss why they believe many hours on social media can cause depression. Have them share their answers. Encourage each pair to write two ways to avoid negative effects from social media. Again, have them share their ideas.

WEBQUEST

Remind students to check two or three websites to confirm their answer. Ask them to find out which famous social media logo is being referred to and what the name of the bird is. Have them describe other famous logos of the social media they use. Ask them to choose their favorite logo. Then, have them rank the social media they use from best to worst and have them justify their answers.

Speaking
Lesson Aim: I can express different points of view.

🔊5.06–5.09 Audioscripts pT142

1 🔊**5.06** Point to the image and ask: *What do you think is happening? Who are they? Does this happen in your house?* Ask students to read and listen to the dialogue. Then ask: *What is the discussion about?* Have students talk about similar situations to this one. Have them answer the question and check answers as a class.

2 Have a volunteer read sentences 1–5. Ask students to, individually, circle the correct option from memory. Then have them read the dialogue to confirm their answers.

Living English

3 Read through sentences 1–3 in the chart with the students. Ask them to find the questions/statements with the same meaning in the dialogue in Exercise 1. Then have students check them against the expressions written above the chart and write them in the corresponding place in the chart.

4 🔊**5.07** Play the audio for students to check their answers. Have students repeat the expressions, focusing on their intonation.

Pronunciation

5 🔊**5.08** Have students listen carefully to the pronunciation of the letter *o* in bold in the sentences. Have them notice that the letter is pronounced in the same way in each sentence.

6 🔊**5.08** Have the class say the sentences along with the audio. Then play the audio again, pausing after each sentence for students to repeat. Have them pay attention to how they move their lips when saying both words with *o*. Finally, have students read the whole sentences.

SPEAKING

EXPRESSING DIFFERENT POINTS OF VIEW

1 🔊 5.06 **Read and listen to a family at breakfast. What are three of the four people doing?** They're looking at screens

Mother	**Breakfast's** ready! Phones down, please.
Son	Why do we have to put our phones down? Dad's **on his computer**.
Father	I'm working.
Daughter	And we're **talking to our friends**.
Father	I know, but that's not the same. I have something urgent to do.
Son	Sure, but I need to **post this comment**.
Daughter	Yeah, and **my friends are important, too**.
Mother	You know, that's a really good point, but **it's family time now. Two minutes. And then ... no one uses a phone or computer!**

2 **Circle the correct options.**

1 The son *agrees* / *disagrees* (circled) with his mother.
2 The father *agrees* / *disagrees* (circled) with his daughter.
3 The son *explains* (circled) / *doesn't explain* his point of view.
4 The daughter *agrees* (circled) / *disagrees* with her brother.
5 The mother *presents* (circled) / *doesn't present* a new point of view.

LIVING ENGLISH

3 **Complete the chart with the expressions below.**

• I know, but ... • Sure, but ... • Yeah, and ...
• You know, that's a really good point, but ...

1 I agree with you, but I want to make a different point.	You know, that's a really good point, but ...
2 That's true, but I don't think it's an important point.	I know, but ...; Sure, but ...
3 I agree with you, and I want to make another point.	Yeah, and ...

4 🔊 5.07 **Listen, check, and repeat the expressions.**

PRONUNCIATION

5 🔊 5.08 **Listen and pay attention to the pronunciation of the *o* in *something* and *wonder*.**

/ʌ/
I have s**o**mething urgent to do.
I w**o**nder why we have to put our phones down.

6 🔊 5.08 **Listen again and repeat.**

7 🔊 5.09 **Circle the letters in bold that have the same sound as the *o* in *something* and *wonder*. Then listen and check.**

1 a M**a**tch the columns. b They don't have m**u**ch. (circled)
2 a S**o**me ads are smart. (circled) b I feel the s**a**me way.
3 a C**u**t the carrots. (circled) b She is c**u**te.
4 a I can r**u**n fast. (circled) b I ran to sch**oo**l.
5 a I'll leave s**oo**n. b Who's your s**o**n? (circled)

8 🔊 5.06 **Listen to the dialogue again. Then practice with three classmates.**

9 **Role play a new dialogue. Follow the steps.**

1 Change the words in blue to write a new dialogue in your notebook.
2 Practice your dialogue with your classmates.
3 Present your dialogue to the class.

YOUR DIGITAL PORTFOLIO
Record your dialogue and upload it to your class digital portfolio.

62

PRACTICE EXTRA

---

7 🔊**5.09** Read through the sentences with the students to check understanding. Individually, have students read the sentences to themselves, paying attention to the pronunciation of the sounds in bold. Have them circle the words that have the same *o* pronunciation.

8 🔊**5.06** Have the class read the dialogue silently. Then play the audio again, pausing after each speaker for the class to repeat what they hear. Finally, have students practice the dialogue in groups of four.

9 Read through the steps with students and check understanding. Encourage them to be creative and use the vocabulary learned in this unit. Try to find time in class for pairs to present their dialogues. If this is not possible, monitor pairs as they practice and provide feedback on intonation.

Your Digital Portfolio

Give students a date for uploading their work and make sure they all listen to one another's dialogues.

Practice Extra

Unit 5

Lesson Aim: I can talk about my favorite type of music.

Warmer

Divide students in groups of three and give them 30 seconds to write down all the different types of music they can think of. Be strict with the timing. When finished, elicit the types they listed. Have students rank their favorites.

THINK!

1 Ask students to look at the image and describe what they see. Ask them: *How do you feel when you are in a place like this? Do you like crowds? Have you been to a concert?*

2 Ask students to sit in pairs in order to answer the second question. Then ask them: *Could you live without music? How often do you listen to music? Do you listen to certain songs when you do certain things? Can you study while listening to music?* Have them share their answers.

6.1 Feel the Music

Summary

The video is about the positive effects of music on our mind and body.

In Class

Ask: *What effect does music have on you? When do you like listening to music? What kind of music to you mostly listen to? Do you believe music has healing powers?* Have students answer these questions in smaller groups and share the answers with the class.

Exercise 1

Ask students to watch the video to answer the questions:

1 *Who is Evelyn Glennie?* Check the answer with the class.
A Scottish musician.

2 *What happened to her when she was 12?* Check the answer with the class.
She lost most of her hearing.

Exercise 2

Play the video again and write the following sentences on the board for students to complete. Then, ask them to watch the video again and make up two more questions to ask their partners.

1 Evelyn plays percussion instruments like __drums__ – they create the strongest __vibrations__.

2 Deaf people cannot enjoy music.
( ) True (✗) False

3 Match the sentence halves.

1 Evelyn lost most of her hearing
2 Music is good for
3 Music is
4 Hospital patients felt better

a (4) after listening to music.
b (3) a mix of sounds.
c (1) when she was just 12.
d (2) your body and your mind.

At Home

Exercise 3

Ask students to research people who have lost one of the five senses and still play some kind of instrument. Have them research the following: their name, where they are from, what they play, and what sense they lost.

Resources

- Teacher's worksheets Unit 6
- Test Generator Unit 6
- Practice Extra Unit 6
- Workbook pages 132–135
- Puzzles and Games page 104

Flipped Classroom

Ask students to choose four countries and research and list their traditional musical instruments and songs. Ask: *Do you think that people from different cultures react to music in different ways?* Have them reflect upon this question while researching each country's traditional songs and instruments.

Unit Aims

Cambridge Life Competencies Framework

I can ...

- use simple techniques to start, maintain, and close conversations of various lengths to describe the kind of music I like. **(Communication)**
- understand essential grammatical terms and concepts: using the present perfect to talk about what I have recently done. **(Learning to Learn)**
- state opposing opinions in a respectful way when discussing my favorite songs. **(Emotional Development)**
- use strategies and techniques for improving my English (e.g., mind maps to organize my thoughts). **(Learning to Learn)**
- give my opinion on other students' contributions respectfully. **(Collaboration)**
- discuss songs that make me feel different emotions. **(Emotional Development)**
- accept others and show respect for cultural differences related to music. **(Social Responsibility)**

Vocabulary in Context
Lesson Aim: I can identify and describe different types of music.

Warmer

Have students sit in pairs. Ask: *If you could be any musician in the world, who would you be and why?* Have students share their answers with the class. Ask them if they believe rock stars have a good life. Have them justify their answers.

Flipped Classroom Check

Have students share their lists and compare the different types of songs and instruments. Have students then vote on the best as a whole class. Alternatively, this could be done using an online survey creator. Then ask students: *Do you prefer listening to songs in your own language or in another language? Why? How do you feel about your country's traditional music?*

6.01–6.02 Audioscript pT142

Target Vocabulary

classical music	/ˈklæs·ɪ·kəl.ˈmju.zɪk/
country music	/ˈkʌn·tri.ˈmju.zɪk/
heavy metal	/ˌhev.i ˈmet̬.l/
hip-hop	/ˈhɪpˌhɑp/
jazz	/dʒæz/
pop	/pɑp/
R & B (rhythm and blues)	/ɑːr.ən.biː/ (/ˌrɪð.m ən ˈbluːz/)
reggae	/ˈreg.eɪ/
rock	/rɑːk/
techno	/ˈtek.noʊ/

1. Have students look at the survey and its title. Read sentences a and b to check understanding. Have students check the correct answer individually. Have them check their answer in pairs.
2. 6.01 Read the instructions so students understand what they are supposed to do. Play the audio and have students match the types of music to the ones listed in the diagram. Have them check their work in pairs.
3. 6.02 Play the audio for students to check their work from Exercise 2. Have them repeat the types of music, checking pronunciation and intonation.

VOCABULARY IN CONTEXT

TYPES OF MUSIC

1 Look at the diagram. Check (✓) its objective.

a ○ to show the best type of music for students at school
b ✓ to show students' favorite types of music in a school

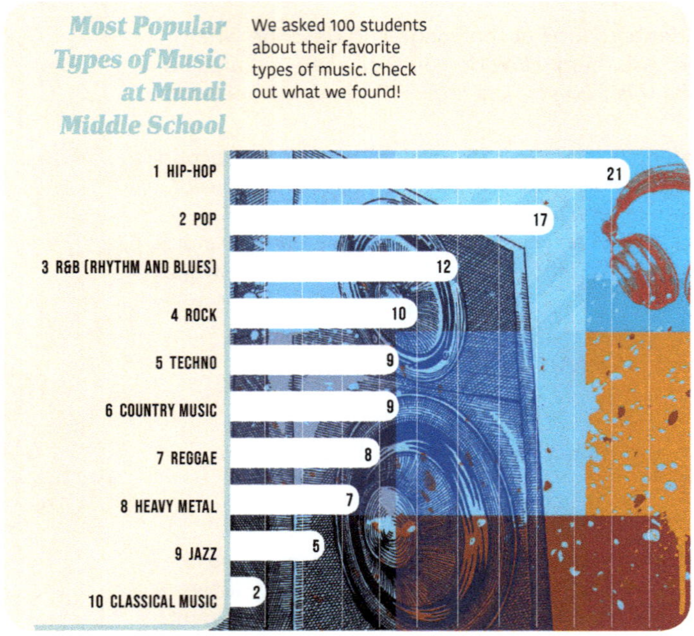

2 6.01 Listen to ten music extracts. Match a–j with the types of music 1–10 in the diagram.

a 6 f 9
b 1 g 7
c 10 h 8
d 4 i 3
e 2 j 5

3 6.02 Listen, check, and repeat the types of music.

64

Vocabulary in Context
Lesson Aim: I can identify and describe different types of music.

4 Ask volunteers to read the words above the images. Have students look at the images and label them. Have them complete the exercise individually, then check in pairs. Ask: *What helped you match the words to the images?*

5 Have students observe the graphic organizer. Individually, have them write two of their favorite types of music, exemplifying with names of artists and songs.

USE IT!

6 Ask students to use the graphic organizer from Exercise 5 to share their favorite types of music, artists, and songs. Draw their attention to the speech bubbles and model the activity with two students. Have them do the activity in small groups and then have them share their favorites with the class.

Homework

Workbook page 133, Exercises 1 and 2

Practice Extra

Unit 6

Fast Finishers

Puzzles and Games page 104, Exercise 3

Extension

As a further practice exercise, have students build a collaborative board with their favorite artists and songs on it. Have them upload the songs so students can have a music library containing all the favorites of their class. Have them describe the type of music using the vocabulary learned from this lesson. If you cannot do this digitally, have each student write a paragraph and display them where everyone can see them.

UNIT 6

4 Label the images from music videos with the types of music below. There is one extra type.

• ~~classical music~~ • country music • hip-hop • jazz • reggae • rock • techno

1 
classical music

2 
country music

3 
rock

4 
jazz

5 
techno

6 
hip-hop

5 Write two types of music that you like in the chart. Then add your favorite artists and songs.

Type of Music | **Artists** | **Songs**

USE IT!

6 Work in small groups. Use the chart in Exercise 5 to talk about your favorite types of music, artists, and songs.

My favorite type of music is pop and I really like Ed Sheeran.

Me too!

Well, he's OK, but I prefer hip-hop.

WORKBOOK p.133 PRACTICE EXTRA

Reading
Lesson Aim: I can read and understand reviews about a famous band's concert.

Warmer

Have students sit in pairs and ask them: *Do you believe the Internet is helping or harming musicians? Do people go to concerts less because of the Internet?* Have them justify their answers.

6.03 Audioscript pT143

1 Have students look at the design and title of the text. Have students predict what they will read about. Ask them to read the sentences 1–3 in Exercise 1 to check understanding and choose the correct description without reading the text, just by using the images and title. Have them check their answers in pairs.

2 6.03 Have a volunteer read the words above the sentences. Individually, have them read the article and complete sentences 1–5 with the corresponding words. Play the audio and have them check their work in pairs. Ask: *Would you attend a concert of a band you don't necessarily like?*

3 Read sentences 1–3 to check comprehension. Draw students' attention to the words: *expect*, *anxious*, and *able*. Have students read the comments to themselves. Ask them to answer the questions with the corresponding name. Check answers with the class and play the final part of the audio for students to check their work.

THINK!

Divide students into small groups to discuss the question. Ask them what the dangers could be of attending a concert. Encourage each group to come up with a response for the worried mother. Have each group report their comment.

Homework

Workbook page 135, Exercises 1, 2, and 3

READING

Home | Music | Pop | Concert reviews

BTS Rocks Green Alliance Arena for a Memorable Night!

Leticia Harris | September 30 | 3 min read

If you don't know the guys in the photo, they are the South Korean band BTS, the most popular Korean pop (or K-pop) group in the world. The seven bandmates have attracted millions of fans from Bangkok to Brazil. Their music is basically pop, but it has always included elements of hip-hop and rock.

I've seen some great concerts, but the one I went to last Saturday was one of the best. BTS didn't disappoint their devoted fans at the Green Alliance Arena. More than 55 thousand teenagers (and some parents) sang and danced to the band's greatest hits. It was an unforgettable concert.

The boys first went onstage to sing the most popular song from their recent album and then sang hits from previous ones. Their performance of ballads was amazing – Jungkook, V, Jimin, and Jin showed all their vocal power. After that, it was RM, Suga, and J-Hope's turn to show their talent with rap.

After two hours of incredible music, the concert came to an end with the boys singing an old favorite, *Mikrokosmos*. The audience held up their phones, using them to light up the dark stadium. It was a great end to a great concert!

3 comments

BTS Dad: *I was one of the parents at the concert last Saturday with my daughter. I've never been a fan of K-pop, but BTS is great!*

JaneT: *My son has never been to a concert. There's another BTS concert this Friday. Will it be safe for him to go with his friends?*

Leticia Harris: *It's safe! But tickets have sold out. Sorry!*

1 Look at the title and the image. Check (✓) the correct description of the text.

1 ○ It's a **biography** of a band.
2 ○ It's an **article** about a band's songs.
3 ✓ It's a **review** of a concert.

2 6.03 Read and listen to the text. Then complete the sentences with the words below.

• ~~band~~ • concert • famous • fans • members • phones • pop • review

1 BTS is a K-pop *band* from South Korea. They are *famous* all over the world.
2 There are seven *members* of the band. They sing *pop* music with elements from other music types.
3 There was a BTS *concert* last Saturday. Thousands of *fans* were there.
4 During the last song the audience turned on the lights on their *phones*.
5 The author of the *review* loved the concert.

3 Read the three comments again and answer the questions.

Who …
1 didn't expect to enjoy the concert? *BTS Dad*
2 is feeling anxious about a concert? *JaneT*
3 probably won't be able to go to the concert on Friday? *JaneT's son*

THINK!
Why do you think JaneT is worried about her son going to a big music concert? How would you reply to her?

66

WORKBOOK p.135

Language in Context
Lesson Aims: I can use the present perfect to talk about concerts I have been to and songs I have heard.

1 Read through the chart with the students. Draw students' attention to the short form used in the present perfect: *I've seen some great concerts.* Give some more examples. Play Track 6.03 again and have students complete the chart. Elicit whether the sentences relate to the past or present. Draw their attention to the affirmative and the negative statements and elicit how we form the present perfect (*have/has* + past participle). Read through the examples and have students make up sentences which are true for them.

2 Remind students how we form the present perfect. Read through sentences 1–6 with them. Individually, have students complete the sentences using the verbs in parentheses. Draw their attention to the negative verbs. Have them check their work in pairs.

LOOK!

Draw students' attention to the *Look!* box. Have a volunteer read the example. Encourage students to give you more examples comparing the present perfect to the simple past. Write the examples on the board and circle the words that point out when the action happened in the past in the simple past examples. Brazilian students tend to use the simple past instead of the present perfect, e.g.: ~~*I have been very tired yesterday.*~~ *I was tired yesterday.* ~~*In the last few years, things changed a lot.*~~ *In the last few years, things have changed a lot.*

3 Read through the verbs with students. Elicit how we form the present perfect using the verbs as examples without completing the sentences, e.g.: buy – have/has bought. Individually, have students complete the text. Check answers with the class by having different students read a sentence each.

USE IT!

4 Read the prompts with the class to check understanding and have them check the things they have already done. Ask them to write two more things they have already done.

UNIT 6

LANGUAGE IN CONTEXT

1 **Look at the examples below. Complete the sentences from the review.**

Present Perfect: Affirmative and Negative

Affirmative (+)	**Negative (–)**
I [1] 've seen some great concerts.	I haven't performed onstage. I [4] have never been a fan of K-pop.
You **have listened** to this song a lot.	You **haven't met** my mom. You**'ve never heard** this band before.
She**'s downloaded** their new album. Their music [2] has always had elements of hip-hop and rock.	JaneT **hasn't watched** any K-pop videos. My son [5] has never been to a concert.
We**'ve learned** to read music at school.	We **haven't bought** tickets for the concert.
The seven bandmates [3] have attracted millions of fans.	They **haven't sung** this song very often.

2 **Complete the sentences with the correct present perfect form of the verbs in parentheses.**

1 The singers have performed (perform) in different countries.
2 I haven't played (not play) the piano in a concert.
3 Mike has learned (learn) to play six different instruments.
4 My mom hasn't listened (not listen) to K-pop.
5 Erica has met (meet) her favorite R & B singer.
6 Our band has never appeared (never appear) in public.

LOOK!

If we say when the action happened, we use the simple past, not the present perfect.
She **has seen** that movie. (= at some time in the past)
She **saw** it **last Saturday**.

3 **Complete the text with the correct present perfect form of the verbs below.**

• buy • never meet • never watch • say • ~~see~~ • win

Beyoncé is my favorite R & B singer. I [1] 've seen her onstage three times, and she's a great performer. She's coming to my city again next week and I [2] 've/have bought a ticket for her concert. But my friend Liz [3] has won a radio competition and she's going to spend an afternoon with Beyoncé! She [4] 's/has never met the R & B diva, of course, and she's really excited about it. The funny thing is that Liz 's/has never watched a live concert and her parents [6] have said they won't let her go to Beyoncé's!

USE IT!

4 **Look at the list. Check (✓) the things you've done.**

○ go to a live concert ○ meet a famous person ○ sing in public
○ listen to K-pop ○ perform on a stage ○ win a competition

5 **Work in pairs and tell your partner what you have and haven't done from Exercise 4.**

I've been to a live concert.
Really? Who did you see?

WORKBOOK p.132 and 134 PRACTICE EXTRA

5 Put students into pairs. Read the examples in the speech bubbles and model the conversation with a student. Have students use the prompts from Exercise 4 and act and react to their partner's comment. Monitor the activity by walking around the class.

Grammar Game

Encourage students to make up five true sentences with the present perfect and a time expression but stop before they say the time expression, e.g.: *I have watched five films this* __________. Their partner has to guess what the correct time expression is by asking: *Have you watched five films this (week)?* Each student writes down five sentences and then pairs take turns to guess the time expression. Monitor the activity by walking around the class.

Homework

Workbook page 134, Exercises 1 and 2

Practice Extra

Unit 6

Listening and Vocabulary

Lesson Aim: I can identify and talk about different musical instruments and songwriters.

Warmer

Ask students if they play any musical instruments. Elicit the instruments played and see which is the most common one. Rank them from most to least played. Ask: *If you could invent a new instrument, what would it sound like?* Have students discuss this in pairs and have them report their answers to the class.

6.04–6.06 Audioscripts pT143

Target Vocabulary

drums	/drʌmz/
flute	/fluːt/
French horn	/ˌfrentʃ ˈhɔːrn/
guitar	/ɡɪˈtɑːr/
keyboard	/ˈkiː.bɔːrd/
saxophone	/ˈsæk.sə.foʊn/
trumpet	/ˈtrʌm.pət/
violin	/ˌvaɪəˈlɪn/

1 **6.04** Read through the words with the students and ask them to mime each of the instruments. Have them label the images. Play the recording to check their work and ask students to repeat, drawing their attention to pronunciation.

2 **6.05** Have students tell you their favorite instrument. Ask them if they have ever been to a classical concert. Play the recording for students to listen to the sound of the different instruments. Have them write down the corresponding instrument. Again, ask them to choose their favorite from among these.

3 **6.06** Ask students if they can name any famous songwriters. Write them on the board. Have them discuss singers who do and singers who don't write their own songs. Ask: *Which instruments do you think songwriters should be able to play?* Have them complete Exercise 3 with four instruments they believe this specific songwriter might play. Have them listen to the audio to check their prediction.

4 **6.06** Ask volunteers to read the questions a–e. Have them notice the verb tense used in each of the questions. Ask them to order the questions from the audio from memory, then play the audio again to check.

LISTENING AND VOCABULARY

1 6.04 **Label the musical instruments with the words below. Then listen, check, and repeat.**

• drums • guitar • flute • French horn
• keyboard • saxophone • trumpet • ~~violin~~

1  violin
2  keyboard
3  guitar
4  trumpet
5  flute
6  drums
7  saxophone
8  French horn

2 6.05 **Listen and write the name of the musical instruments you hear.**

1 drums 3 guitar 5 saxophone 7 French horn
2 flute 4 keyboard 6 violin 8 trumpet

3 6.06 **You're going to listen to a talk show with a songwriter. Which four instruments from Exercise 1 do you think she plays? Listen and check your predictions.**

1 guitar 2 drums 3 flute 4 keyboard

4 6.06 **Listen to the talk show again. Number the questions in order (1–5).**

a Have you ever fallen in love? 4
b How many songs have you written? 5
c Was it about a specific person? 3
d Has music always been important in your life? 2
e What instruments do you play? 1

5 **Circle the correct options.**

1 Kate Queen was (14) / 16 when she wrote her first song.
2 Her (friends') / parents' relationships inspired Kate to write her first song.
3 Kate wrote her first song using her *guitar* / (*keyboard*).
4 A lot of her *dance* / (*love*) songs have been number one.
5 She has written (*more*) / *less* than 100 songs.

68

WORKBOOK p.133

5 Have students circle the options individually. If necessary, play the audio again. Have them check in pairs. If time allows, ask students to tell their partner something interesting about a famous singer or songwriter.

Homework

Workbook page 133, Exercises 3 and 4

Language in Context
Lesson Aim: I can ask and answer *Wh–* questions and *Yes/No* questions using the present perfect.

1 Play Track 6.06 again to help students complete the chart. After checking answers, have pairs of volunteers read out a question and answer each. Draw attention to how *Wh–* and *Yes/No* questions are formed in the present perfect.

2 Have students look at the scrambled questions and ask them to first notice whether they will be *Wh–* questions or *Yes/No* questions. Draw their attention to the answers a–e. Individually, have them put the words in order and then match them to the corresponding answers. Have them check their work in pairs

USE IT!

3 Draw students' attention to the examples in the speech bubbles. Have students read through the verbs and look at the images and their captions. Have one or two volunteers model the activity using the speech bubbles for support. Put students into pairs to practice. Encourage students to go beyond just answering *Yes, I have*. Encourage them to ask for further information, using the simple past, e.g.: *Where did you go? What did you eat? What show did you watch?* etc.

Homework
Workbook page 134, Exercises 3 and 4

Practice Extra
Unit 6

Fast Finishers
Puzzles and Games page 104, Exercise 4

Grammar Game
Play a truth or lie game with the students. Individually, have students make a list of actions to interview their partner using *Have you ever …?* In pairs, students ask their questions. They must answer all questions with *Yes*. Their partner can then ask them three *Wh–* questions in the simple past and try to spot from their answers and body language if they are telling the truth or lying.

LANGUAGE IN CONTEXT

1 Complete the questions and answers from the talk show in the chart. Use the words below.

• be • ~~fall~~ • write

Present Perfect: Questions and Short Answers		
Yes/No Questions (?)	[1] Have you ever fallen in love? [2] Has music always been important in your life? Have many people **heard** Kate's songs?	Yes, I [3] have. / No, I **haven't**. Yes, it [4] has. / No, it **hasn't**. Yes, they **have**. / No, they **haven't**.
Wh– Questions (?)	How many songs [5] have you written? What **has** Kate **done** recently? How **have** her songs **influenced** other musicians?	

2 Put the words in order to make questions. Then match the questions with the answers.

1 have / where / recently / Marina and Ana / been ?
Where have Marina and Ana been recently? d

2 you / for the concert / tickets / bought / have ?
Have you bought tickets for the concert? c

3 Jake / how many times / seen / has / Kate onstage ?
How many times has Jake seen Kate on stage? a

4 my saxophone / have / ever / you / I / shown ?
Have I ever shown you my saxophone? e

5 Kate / has / an interview / why / given ?
Why has Kate given an interview? b

a Only once or twice, I think.
b Because her fans want to know more about her.
c Yes, I have. I used my debit card.
d To their grandma's house in the country.
e No, you haven't. Can I see it?

USE IT!

3 Work in pairs. Take turns asking and answering questions with *Have you ever …?* using the verbs below.

• eat • go to • have • listen to • watch • travel

Have you ever traveled by plane?

No, I haven't. What about you?

by plane

Indian food

a classical music concert

a talk show

jazz

guitar lessons

WORKBOOK p.132 and 134 PRACTICE EXTRA

A *Have you ever eaten frog's legs?*
B *Yes, I have*
A *Where did you eat them?*
B *In Thailand.*
A *Who were you with?*
B *My parents.*
A *What do they taste like?*
B *Chicken.*
A *OK … It is true.*

Have you ever eaten Indian food?
Have you every been to a classical music concert?
Have you every watched a talk show?
Have you ever listened to jazz?
Have you ever had guitar lessons?

Extension

Ask students to write a small paragraph about how the music industry has changed in the last ten years. Have them describe the following:

- how the songs have changed
- if the style has changed
- if concerts have changed
- any other topic concerning the music industry.

Across the Curriculum
Lesson Aim: I can understand and discuss a text about hip-hop.

6.2 The Schuhplattler

The video on page 71 and accompanying exercises below can be used as a lead-in to the topic of the Across the Curriculum text, or after the reading activities to complete the unit.

Summary

The video is about a traditional folk dance from eastern Germany.

In Class

Tell students they are going to watch a video about a traditional dance from Europe. Ask them to list some of the traditional dances in Brazil. Ask them if they know of traditional dances from different parts of Brazil. In small groups, see who can list the most. Have them share their work. Finally, have students answer the last question in the video: *How does music make you feel?*

Exercise 1

Ask students to watch the video to answer the questions.

1. *What is* Schuhplattler? Check the answers with the class.
   It is a traditional folk dance.
2. *Where is it from?* Check the answer with the class.
   Bavaria in southeastern Germany.

Exercise 2

Write the following sentences on the board and have students answer them. Then, ask students to make up two more questions to ask their partners. Play the video again for students to check their answers.

1. The dance called the *Schuhplattler* includes ___clapping___, ___stamping___ and ___hopping___.
2. It initially started as a dance
   ( ) for older people.
   (✗) for two.
   ( ) for groups.
3. The *Schuhplattler* has the following characteristics. Check all that apply.
   (✗) The girls spin across the stage.
   ( ) It is a breakdance.
   ( ) It is easy.
   (✗) The boys stamp their feet and clap.
   (✗) Modern pop groups are using the *Schuhplattler* in their performances.

ACROSS THE CURRICULUM

MUSIC

The Early History of HIP-HOP

Hip-hop is a cultural movement that started in the 1970s, in African-American and Latino neighborhoods in New York. Its main art form is rap music, but hip-hop also involves DJing, graffiti painting, and breakdancing. Rapping – speaking words rapidly in rhythm – is the way hip-hop artists perform most of their songs. Check out some important events in the movement in the 20th century.

1973 "The father of hip-hop," *DJ Kool Herc*, aged 16, DJs a party for his sister's birthday in the Bronx, a poor neighborhood in New York.

1977 Hip-Hop spreads outside poor areas, with rappers performing all over New York.

1979 Sugarhill Gang records the first commercial hip-hop song, *Rapper's Delight*.

1981 A national news magazine program reports the "rap movement" for the first time.

1982 Hip-Hop arrives in Hollywood! *Wild Style* is the first movie to show hip-hop and graffiti artists.

1986 Run-DMC, a famous hip-hop group, records *Walk This Way*, a classic from rock band Aerosmith. Run-DMC is the first hip-hop group to be nominated for a Grammy.

1990 Hip-hop hits the popular TV screen with *The Fresh Prince of Bel-Air*, a series starring Will Smith.

1992 Artists from California start to dominate the hip-hop scene. Dr. Dre, one of the most famous West Coast rappers, records his first solo album.

1998 Jay-Z and Eminem release albums and increase the popularity of hip-hop.

1999 Singer Lauryn Hill's album *The Miseducation Of Lauryn Hill* is the first hip-hop album to be Album Of The Year at the Grammy Awards.

2000 Hip-hop is the most popular type of music in the United States and a global phenomenon.

70

At Home

Exercise 3

Ask students to choose one of the traditional dances they listed at the beginning of the class. Have them research more about it: *When did it start? What are its main characteristics? Where is it originally from? What type of dance is it? Who takes part in the dance?*

Background Information

The five elements of hip-hop are beats, rhymes, dance, graffiti, and social consciousness. Some say rap and hip-hop are the same but there are some minor differences. Rap is a form of popular music that grew out of hip-hop culture. Hip-hop has a more cultural view.

6.07 Audioscript pT143

1 Ask students what they know about hip-hop. Draw a KWL chart on the board consisting of three columns with the headings: 1) *What I Know,* 2) *What I Want to Know,* and 3) *What I Learned.* Ask students to copy it into their notebooks and complete the first two columns about hip-hop music. Have them look at the images in their books and the organization of the article. Have a volunteer read the sentence in Exercise 1. Have them complete the sentence individually. Once they finish, check answers with the class.

2 6.07 Have volunteers read sentences 1–5. Ask them to read the article and write whether the sentences are true or false. Have them check in pairs before playing the audio to check their answers.

3 Have a volunteer read questions 1–6 to check understanding. Individually, have them answer the questions. Have them complete the third column of the KWL chart with information they learned from the article. Have students compare their work and add any other information they know regarding hip-hop. Have them check if all their questions were answered from the second column. If not, have them research on the Internet.

Words in Context

4 Ask students to find words 1–4 in the text. This should help them work out their meaning. Then have them read the definitions a–d and match the words to their meanings. Check answers with the class.

---

1 Look at the organization of the article and complete the sentence with the words/phrases below. There are two extra words/phrases.

• a conclusion • alphabetical • an introduction • chronological

The article has a paragraph as [1] an introduction and then the information is presented in [2] chronological order.

2 6.07 Read and listen to the article. Write *T* (true) or *F* (false).

1 Hip-hop is a cultural movement that includes different art forms. T
2 Rapping is the way hip-hop artists sing and play musical instruments. F
3 Before 1979, there weren't any commercial recordings of hip-hop songs. T
4 In 1986, Aerosmith recorded Run-DMC's song. F
5 In the 1990s, Dr. Dre, Jay-Z, and Eminem become famous hip-hop artists. T

3 Read the article again and answer the questions.

1 Who is "the father of hip-hop"?
DJ Kool Herc is "the father of hip-hop".
2 When did Sugarhill Gang record *Rapper's Delight*?
in 1979
3 What was the first movie to show hip-hop?
Wild Style
4 Which TV series brought hip-hop to a wider audience?
The Fresh Prince of Bel-Air
5 Who was the first hip-hop artist to get a Grammy for Album Of The Year?
Lauryn Hill
6 When did hip-hop become the most popular type of music in the US?
in 2000

WORDS IN CONTEXT

4 Match the expressions from the article with their definitions.

1 spread b	a make a recording available to the public to buy
2 nominated d	b reach a wider area
3 release a	c prize
4 award c	d included in a competition for a prize

THINK!

How popular are hip-hop and hip-hop artists in your country? What's your opinion of this type of music?

WEBQUEST

Learn more! Check (✓) the correct answer.
In hip-hop concerts, the MC is the person who performs the rap. What is the original meaning of "MC"?

- ○ Master of Charts
- ○ Mic Controller
- ✓ Master of Ceremonies

VIDEO 6.2

1 What is *Schuhplattler*?
2 Where is it from?

71

THINK!

Encourage students to use the thinking routine *think–pair–share* for this activity. This involves posing a question to students, asking them to take a few minutes to think about it, and then turning to a nearby student to share their thoughts. Then put students into groups to discuss the questions. Have them share their ideas with the class. Ask them to think about whether hip-hop artists are popular in their country, and have them reflect on whether they like this kind of music or not. Have them share their thoughts. Having finished the discussion, do a quick survey to see how many students like hip-hop music in the class.

WEBQUEST

Encourage students to make a note of the sources they use. Then, in class, ask them to share the websites. Ask them to tell you why these sites are reliable. Have them answer the question and ask them if they know any other meanings of *MC* (Master of Ceremonies, Member of Congress, Medical Corps, Microphone Controller).

Writing
Lesson Aim: I can read and write reviews of famous songs.

6.08 Audioscript pT143

1 6.08 Have students skim the reviews and tell you what they think they are about. Ask students where they can read reviews like these. Have them read the reviews silently and check the correct answer. Check answers with the class by playing the audio. Ask them if they know this song and if anyone would like to sing it for the class.

2 Have a volunteer read sentences 1–5. Have them match the sentences with the corresponding person from memory. Have them check in pairs. Then have them read the reviews again to check their answers.

3 Have students read the notes in the *Look!* box before doing this activity. Ask them to read through sentences 1–4 to check understanding. Encourage students to follow the steps and use the reviews in Exercise 1 as a model. Allow them to work in pairs or small groups to brainstorm ideas. Give students time to make notes and organize their ideas.

LOOK!

Draw attention to the *Look!* box. Remind students what facts must be part of a review. Have a volunteer read the paragraph. Encourage students to look up other reviews for reference.

4 When they peer correct, ensure students focus on the items in the checklist. Monitor and help as necessary. Make sure students' feedback is respectful and clear. Have students write their final version.

WRITING

1 6.08 **Read and listen to the reviews. Check (✓) what they are about.**

a ☑ songs b ◯ concerts c ◯ movies

Somewhere Over the Rainbow

Singer: Judy Garland
Year of recording: 1939

Judy Garland sang *Somewhere Over the Rainbow* in the 1939 movie *The Wizard of Oz*. She played the role of Dorothy in the movie when she was only 16 years old. Garland sang it with the orchestra of the movie studio, which was usual in musicals at that time. The performance and the beautiful lyrics about hope and optimism make *Somewhere Over the Rainbow* one of the greatest songs of the 20th century. Hundreds of other artists have recorded the song.

Cover singer: Ariana Grande
Year of cover recording: 2017

Ariana Grande sang *Somewhere Over the Rainbow* for the first time in the *One Love Manchester* charity concert in England, in June 2017, 11 days after her earlier concert in Manchester ended in tragedy. Her performance is very emotional and includes elements from jazz, with just a keyboard as a musical instrument. The song has had millions of downloads and has raised millions of dollars for charity.

2 **Read the reviews again. Write *JG* for Judy Garland and *AG* for Ariana Grande.**

1 She recorded the song in the 21st century. AG
2 She recorded the song for a movie. JG
3 There were a lot of musicians in the recording of her song. JG
4 She performed the song in a live concert. AG
5 People have donated a lot of money in order to listen to her song. AG

3 **Write a review of a famous song and a review of its cover version.**

1 Choose an original song that has a cover version and listen to the songs.
2 Collect information about the original song and its cover version.
3 Find or draw images of the two singers.
4 Write the first version of your reviews. Use vocabulary from Unit 6.

LOOK!
In a song review, we usually include facts about the artist(s) and when/where the song was recorded. We also give opinions about the style and feeling of the performance.

4 **Switch your reviews with a classmate and check his/her work. Use the checklist below.**

◯ an original song and its cover version
◯ information about the artists and when/where the recordings took place
◯ images of the singers
◯ opinions about the style and feeling of each performance
◯ verbs in the present perfect

YOUR DIGITAL PORTFOLIO
Edit your review, then publish it. Upload it to the class portfolio for everyone to see!

72

Your Digital Portfolio

Give students a date for uploading their work and make sure they all look at one another's work.

Practice Extra

Unit 6

Lesson Aim: I can review what I have learned and reflect on my progress.

Tell students that the exercises on these pages review the vocabulary and language they have learned in Units 5 and 6. Point out that they can also check their progress and reflect on what they can do.

Vocabulary

1 Draw students' attention to the words in italics. Remind them of the adjectives learned in Unit 5. Have them read through sentences 1–5. Individually, ask them to circle the best alternative. Check their work and brainstorm other adjectives with the class by asking them to make up more sentences.

2 Read the incomplete sentences with students. Elicit from them the internet words learned in Unit 5. Have them decide which word completes each gap according to the context. Check answers with the class.

3 Review the vocabulary for different types of music and have students look at the scrambled words. Have them read through the descriptions of the types of music and unscramble the words in order to complete the different types from context. Encourage them to describe their favorite types.

4 Look through the images with the class. Remind students of the different instruments. Individually, have them label the images. After checking answers, encourage students to tell you their favorite instrument.

REVIEW
UNITS 5 AND 6

VOCABULARY

1 Circle the correct options.

1 Brr! It's difficult to get up early for school when the weather is *crazy* / *freezing*.
2 Marie Curie was a *brilliant* / *silly* scientist. She got two Nobel prizes.
3 The photos of Ben's accident were *shocking* / *useless*! I'm happy he's OK.
4 There are seven bedrooms at Sofia's house. It's a *huge* / *weird* place.
5 The view of the mountains from our hotel room was *spectacular* / *ugly*.

2 Complete the sentences with the correct internet words.

1 You can't d o w n l o a d a large f i l e now. The internet connection is too slow at the moment.
2 I took a s c r e e n s h o t of Santiago's last t w e e t before he deleted it from Twitter.
3 You don't need a username and p a s s w o r d to s e a r c h for information on that website.
4 To p o s t your photos on the online album, first you need to u p l o a d them to the website.

3 Put the letters below in the correct order. Then match the words with the descriptions.

• cork • gargee • ~~ohtnce~~ • sisccalal ciums • veyha tamel

1 fast electronic dance music techno
2 popular music from Jamaica reggae
3 began as rock and roll in the 1950s rock
4 Beethoven and Mozart played it classical music
5 very loud rock music with electric guitars heavy metal

4 Can you guess the musical instruments? Label the images.

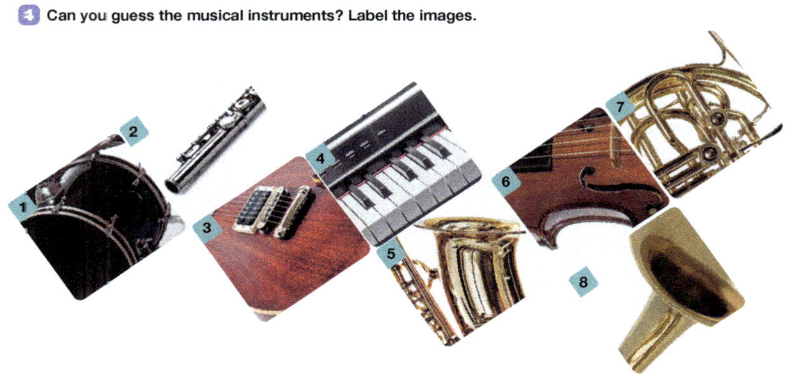

1 drums
2 flute
3 guitar
4 keyboard
5 saxophone
6 violin
7 French horn
8 trumpet

73

Lesson Aim: I can review what I have learned and reflect on my progress.

Language in Context

5 Review the second conditional with the class. Elicit examples of all the different conditionals and write them on the board. Then draw students' attention to the sentences and have them complete them using the second conditional. Check answers with the class. Put students into pairs and ask them to make up sentences regarding hypothetical situations. Encourage students to refer to the chart on page 57 if they have any uncertainties.

6 Have students refer to the chart on page 59, if necessary. Have them read the words above the exercise and remind them of the indefinite pronouns. Draw students' attention to the dialogue and have them read through it in pairs. Encourage them to complete it together, using the words from above the dialogue. Check as a class. Encourage pairs to build another dialogue about a lost object, using this one as reference.

7 Ask students how we form the present perfect and when we use it. Have them check the chart on page 67 if they still have uncertainties. Elicit examples of affirmative and negative sentences and write them on the board, highlighting the structure. Write four different time frames on the board and ask them to make sentences using the present perfect (*today, this week, this month, this year*), e.g.: *I have not been to the movies this year.* Draw students' attention to the sentences. Have them complete them individually using the given verbs in the correct form. To check answers, ask students to take turns reading sentences.

8 Elicit from students how we form the interrogative of the present perfect. Ask students to look at the chart on page 69, if necessary. Have students look at the affirmative statements they wrote in Exercise 7 and ask them to use them as prompts to make up sentences in the interrogative form to interview their classmates, e.g.: *Have you sung in public?* Have students order the rest of the sentences. Check answers with the class.

LANGUAGE IN CONTEXT

5 **Complete the second conditional sentences with the correct form of the verbs in parentheses.**

1 If Haru *knew* (know) how to cook, he *wouldn't eat* (not eat) so much junk food.
2 If the students *had* (have) tablets in class, they *would be* (be) able to look for information.
3 If Bia *bought* (buy) a new cell phone, she *would take* (take) better photos.
4 Mateo *wouldn't go* (not go) to the movies tonight if he *needed* (need) to study.
5 I *wouldn't be* (not be) happy if I *didn't listen* (not listen) to music every day.

6 **Complete the dialogue with the words below.**

• anything • ~~anywhere~~ • no one • someone • something • somewhere

Hailey: Have you seen my phone? I can't find it [1] *anywhere*.
Diego: No, I don't know where it is.
Hailey: Well, I'm sure I left it [2] *somewhere* in this room. I think [3] *someone* has taken it.
Diego: Don't be silly. There's [4] *no one* here except me and I don't have it.
Hailey: Well, where is it, then? This is terrible. I can't do [5] *anything* if I don't have a phone.
Diego: Wait a minute – there's [6] *something* in your pocket. What's that?
Hailey: Oh! It's my phone. Great! Thanks, Diego.

7 **Complete the sentences with the correct present perfect form of the verbs below.**

• buy • not have • never listen • perform • ~~sing~~

1 Mariela is a great singer. She *has sung* in public many times.
2 I *have bought* tickets for the hip-hop festival on Saturday.
3 My sister *hasn't had* lessons, but she plays the guitar really well.
4 Our band *has performed* on stage three times.
5 My best friend loves jazz, but I *have never listened* to that type of music.

8 **Put the words in the correct order to write questions.**

1 you / a / seen / live / you / have / concert / ever ?
Have you ever seen a live concert?
2 times / traveled / how / by / have / many / plane / you ?
How many times have you traveled by plane?
3 how / money / spent / you / much / today / have ?
How much money have you spent today?
4 family / in / has / ever / your / country / lived / another ?
Has your family ever lived in another country?

CHECK YOUR PROGRESS

I CAN...

- describe things with strong adjectives and talk about the Internet 🙂 ○ ☹ ○
- use the second conditional and indefinite pronouns 🙂 ○ ☹ ○
- talk about different types of music and musical instruments 🙂 ○ ☹ ○
- use the present perfect for experiences. 🙂 ○ ☹ ○

LEARN TO LEARN

Writing new words in example sentences

Use your notebook to write sentences using new words. Try to make the sentences meaningful to you – they can be about personal experiences or people who are important to you. Review your sentences regularly.

I started learning to play the flute when I was 11.

When we use the school computers, we can't download anything.

74

Check Your Progress

This section gives students an opportunity to reflect on what they have learned. Read each statement with the class. Elicit examples and/or information students remember. Alternatively, students could go through the statements in pairs or groups. If necessary, have them go back to the relevant unit and section to review each topic. Students then do the task in the Check Your Progress box individually. When they finish, ask: *What can you practice more? What is easy/difficult/interesting?* Invite students to give feedback.

Learn to Learn

Throughout the course, students do a variety of *learn to learn* activities, which offer them techniques for retaining vocabulary. Draw student's attention to the box. Have a volunteer read through the text. Have them explain what they read in their own words. Encourage students to make up sentences which are true for them, using the structures and vocabulary learned in these two units. Have them write them in their notebooks. Encourage students to review the sentences regularly.

Unit 7 Africa: Past, Present, and Future

Lesson Aim: I can discuss some interesting facts about Africa.

Warmer

Write the word *continents* on the board. Put students into pairs and ask them to list all the continents. Have them write at least two interesting facts they know about each of them. Have them share their list and facts with the whole class.

THINK!

1 In pairs, have students draw a KWL chart in their notebooks and complete the first two columns regarding the topic.

2 Encourage students to look through the unit and observe the images and topics. Have them check their KWL chart and see if the unit content matches their idea of Africa.

7.1 Amazing Africa

Summary

The video is about the continent of Africa.

In Class

Have students look back at their KWL chart. Have them sit in small groups and discuss the following questions: *Is Africa as big as Brazil? Is the population similar in size? What is the first thing that comes to your mind when you think of Africa?* Ask them to share their ideas with the other groups.

Exercise 1

Ask students to watch the video to answer the questions:

1 *How many countries are there in Africa?* Check the answer with the class.
54 countries

2 *How many languages do people speak in Africa?* Check the answer with the class.
More than 2000

Ask students the last question from the video: *What else would you like to know about Africa?* Discuss the answer as a class as they add more ideas to the second column in the KWL chart.

Exercise 2

Play the video again, write the following statements on the board and have students complete them. Then, ask them to watch the video again and make up two more questions to ask their partners.

1 More than __1.1 billion__ people live in Africa.

2 Watch the video and list three facts about the Congo river.
It is the deepest river in the world; it is in the world's second largest rainforest; it's an important habitat for many endangered species, including forest elephants and mountain gorillas.

At Home

Exercise 3

Encourage students to choose one country in Africa to explore a little more deeply. Have them bring some interesting facts about that country: population, important traditions, localization, weather, cultural facts, etc. Have them share their findings on a collaborative platform.

Resources

- Teacher's worksheets Unit 7
- Test Generator Unit 7
- Practice Extra Unit 7
- Workbook pages 136–139
- Puzzles and Games page 105

Flipped Classroom

Challenge students to research more facts about Africa. Ask: *Can you name some things Africa has given to the world? How about something the world has given to Africa? Can you name some of Africa's most famous people?* Ask students to research some of these facts and any other interesting ones and present them in the next class.

Unit Aims

Cambridge Life Competencies Framework

I can …

- use simple techniques to start, maintain, and close conversations of various lengths to talk about Africa. **(Communication)**
- understand essential grammatical terms and concepts: using the present perfect with *just, since, for, already* and *yet* to talk about Africa. **(Learning to Learn)**
- state opposing opinions in a respectful way when discussing my ideas. **(Emotional Development)**
- use strategies and techniques for improving my English (e.g., mind maps to organize my thoughts). **(Learning to Learn)**
- create questions about a video and discuss its content. **(Creative Thinking)**
- accept others and show respect for cultural differences. **(Social Responsibility)**
- make informed comparisons between my own society and other societies. **(Social Responsibility)**

Vocabulary in Context
Lesson Aim: I can understand information and talk about ancient Africa.

Warmer

Ask students if they remember how many countries there are in Africa. In pairs, have them write the number and list as many as they can. Give them one minute to do this. Share as a class and see if they were able to reach the right number (54).

Flipped Classroom Check

Put students into groups and have them share their information about Africa and its famous people. Have them write down the most interesting facts and have each group share one fact with the class. Have them complete the last column of their KWL chart with facts they learned from their peers and from the video.

7.01 Audioscript pT143

Target Vocabulary

achieve	/əˈtʃiv/
achievement	/əˈtʃiv·mənt/
construct	/kənˈstrʌkt/
construction	/kənˈstrʌk·ʃən/
develop	/dɪˈvel·əp/
development	/dɪˈvel·əp·mənt/
discover	/dɪˈskʌv·ər/
discovery	/dɪˈskʌv·ə·ri/
organize	/ˈɔr·gəˌnɑɪz/
organization	/ˌɔr·gə·nəˈzeɪ·ʃən/
produce	/prəˈdus/
production	/prəˈdʌk·ʃən/
survive	/sərˈvɑɪv/
survival	/sərˈvɑɪ·vəl/

VOCABULARY IN CONTEXT

ACHIEVEMENTS

1 7.01 **Circle the correct options to complete the fact file. Then listen and check.**

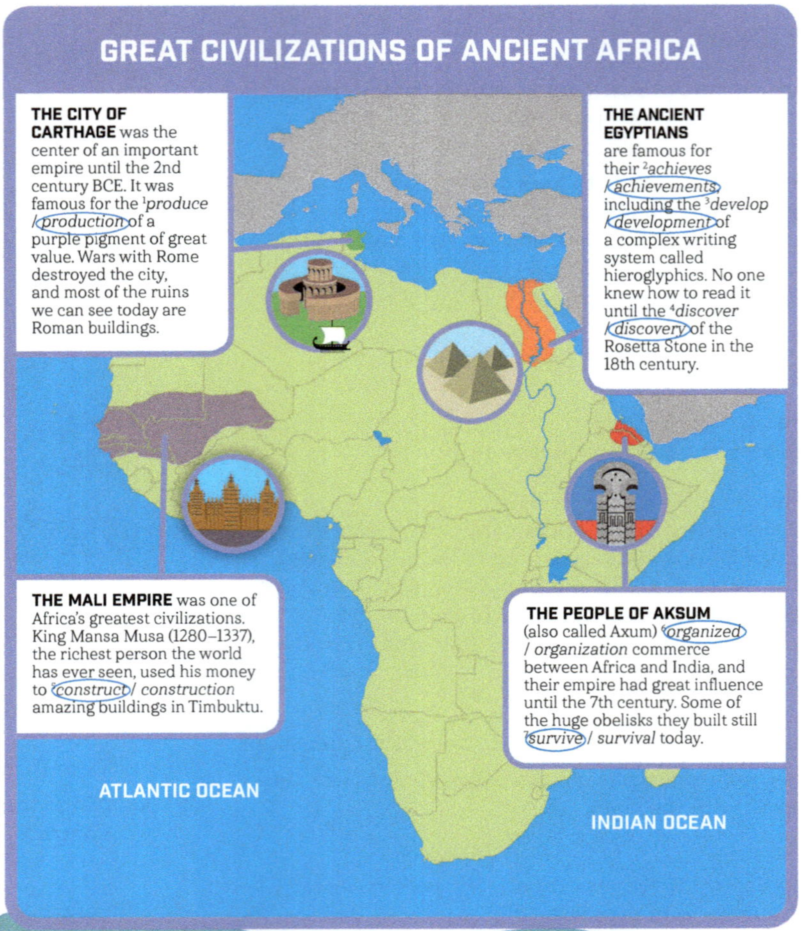

76

1 7.01 Write the following titles on the board: *The City of Carthage, The Ancient Egyptians, The Mali Empire,* and *The People of Aksum*. Have students write them in their notebooks as headings. Ask students if anyone can say anything about any of them. Have students look at the fact file and invite volunteers to read each of the facts about the different civilizations. As their peers read, ask the rest of the students to take notes of at least one important fact about each of the civilizations and write them in their notebooks. Have them share their notes. Individually, have students circle the correct alternative. Play the audio for students to check their work and repeat the words. Discuss with students the importance of each of the civilizations.

Vocabulary in Context
Lesson Aim: I can understand how to change verbs into nouns to talk about achievements.

7.02 Audioscript pTXXX

2 **7.02** Read through the words 1–7 with the students. Draw their attention to the heading of each chart. Have students refer to the fact file to complete the charts. Check answers with the class by playing the audio. Have them give you other examples of verbs and their corresponding noun. Encourage them to make sentences which are true for them using the words in Exercise 2.

3 Invite students to read each sentence individually and analyze the words listed below each sentence. Have them notice whether the words are nouns or verbs. Have students check the correct alternative. Students check their work in pairs. Have them justify their choices.

USE IT!

4 Read through the statements with the students. Individually, have them complete the chart with facts that are true for them.

5 Have students look at the statements in the left column in Exercise 4 and make them into questions, as in the first speech bubble. Model the exercise with a student, using the examples in the speech bubbles. Put students into pairs to ask and answer the questions. Encourage them to ask for extra information.

Homework

Workbook page 137, Exercises 1 and 2

Practice Extra

Unit 7

Fast Finishers

Puzzles and Games page 105, Exercise 1

UNIT **7**

2 7.02 **Complete the charts. Then listen, check, and repeat.**

Verbs	Nouns Ending in *–ment*
1 achieve	achievement
2 develop	development

Verbs	Nouns Ending in *–tion*
4 construct	construction
5 organize	organization
6 produce	production

Verbs	Nouns Ending in *–y*
3 discover	discovery

Verbs	Nouns Ending in *–al*
7 survive	survival

3 **Check (✓) the correct missing words in the sentences.**

1 The . . of the Cape Town Stadium took almost three years.
a ○ achievement b ✓ construction c ○ survival
2 Kenyan runners have … great success in the Olympic Games.
a ✓ achieved b ○ discovered c ○ organized
3 The . . of gold in the late 19th century brought thousands of people to South Africa from all over the world.
a ○ organization b ○ development c ✓ discovery
4 Factories use robots for the … of cars.
a ○ achievement b ✓ production c ○ survival
5 To … pandas need to eat 12–38 kg of bamboo every day.
a ✓ survive b ○ achieve c ○ organize
6 Albert Sabin …. the oral polio vaccine in the 1950s.
a ○ organized b ○ constructed c ✓ developed

USE IT!

4 **Complete the chart using your own ideas.** Students' own answers

Something you've achieved this year	
A discovery you've made recently	
An organization you belong to	
Something that's necessary for your survival	
The most important item your country produces	

5 **Work in pairs. Take turns asking and answering questions about your information and your partner's information.**

What have you achieved this year?
I've learned how to write a rap.
When did you do that?

WORKBOOK p.137 PRACTICE EXTRA 77

Extension

Encourage students to look back at the lesson and build an infographic about what they have learned about Africa so far. Have them refer to the KWL chart they built during the Unit Opener and have them use the *What I Learned* column when building their infographic. Have them share their infographics with the class.

Reading
Lesson Aim: I can read and understand an article about innovations.

Warmer

As a whole-class activity, invite students to list some technological innovations they are looking forward to (human cloning, time traveling, eternal life pill, cancer cure, teleportation, etc.). As they report them, write their ideas on the board.

7.03 Audioscript pT144

1 Draw students' attention to the text, its title and headings, and the images. Have them circle the correct options just by reading the title and looking at the images. Have them share their work.

2 7.03 Ask a volunteer to read through 1–4 in Exercise 2 before reading the text. This will give students a clear objective while reading. Have them complete the exercise, keeping in mind there is one extra answer. Play the audio for students to check their answers. Ask them to tell you why these innovations were important for each person.

3 Have volunteers read sentences 1–6. Students should do the exercise individually. Having read the statements and written *T* or *F*, ask students to underline the true statements in the text and correct the false statements in their notebooks. (2 Allela's invention produces an audio message on a phone screen. 4 Gnikou wants to use these printers to make medical equipment to help disabled people. 5 Majik Water uses a chemical process to take water from the air and convert it into drinking water. 6 The three inventors have not done everything they wanted to achieve.) Check answers with the class.

THINK!

Put students into pairs to discuss the question. Ask students to come up with at least two inventions. Have students discuss how useful each invention would be for humanity.

Homework

Workbook page 139, Exercises 1, 2, and 3

READING

1 **Look at the title, headings, and images in the article. Circle the correct options in the sentence below.**

The article is about *technological inventions* / *survival techniques* that some people *have developed* / *might develop* in a *country* / *continent*.

LOOKING FOR INNOVATION? HERE'S AFRICA FOR YOU

A large and young population that wants change. Countries like Rwanda and Ethiopia, examples of the world's fastest growing economies. Many problems to solve. These ingredients make Africa the perfect place for innovation. In fact, some recent African developments have already surprised the world.

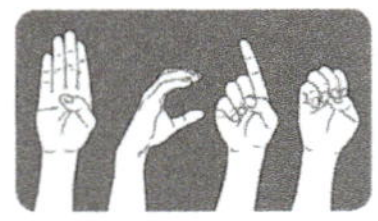

SMART GLOVES FOR SIGN LANGUAGE

Roy Allela's niece was born deaf and has to use sign language. Because no one in Allela's family could communicate with her, he designed a translation glove: his niece wears the glove and connects it to a phone. The phone then translates her hand movements into an audio message. Allela's dream is to see these gloves in all Kenyan schools that have deaf students. He hasn't achieved this objective yet, but he's working hard on it.

3-D PRINTERS FROM E-WASTE

Electronic waste from around the world is one of Africa's big problems. Afate Gnikou from Togo has decided to do something with it: he has constructed 3-D printers using parts of old computers, scanners, and other electronics. He now works with a lab which has given these printers to local schools. In the future, Gnikou wants to use these printers to make medical equipment to help disabled people.

WATER FROM THE AIR

There is six times more water in the air than in all the rivers on Earth. During a drought in 2016, when Kenya had almost no rain, Beth Koigi had a brilliant idea: her Majik Water invention uses a chemical process to take water from the air and convert it into drinking water. She has already produced a prototype of her invention.

2 7.03 **Read and listen to the article. What motivated these people to create something? Write *A* (Allela), *G* (Gnikou), or *K* (Koigi). There is one extra answer.**

1 a problem with old objects G
2 money difficulties –
3 a problem in the family A
4 extreme weather conditions K

3 **Write *T* (true) or *F* (false).**

1 The article lists three reasons to explain why there are many innovations in Africa. T
2 Allela's invention produces a written message on a phone screen. F
3 For his 3-D printer Gnikou uses materials that people have thrown away. T
4 Students near the lab Gnikou works with are making medical equipment with their printers. F
5 Koigi's Majik Water produces cleaner drinking water from rivers. F
6 The three inventors have done everything they wanted to achieve. F

THINK!
Each of these innovators invented something to solve a problem. What problems do you see around you and what inventions might help solve them?

78

WORKBOOK p.139

Language in Context
Lesson Aims: I can use the present perfect with the expressions *already, just,* and *yet.*

1 Have students read the sentences in the chart. Ask them to refer to the article on page 78 to complete it. Draw their attention to the three headings *Already, Just,* and *Yet.* Explain that *already* is used to talk about something that has been done, e.g.: *She has already finished studying. Just* is used to talk about something that happened a few moments ago, e.g.: *I have just arrived. Yet* is used to say that something is going to happen very soon, e.g.: *I have not called him yet.* Draw students' attention to the fact that in the US, *already, just,* and *yet* are often used with the simple past.

2 Have students do the activity individually. Remind them how we structure the present perfect tense. They can use the grammar chart in Exercise 1 to help them. Draw their attention to the words *already, just,* and *yet.* Students check their answers in pairs. Then check answers with the class.

LOOK!

Draw attention to the sentences in the *Look!* box. Remind students that the words *just* and *already* always come after the verb *has/have.* Students tend to change the order: ~~*I just have received your letter.*~~ *I have just received your letter.*

3 Have a volunteer read the sentences 1–5. Draw student's attention to the check marks beside each phrase of Tamara's checklist. Ask: *What has Tamara already done? What hasn't she done yet?* Have them write sentences about Tamara using the words *already, just,* and *yet.* Have them check and compare their answers in small groups.

USE IT!

4 Have a volunteer read the prompts for the sentences. Have a student give an example by using one of the words: *already, yet,* or *just.* Have students use the prompts to make up more sentences or have them come up with other ideas. Draw students' attention to the expression *turn 15.* Explain its meaning and have them practice it by asking when their birthdays are and when will they turn 14 or 15.

UNIT 7

LANGUAGE IN CONTEXT

1 **Look at the examples below. Complete the sentences from the article.**

Present Perfect with *Already, Just,* and *Yet*

Already	*Just*	*Yet*
I **have already finished** my homework. Beth Koigi [1] has already produced a prototype. Some African developments [2] have already surprised the world.	I know Felipe is at home. I**'ve just spoken** to him. It**'s just started** raining. Let's stay here. My brothers **have just gone** out. They left five minutes ago.	We **haven't uploaded** the file **yet.** Roy Allela [3] hasn't achieved this objective yet. **Have** you **met** my cousin **yet?** **Have** scientists **discovered** a cure **yet?**

2 **Put the words in the correct order to make sentences and a question.**

1 lives / invention / already / This / improved / our / has
This invention has already improved our lives.
2 have / posted / I / photos / some / online / just
I have just posted some photos online.
3 haven't / The / the / downloaded / students / yet / file
The students haven't downloaded the file yet.
4 We / the / events / organized / have / sports / already
We have already organized the sports events.
5 yet / company / developed / Has / an / the / app ?
Has the company developed an app yet?

LOOK!
Use *already* and *just* after *have/has*.
I **have just** received your email.
She **has already** written the summary.

3 **Tamara has to write a blog post about an African invention. Look at her checklist and write what she has and hasn't done. Use *already, just,* and *yet.***

1 She has already chosen the invention.
2 She has already searched for information.
3 She has just written the first draft.
4 She hasn't asked a friend for feedback yet.
5 She hasn't produced the final version yet.

1 choose the invention ✓
2 search for information ✓
3 write the first draft ✓
4 ask a friend for feedback
5 produce the final version

USE IT!

4 **Write sentences about yourself with *already, just,* and *yet* in your notebook. Use the ideas below or your own ideas.**

- do all my homework for tomorrow
- learn how to use *already, just,* and *yet*
- finish Exercise 3
- take driving lessons
- have lunch
- turn 15

5 **Work in groups. Take turns reading your sentences to the group. Discuss the sentences and then tell the class some information about your group.**

Adriana has already done all her homework for tomorrow.

Pedro and I haven't finished Exercise 3 yet.

WORKBOOK p.136 and 138 PRACTICE EXTRA

5 Put students into groups and have them share the sentences each one wrote. Draw students' attention to the speech bubbles. Invite two students from different groups to model the activity. Then, invite individuals within the group to report information that they've learned to the class, as in the example given.

Grammar Game

Play the game "My Lying Bucket List." Encourage students to create a bucket list (a list of experiences or achievements that a person hopes to do or accomplish during their lifetime). Individually, have each student write six items on their bucket list in their notebooks. Have students swap notebooks with a partner. Students should then read their partner's bucket list and interview them regarding all they have accomplished by asking further questions and getting more information. The partner should convince his interviewer that he has already done the whole list. Encourage students to use the words *just, already,* and *yet.*

Homework

Workbook page 138, Exercises 1 and 2

Practice Extra

Unit 7

Listening and Vocabulary

Lesson Aim: I can understand a podcast about an extreme sport; I can understand people saying how they feel about certain sports.

Warmer

Put students into groups of three. On *Go!* have students list as many unusual or extreme sports as they can think of. The group that names the most in five minutes wins.

7.04–7.06 Audioscripts pT144

Target Vocabulary

afraid of	/əˈfreɪd.ʌv/
famous for	/ˈfeɪ·məs.fɔr/
good at	/gʊd.æt/
interested in	/ˈɪn·trə·stɪd.ɪn/
proud of	/praʊd.ʌv/
tired of	/taɪərd.ʌv/

1 Invite students to look at the image. Read the questions with students and have them answer in pairs. Have them report their answers to the class. Discuss other lesser-known sports with the class.

2 7.04 Have a volunteer read the first half of sentences 1–4. Individually, have students try to match the sentences by using the context. Have them compare their answers in pairs. Play the audio to check their work.

3 7.05 Read through sentences 1–6 with students. Play the audio and have them circle the correct alternatives individually while listening. Have them check in pairs. Play the audio once more if necessary.

4 7.06 Invite students to read all the **a** sentences individually. Have them then read the words in each box. Have them try to match the words to make expressions. Then have them complete the **b** sentences using the expressions. Remind them that the meaning of both sentences needs to be the same. Play the audio for them to check their work. Have them repeat the sentences. Encourage them to make up more sentences using the expressions.

LISTENING AND VOCABULARY

1 **Look at the image of a man skimboarding. Then work in pairs and discuss the answers to the questions.**

1 Have you ever heard of skimboarding? Have you ever done it?
2 Do you think skimboarding is a cool thing to do? Why / Why not?

2 7.04 **Listen to the beginning of a podcast. Match 1–4 with a–d.**

1 The name of the podcast is ___c___
2 Today's episode is about ___a___
3 The title of the movie is ___b___
4 The director of the movie is ___d___

a a movie about a skimboarder.
b *Skimboarding Pro.*
c Dlamini Pod.
d Sofia Vieira.

3 7.05 **Listen to the whole podcast and circle the correct options.**

1 Sofia has made several movies about *Angola / surfing.*
2 Pedro spent a lot of time *watching the surfers / skateboarding near the beach.*
3 When he started skimboarding he *knew a lot / didn't know anything* about the sport.
4 In 2019 *a movie director / some sports people* saw that Pedro was good at skimboarding.
5 The movie has received *positive / negative* reviews.
6 The critic believes Sofia's movies are successful because she loves *Angola / telling stories.*

4 7.06 **Complete the b sentences using a word from each box so that they mean the same as the a sentences. Then listen, check, and repeat the phrases.**

• afraid	• famous	• good
• interested	• proud	• ~~tired~~

• at	• for	• in
• ~~of~~	• of	• of

1 a Waiting for the bus always makes me feel impatient.
b I'm ___tired of___ waiting for the bus.

2 a My brother sings well.
b My brother is ___good at___ singing.

3 a Everyone knows about Brazil's beaches.
b Brazil is ___famous for___ its beaches.

4 a Spiders don't make me feel scared.
b I'm not ___afraid of___ spiders.

5 a I don't like kayaking anymore.
b I'm not ___interested in___ kayaking anymore.

6 a My dad's paintings make him feel good about himself.
b My dad is ___proud of___ his paintings.

80

WORKBOOK p.137

Homework

Workbook page 137, Exercises 3 and 4

Language in Context

Lesson Aim: I can use the present perfect with the expressions *since* and *for*.

1 Draw students' attention to the use of the present perfect and the words *since* and *for* in the sentences in the chart. Tell them we use *for* when we measure the duration of an action and we use *since* when we give the starting point of an action, event, or state. If necessary, play Track 7.05 again to help students complete the chart. Check by having students read their sentences.

2 Students can use the grammar chart in Exercise 1 for help. Have them work individually. Have them check their work in pairs.

LOOK!

Draw attention to the sentence in the *Look!* box. Have a volunteer read the sentence and then give more examples which are true for them. Elicit more examples from the class. Remind them to always use the present perfect, e.g.: ~~*I studied English since I was four.*~~ *I have studied English since I was four.*

3 Have students work individually, trying to order the questions using the prompts and then answering them appropriately using the word in parentheses. Refer them to the grammar chart, if necessary.

USE IT!

4 Invite students to read the questions and check the column which is true for them. Have them come up with two more questions.

5 Model the conversation in the speech bubbles with a student. Put students into pairs to do the exercise. Encourage them to answer using both *since* and *for*.

Homework

Workbook page 138, Exercises 3 and 4

Practice Extra

Unit 7

Fast Finishers

Puzzles and Games page 105, Exercise 2

LANGUAGE IN CONTEXT

1 Complete the sentences from the podcast in the chart. Use the words below and *since* or *for*.

- 's been ... a few weeks
- 's received ... the opening night
- 've been ... many years

Present Perfect with *Since* and *For*

Since	*For*
I've **lived** in Angola **since 2021**.	I [2]'ve been a big fan for many years.
You've **studied** French **since February**.	You've **been** my English teacher **for a long time**.
Sofia **has made** movies about Angola **since** she left college.	It [3]'s been in movie theaters for a few weeks.
It [1]'s received excellent reviews since the opening night.	We've **watched** TV **for two hours**.

How long have you known Marco? I've known him **since I was 11**. / I've known him **for four years**.
How long has your sister played the guitar? **Since last year**. / **For ten months**.

2 Complete the sentences with *for* or *since*.

1 My father has liked painting since he was a teenager.
2 I've played the piano since I was six years old.
3 Here's a snack. You haven't eaten anything for hours!
4 My cousins have had a vlog for two years.
5 South Africa has been an independent country since 1910.
6 This company hasn't developed a new product for a long time.

LOOK!
Use the present perfect with *since*.
I **have known** my best friend **since** I was five. (= We have been friends for ten years.)

3 Write questions with *how long* and answer the questions.

1 Brasília / be / the Brazilian capital? (since)
How long has Brasília been the Brazilian capital? It's been the Brazilian capital since 1960.
2 you / live / in your neighborhood? (for)
How long have you lived in your neighborhood? I've lived in my neighborhood for ... years/months/weeks.
3 you / know / your best friend? (since)
How long have you known your best friend? I've known him/her since I was eight / last year / etc.
4 your English teacher / be / in the classroom? (for)
How long has your English teacher been in the classroom? He's/She's been in the classroom for 20 minutes / an hour / etc.

USE IT!

4 Check (✓) *Yes* or *No* so that the answer is true for you.

Students' own answers	Yes	No
Do you play a musical instrument?		
Do you have a pet?		
Are you interested in sports?		
Do you have a smartphone?		

Do you play a musical instrument?
Yes, I play the guitar.
How long have you played it?

5 Work in pairs. Take turns asking the questions in Exercise 4. When your partner answers *Yes*, find out more information by asking a question with *How long*.

WORKBOOK p.136 and 138 PRACTICE EXTRA

Grammar Game

Students play a game of "Call My Bluff." Divide students into teams of four. Teams will play against each other. Players have to trick the opposing side using a present perfect statement about themselves. Team A chooses one of the words (*since, for, just, already*, and *yet*) and tells Team B the word. Then, each member of Team B makes up a sentence about themselves using this word. It can be a true or false statement. Team A must then ask questions in order to find out if each statement is true or not. Team A is awarded one point for every grammatically correct question asked. Teams take turns.

Extension

Each student should write two sentences about themselves using the present perfect with *since, for, just, already*, and *yet*. Have students put their pencils and pens down and close their eyes. In turns, all students should read out one of their sentences. When all students have read their sentences, students can open their eyes and should try to remember who said which sentence and write it down.

Around the World

Lesson Aim: I can understand a text about Himba culture.

7.2 Fashion from Africa

The video on page 83 and accompanying exercises below can be used as a lead-in to the topic of the Around the World text, or after the reading activities to complete the unit.

Summary

The video is about the world of fashion in African countries.

In Class

Tell students they're going to watch a video about how amazing the fashion world is in Africa. Although we are talking about one continent, its fashion varies immensely from country to country. Not only its fabrics, but its colors and patterns. Ask: *What do you imagine African fashion is like? What do people wear in Africa?*

Exercise 1

Ask students to watch the video to answer the questions.

1 *What is a* djellaba *and where do people wear them?* Check the answer with the class.
It is a type of tunic that men wear in Morocco.

2 *What is the name of the fashion show that appears in the video?* Check the answer with the class.
Dakar Fashion Week

Exercise 2

Write the following sentences/questions on the board. Play the video again and have students answer them. Then, ask them to watch the video again and make up two more questions to ask their partners.

1 A type of blanket, worn by the Maasai people in Kenya is called a ___shuka___.

2 The countries and cultures in Africa all have the same traditional clothes and styles.
( ) True (✗)False
Have students justify their answers with examples from the video.

3 Order the sentences according to when they are mentioned in the video.
(4) The colors and patterns on the cloth are printed with mud.
(2) A *djellaba* is a tunic that men wear.
(1) Africa is so diverse.
(5) Dakar Fashion Week happens every year in Senegal.
(3) Every color in *kente* has a meaning.

AROUND THE WORLD

The Himba

The Himba almost disappeared in the 1980s because of war and drought. Since then, their population has grown. People think there may be more than 25,000 Himba in Namibia today.

1

2

Himba ways

In Himba society the men make political decisions and look after the cows and goats. The women milk the animals, carry water to the village, cook, and build their huts.

3

4

Himba women and men are famous for their complex hairstyles. Girls, women, older boys, and men all wear their hair in braids, but in different styles. Some young girls wear braids over their faces and older girls start wearing a headpiece made of goat skin, which looks like three leaves. After getting married or having a child, they wear a different headpiece. Himba women also cover their bodies with butterfat – the fat from cow's milk – and red coloring.

Good thinkers

The modern world hasn't had much influence on traditional Himba culture. That's why scientists are interested in studying the Himba. One of the questions scientists want to answer is: "Do the Himba think in the same way as people in other societies?" The results of some studies have shown that the Himba are better at finding creative ways to solve problems. Also, their attention to detail is amazing and they achieve better results on tests like the Ebbinghaus illusion than many other people.

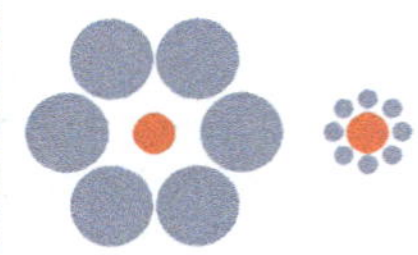

The Ebbinghaus illusion: which orange circle is bigger?

Tradition and modern life

Since Namibia's independence in 1990, some things have changed for the Himba. Some young people have already left their villages to get a job or go to school. Some haven't come back. In the villages, some Himba think integration with the modern world is necessary, while others think it will destroy their culture. Time will tell.

5

82

At Home

Exercise 3

Ask students to make an infographic depicting the different traditions in fashion in Africa. Encourage them to add details such as country, color, patterns, and meanings. Have them research more on the Internet and add images, if possible. Have them share their work on a collaborative platform.

Background Information

All over Africa, some tribes like the Himba still respect and live according to the traditions of their ancestors. Himba culture has nearly disappeared a dozen times due to war, droughts, and other conditions. It is a tribe located in northwestern Namibia.

7.07 Audioscript pT144

1 Ask a volunteer to read sentences 1–2 and their three alternatives before reading the text on page 82. Draw their attention to the title and the images to help them choose the correct alternative. Have them justify their choices.

2 7.07 Again, ask a volunteer to read sentences 1–4. Then invite students to read the text and underline information related to sentences 1–4. Have them correct the one false statement while listening to the audio. Check answers with the class. Draw their attention to the expression *time will tell* at the end of the text. Have them infer its meaning (it means that it will not be known whether it is true or not until sometime in the future).

3 Have students take turns to read out sentences 1–6. Individually, have them circle the correct alternative from memory. Ask them to check their work in pairs by reading the text again.

Words in Context

4 Ask students to find the words in the article. Have them label the images accordingly. Check answers with the class. Encourage them to come up with a paragraph using all the words, about the Himba community. Have them share their paragraphs.

5 Encourage students to use the paragraphs they made up in Exercise 4 and the information from the text to make a caption for each of the images in the text. Have them share their captions.

1 **Look at the text. Check (✓) the correct options.**

1 The text is from …
a ◯ a story book for children.
b ✓ an encyclopedia for young people.
c ◯ a history textbook for teenagers.

2 The objective of the text is to …
a ◯ tell a story about an African family.
b ◯ explain how some African people lived in the past.
c ✓ give information about an African society.

2 7.07 **Read and listen to the text. Check (✓) the false sentence.**

1 ◯ Most Himba people have kept their traditional culture.
2 ◯ In Himba society, hairstyles have important meanings.
3 ◯ Scientists have tested the way Himba people think.
4 ✓ The Himba population today is smaller than in the 1980s.

3 **Circle the correct options.**

1 In Himba society men and women *share* / *don't share* the same responsibilities.
2 Himba men don't have to *take care of animals* / *construct homes*.
3 Women change their *hairstyle* / *skin color* when they get married.
4 The Himba have shown that they can *develop illusion tests* / *think creatively*.
5 The Himba are *good at* / *proud of* concentrating on details.
6 *All* / *Not all* Himba who get a job come back to their village.

WORDS IN CONTEXT

4 **Find these words in the text and label the images.**

• goat • hut • leaves • braids

a 
goat

b 
braids

c 
leaves

d 
hut

5 **In your notebook, write captions for images 1–5 in the text. Use the words in Exercise 4 and information from the text.**

THINK!

Think about an indigenous society you know (from Africa or from another continent). What are the people good at? What can they teach other societies?

WEBQUEST

Learn more! Check (✓) the correct answer.
Which orange circle is bigger in the Ebbinghaus illusion? What other illusions like this can you find?

◯ **the circle on the left**
◯ **the circle on the right**
✓ **the circles are the same size**

VIDEO

7.2

1 What's a djellaba and where do people wear them?
2 What is the name the fashion show that appears in the video?

THINK!

In small groups, encourage students to make a list of indigenous societies they have heard of. If time allows, have them research more about these societies and write down at least five interesting facts about them and where they are from. Have students reflect on whether these societies can teach other societies.

WEBQUEST

Remind students of how to keep safe while searching for information on the Internet. Ask them to tell you two things they should do to make sure their search is safe and accurate. Have students research the Ebbinghaus illusion. Ask them to discuss how the visual system works and why this is an illusion. Have them bring their research to class and share their findings.

Speaking
Lesson Aim: I can present new information about an app.

7.08–7.11 Audioscripts pT144

1 7.08 Have students look at the image. Ask: *What can you see? What is the girl doing? What do you think is happening?* Have students read 1–3 and match them with a–c by using the context of the sentences. Then have then them read and listen to Rafaela's vlog to confirm their answers.

Living English

2 Check understanding of the three expressions. Ask students to find them in Rafaela's vlog in Exercise 1 and see how she uses each expression. Play Track 7.08 again if necessary, so that students can focus on pronunciation and intonation. When students have completed the chart, invite students to read out their answers. Have students think of similar expressions in their own language.

3 7.09 Play the audio, pausing after each expression for the class to repeat. Then ask individual students to say the expressions. Encourage them to exaggerate the intonation.

Pronunciation

4 7.10 Play the audio. Encourage students to listen carefully to the different pronunciations of the ending *–ed*. Point out that the endings are pronounced differently: *worked* and *liked* have a /t/ sound, *started* and *wanted* have an /ɪd/ sound, and *listened* and *arrived* have a /d/ sound at the end. Play the audio again so students can hear the difference. Write down more examples of verbs ending in /t/, /ɪd/, and /d/ on the board.

5 7.10 Have students listen and repeat the words quickly and naturally, focusing on the pronunciation of the endings. Ask them to look for other words ending *–ed* in their books and practice the pronunciation.

6 7.11 Have students read the words above the chart. Play the audio so students can listen to the sentences. Have them complete the chart according to the pronunciation of the ending of each word. Have students check their work in pairs. Then play the audio again for them to check.

7 7.08 Have the class read the vlog along with the audio. Then play the audio again, pausing for the class to repeat what Rafaela says. Finally, in pairs, have students practice reading the vlog to each other.

8 Read through the steps with students and check understanding. Tell them to use the vocabulary and expressions they have learned from this and previous units. Have them use the vlog in Exercise 1 as reference. Try to find time in class for pairs to present their vlogs. If this is not possible, monitor pairs as they practice and provide feedback on intonation for presenting new information.

Your Digital Portfolio

Give students a date for uploading their work and make sure they all listen to one another's vlogs.

Practice Extra

Unit 7

SPEAKING

1 7.08 **Read and listen to the vlog. Then match 1–3 with a–c.**

Rafaela Hi, I'm Rafaela and welcome to my music channel.
OK, so for a long time I've wanted to find a way to hear the best of new African music. And guess what? I've just found out that there's the perfect app – it's called Music&More. Basically, you choose the country or type of music you like. Then the app shows what teenagers around the world have listened to and liked recently. This is how it works …

1 The vlog is about c
2 In Music&More you can select a
3 The app shows b

a "Nigeria" and "rap," for example.
b the music other teenagers have enjoyed.
c an app that introduces you to new music from Africa.

LIVING ENGLISH

2 **Complete the chart with the expressions below.**

• basically, … • guess what? • I've just found out …

Expression used to introduce …	
1 a summary of the main information	basically
2 something exciting	guess what?
3 information you've discovered recently	I've just found out

PRONUNCIATION

4 7.10 **Listen and pay attention to the different pronunciations of *–ed*.**

/t/ liked /d/ listened /ɪd/ wanted

5 7.10 **Listen again and repeat.**

3 7.09 **Listen and repeat the expressions.**

6 7.11 **Listen and complete the chart with the correct words below.**

• decided • lived • played • posted • ~~searched~~ • walked

/t/	/d/	/ɪd/
searched	lived	posted
walked	played	decided

7 7.08 **Listen to the vlog again. Then take turns reading the vlog to a partner.**

8 **Role play a vlog about an app you've started using recently. Follow the steps.**

1 Decide on the topic of your app: music, food, movies, art, or sports.
2 Write the text for your vlog in your notebook. Use the vlog in Exercise 1 for ideas.
3 Take turns reading your vlog to a partner and comment on your partner's vlog.

YOUR DIGITAL PORTFOLIO
Record your dialogue, then upload it to your class digital portfolio.

84

PRACTICE EXTRA

What's Important to Me?

Lesson Aim: I can talk about things that are important to me.

Warmer

Put students into groups and have them list five worries they have about the future. Ask them to classify their worries between family, work, and health. Have them share their ideas with the class.

THINK!

1 Ask students to look at the image and describe what they see. Ask: *Does he look happy? Worried? Thoughtful?* In pairs, have students write down what they believe the boy might be thinking about. Have them share their thoughts.

2 Have students read the question and discuss with a partner what they do when they have to make an important decision. Ask: *Do you talk to your parents? Friends?* Have them share their ideas with the class.

8.1 What Motivates You?

Summary

The video is about activities that motivate us.

In Class

Tell students they are going to watch a video about different activities people do that motivate them. In pairs, have students write a list of things that motivate them. Have them share their list with the class. Ask: *Do you find that motivated people are more successful than unmotivated people? Are you very motivated to do things or do you need motivation?*

Exercise 1

Ask students to watch the video to answer the questions.

1 *What three sports are there in a triathlon?* Check the answer with the class.
swimming, cycling, and running

2 *Name three types of motivation in the video.* Check the answer with the class.
to be the best; winning prizes, awards, or qualifications; a feeling of satisfaction; helping other people

Exercise 2

Write the following sentences/questions on the board. Play the video again and have students answer them. Then, ask them to watch the video again and make up two more questions to ask their partners.

1 A triathlon consists of
( ) a 3.8-kilometer swim, a 180-kilometer bike ride, and a 21-kilometer run
(✗) a 3.8-kilometer swim, a 180-kilometer bike ride, and a 42-kilometer run
( ) a 5-kilometer swim, a 42-kilometer bike ride, and a 180-kilometer run

2 Some people need a *physical challenge* to motivate them.

3 The following activity was not mentioned in the video
( ) volunteer work
( ) running a triathlon
( ) playing an instrument
(✗) reading to the elderly
( ) cleaning up the environment

At Home

Exercise 3

Have students write down their motivation to learn English. Ask: *Do you have an English goal?* Have them write a list of things they can do to reach their goal.

Resources

- Teacher's worksheets Unit 8
- Test Generator Unit 8
- Practice Extra Unit 8
- Workbook pages 140–143
- Puzzles and Games page 105

Flipped Classroom

Ask students if their have heard of the acronym FOMO (Fear Of Missing Out). Ask students to research it on the Internet and build a mind map explaining some of the causes and consequences.

Unit Aims

Cambridge Life Competencies Framework

I can …

- use simple techniques to start, maintain, and close conversations of various lengths to talk about what's important to me. **(Communication)**
- understand essential grammatical terms and concepts: using and understanding the difference between subject and object questions. **(Learning to Learn)**
- state opposing opinions in a respectful way when discussing my ideas. **(Emotional Development)**
- use strategies and techniques for improving my English (e.g., mind maps to organize my thoughts). **(Learning to Learn)**
- understand how personal habits and behaviour have the capacity to affect others. **(Social Responsibility)**
- give supportive feedback to other students' comments. **(Collaboration)**

Vocabulary in Context
Lesson Aim: I can talk about my worries and important decisions I have to make about my lifeworld.

Warmer

Put students into pairs. Ask Student A to choose one of the following topics and ask a question to Student B using the present perfect, simple present, or simple past tenses.

- health
- school
- home
- relationships
- parents
- bullying
- sports
- shopping

Possible questions: *Have you had problems recently at home? Do you have a girlfriend? Have you been bullied? Do you play sports? Is sports an important topic in your life?*

Model the conversation with a student before they begin. Have students change roles and repeat.

Flipped Classroom Check

Ask students to share their understanding of FOMO, and have them talk about their hopes and fears related to it. Ask them to share their mind maps and encourage them to add on ideas mentioned by their colleagues.

8.01 Audioscript pT144

Target Vocabulary

do your best	/du.jʊr.best/
do physical activities	/du.ˈfɪz·ɪ·kəl. æk'tɪv·ə·t̬iz/
do the shopping	/du.ðə.ˈʃɑp·ɪŋ/
do volunteer work	/du.ˌvɑl·ən'tɪər. wɜrk/
do well	/du.wel/
have an opportunity	/hæv.ən.ˌɑp·ər' tu·nɪ·t̬i/
have time	/hæv.taɪm/
have trouble	/hæv.ˈtrʌb·əl/
make a difference	/meɪk.ə.'/ dɪf·rəns
make decisions	/meɪk. dɪ'sɪʒ·ənz/
make mistakes	/meɪk. mɪ'steɪks/
make money	/meɪk.ˈmʌn·i/

VOCABULARY IN CONTEXT

PHRASES WITH *DO*, *HAVE*, AND *MAKE*

1 Look at the images and read the labels. Then circle the correct options.

What do teens worry about?

1

Having / *Making* good **decisions** about the subjects they will study

2

Doing / *Making* **their best** at school

3

Having / *Doing* enough **time** to *do* / *make* **physical activities**

4

How they can avoid doing / *making* **mistakes** in their relationships

5

Responsibilities they have at home, like cooking and *doing* / *having* **the shopping**

6

How to avoid *doing* / *having* **trouble** with bullies at school

7

How they can *do* / *make* **well** at sports

8

How to make sure they *have* / *make* an **opportunity** to *do* / *make* **money** in the future

9

Finding ways to *have* / *make* **a difference** in other people's lives, such as *doing* / *having* **volunteer work**

86

1 Read the title with the whole class. In pairs, have students look at the images and have them guess what each image portrays. Then invite students to read through the sentences below the images individually. Have them check any uncertainties about the vocabulary, at first with a partner, and then with you. Ask if any of the images relate to the topics mentioned in the Warmer. Then have students circle the correct alternative in each sentence. Have them check in pairs.

Vocabulary in Context
Lesson Aim: I can use expressions with the words *do*, *have*, and *make* when talking about important decisions in my life.

8.01 Audioscript pT144

2 8.01 Draw students' attention to the images of the four teenagers. Read through the words above each speech bubble and have students complete them by combining the words with *do*, *have*, or *make*. Encourage students to check the sentences which are also true for them. Help with vocabulary as necessary. Play the audio to check their work.

3 Draw students' attention to the headings in the chart. Have them analyze the sentences they completed in Exercise 2 and classify the phrases under the correct heading. Have them compare their work in pairs.

USE IT!

4 Students answer questions related to important decisions in their lives. Encourage them to make additional questions of their own to ask their peers.

5 Model one question and answer with a student, then put students into pairs to ask and answer the questions. If they wrote additional questions in Exercise 4, they should ask and answer those, too. Ask volunteers to ask and answer their questions in front of the class.

Homework

Workbook page 141, Exercises 1 and 2

Practice Extra

Unit 8

Fast Finishers

Puzzles and Games page 105, Exercise 3

Extension

Have students look back at Exercises 2 and 4 for reference. Have them write a short paragraph using the teenagers' statements as examples and their answers in Exercise 4 as input. Have them expand on their answers from Exercise 4 with more detail or choose another related topic to talk about. Remind them to focus on using the expressions learned in this lesson. Have them share their work with a peer.

UNIT 8

2 8.01 **Complete the four descriptions with *do*, *have*, or *make* and the words below. Then listen, check and repeat the phrases.**

• a difference • the shopping • ~~volunteer work~~

I [1] *do volunteer work* every week at our community center. I [2] *do the shopping* for people who can't leave their homes. I want to [3] *make a difference* in the world.

• an opportunity • physical activities • time

Studying is important to me. I don't [4] *do physical activities* very often – only in PE classes at school – and I don't [5] *have time* to go out every weekend. But I know that if I focus on my goals, I'll [6] *have an opportunity* to study abroad when I'm older.

• decisions • trouble • well

I'm a "study buddy" at school. When students [7] *have trouble* with a school subject, they can come and talk to me. I also help them [8] *make decisions* about which elective classes to take. I like to help other students to [9] *do well* at school.

• mistakes • money • your best

I own an online channel about computer games, and I [10] *make money* from it! I think it's important to [11] *do your best* and I want to start my own game company one day. I'm learning a lot about the industry – even when I [12] *make mistakes*, I learn something from them.

3 **Write the phrases from Exercise 2 in the chart.**

do	have	make
volunteer work	*time,*	*a difference,*
the shopping,	*an opportunity,*	*decisions, money,*
physical activities, well	*trouble,*	*mistakes*
your best		

USE IT!

4 **Write answers to the questions using your own ideas.** *Students' own answers*

1 Who do you talk to when you have trouble at home?

2 How important is it to you to make a lot of money in the future?

3 Have you ever done volunteer work? If so, where?

4 How can teenagers make a difference in the world?

5 **Work in pairs. Take turns asking and answering the questions in Exercise 4.**

WORKBOOK p.141 PRACTICE EXTRA

Reading
Lesson Aim: I can read, understand, and give advice on solving teen dilemmas.

Warmer

Write down the word *dilemma* on the board. Check understanding of the word with students. Ask them to give you an example of a typical dilemma. Have each student write down at least two dilemmas they have had recently regarding something that happened in their lives. Give them an example, e.g.: *Your sister is driving you to school. At a traffic light, she takes out her cell phone and starts texting, but you both know it's illegal to use it while driving. What do you do?* Have students bring up different dilemmas they have had recently and have them share them with the class.

8.02 Audioscript pT144

1 Have students look at the pamphlet. Draw their attention to the title. Ask them to read the first paragraph and infer what the text could be about. Ask them to read the alternatives and check the correct one. Check answers with the class.

2 **8.02** Have volunteers read the dilemmas with both possible solutions to check understanding. Invite students to read the text in order to complete the sentences. Draw students' attention to some words they might not know: *shelter, bead,* and *cheated*. Have them try to infer the meaning. If necessary, have them check the dictionary. Play the audio to check their work. Have them check to see if any of the dilemmas they wrote down in the Warmer were similar to the ones described in the pamphlet. Ask: *Would you play this game?* Have them justify their answer.

3 Have a volunteer read through sentences 1–4. In pairs, have students match the sentences to the dilemma cards. Have them justify their choices. If time allows, have students give suggested solutions to their friends' dilemmas from the Warmer.

READING

DILEMMA TEENS

In this fun game, you and your friends try to suggest solutions to dilemmas that teens might face. Do you think you know your friends well? Play **Dilemma Teens** and find out!

Check out some dilemmas you will face in **Dilemma Teens!**

D1
Your best friend has had a jewelry business for a few months – she uses beads to make necklaces and bracelets. You have always thought her pieces are awful, but you have never said anything. Yesterday, she asked you to write a review of her jewelry for her blog. You agreed to do it.
What do you do? Do you lie in your review?

D2
You did volunteer work at an animal shelter last year. Although you love animals, you decided to leave after six months because the coordinator always shouted at everyone. She called you yesterday asking for help. All the other volunteers have stopped working there. She was very insistent on the phone.
What do you do? Do you go and help at the shelter?

D3
You're a "study buddy" at school. A student has had a lot of trouble with math and she didn't do well last semester. You helped her study for a math test, but she still made a lot of simple mistakes the day before. The teacher gave the test scores yesterday and this student got an A. You think she cheated on the test.
What do you do? Do you tell the teacher?

You can play **Dilemma Teens** face-to-face or download the app and challenge your friends anywhere, anytime!

1 Look at the pamphlet. Check (✓) its purpose.

1 ✓ to advertise a game 2 ◯ to review a game 3 ◯ to give instructions for a game

2 8.02 Read and listen to the pamphlet. Complete the sentences with the phrases below.

- avoiding a difficult person
- being honest
- causing trouble
- keeping quiet
- taking care of animals
- ~~telling a lie~~

1 In card D1, the choice is between telling a lie and being honest about a friend's work.
2 In card D2, the choice is between taking care of animals/avoiding a difficult person and avoiding a difficult person/taking care of animals
3 In card D3, the choice is between causing trouble/keeping quiet for someone and keeping quiet/causing trouble.

3 Read the thoughts of four players. Match them with the dilemma cards. There is one extra thought.

a "Hmm ... I can't stand people shouting at me, but the poor dogs and cats need help." D2
b "What a difficult situation! Why ever did I agree to do that?" D1
c "Gosh ... should I tell a lie about my bad grade? Or should I tell the truth?" c –
d "Well, the teacher trusts me, but I'm not completely sure she copied her answers from another student." D3

THINK!
Work in pairs. Take turns answering the questions on the dilemma cards. Explain your suggested solutions.

88

WORKBOOK p.143

THINK!

Put students into pairs and encourage them to answer the dilemma cards from the pamphlet. Have them justify their answers. Take feedback from the whole class. Take a survey to choose the best answer.

Homework

Workbook page 143, Exercises 1, 2, and 3

Language in Context
Lesson Aims: I can use the present perfect and simple past, and understand the difference between them.

1 Encourage students to look back at the pamphlet on page 88 to help them complete the chart. Draw their attention to the headings in each row. When they finish, have volunteers read the sentences aloud. Have them explain the differences between the tenses.

2 Students can use the grammar chart in Exercise 1 for help. Invite them to read through sentences 1–5 and the verbs in parentheses. Ask students to identify clues which will tell them whether they should use the present perfect or the simple past. To check answers, invite individual students to read out a sentence each.

LOOK!

Draw attention to the *Look!* box. Write the words/phrases *yesterday, in 2018*, and *five days ago* on the board. Have students make up sentences using them. Draw their attention to the verb tense they used. Have a volunteer read the sentences in the *Look!* box. Have them identify the sentences with the simple past in Exercise 2.

3 Invite students to look at the photograph and read the small write-up about the inventor of *Dilemma Teens*. Individually, have students put the sentences in order, taking into consideration the time the action happened, so they know which tense to use. Have them check in pairs.

USE IT!

4 Encourage students to use the present perfect to write two true sentences and one false one about something they have recently done.

5 Read the sentences and questions in the speech bubbles with a student to model the activity. Put students into pairs. Student A reads their first sentence. Student B asks a question to try to guess whether the statement is true or false. Student A should answer Student B's questioning until they are able to guess. Students then swap roles and repeat.

UNIT 8

LANGUAGE IN CONTEXT

1 Look at the examples below. Complete the sentences from the pamphlet.

Present Perfect vs. Simple Past	
Unspecified Time in the Past	Your best friend [1] has had a jewelry business for a few months. You [2] have always thought her pieces are awful, but you [3] have never said anything. A student [4] has had a lot of trouble with math.
Specific Time in the Past	**Yesterday**, she [5] asked you to write a review of her jewelry for her blog. You [6] did volunteer work at an animal shelter **last year**. She [7] didn't do well **last semester**.

2 Complete the sentences with the present perfect or simple past form of the verbs in parentheses.

1 This a great game! We have played (play) it a lot.
2 Alice and her sister started (start) their jewelry business when they were 13.
3 Juan and I didn't have (not have) any trouble using the app on the weekend.
4 Martin is a math tutor at school. He has/'s helped (help) a lot of students with their work.
5 The students have (never work) at an animal shelter before.

LOOK!
If there is a word/phrase saying when the action happened, for example *yesterday, last week, two days ago*, we don't use the present perfect.
She called you **yesterday** asking for help.

3 Write sentences with the prompts about the inventor of Dilemma Teens.

Emily Lopez, inventor of **Dilemma Teens**, a game with moral dilemmas for teens

1 Emily / invent / the game when she was 15
Emily invented the game when she was 15.
2 her father / help / her sell the first version in 2019
Her father helped her sell the first version in 2019.
3 her game / be / in toy stores since 2020
Her game has been in toy stores since 2020.
4 the game / already / sell / 25,000 copies
The game has already sold 25,000 copies.
5 Emily / create / an app for the game last year
Emily created an app for the game last year.

USE IT!

4 Write two true sentences and one false sentence about things you have done.

1 Students' own answers
2
3

I've met Cristiano Ronaldo.

5 Work in pairs. Take turns sharing your sentences from Exercise 4. Ask your partner questions to find out which sentence is false.

Really? Where did you meet him?

WORKBOOK p.140 and 142 PRACTICE EXTRA

Grammar Game

Play "Hot Potato" with your students. Bring two balls that are soft into class. If you have a large class, divide it into two teams and have them sit in a circle. (If this is not possible, have them pass the ball backwards or forwards in their seats.) Play a song and have students pass the ball around in a circle as fast as possible. When you stop the song, the person holding the ball must come up with a question using the present perfect and choose another student to answer (by tossing the ball to them). Then, a third student should ask for more information using the simple past. Start the song and play various rounds.

Homework

Workbook page 142, Exercises 1 and 2

Practice Extra

Unit 8

Fast Finishers

Puzzles and Games page 105, Exercise 4

Listening and Vocabulary

Lesson Aim: I can understand and talk about the importance of voluntary work.

Warmer

In pairs, have students list different types of volunteer work they can think of. Elicit them from the class and write them on the board. Then have students check the ones they would be able to do while studying. Ask if anyone has ever done any volunteer work.

8.03–8.04 Audioscripts pT145

Target Vocabulary

belong to	/bɪˈlɔŋ.tə/
care about	/keər.əˈbaʊt/
deal with	/dil.wɪθ/
fight for	/faɪt.fɔr/
suffer from	/ˈsʌf·ər.frʌm/
work for	/wɜrk.fɔr/

1 8.03 In pairs, have students look at the image and infer what is happening. Ask a volunteer to read sentences 1 and 2 to check understanding before they check the correct alternative. Play the audio to check their work. Draw their attention to the phrasal verb *passed away* and have them infer the meaning. Ask: *Have you ever been interviewed?*

2 8.03 Have students read the questions in the chart, individually. Play the audio again and have them check the correct column. Have them list the different volunteer jobs mentioned and compare them to the ones they listed in the Warmer.

3 8.03 Have volunteers read the sentences. Ask them to try to correct them from memory. Play the audio again to check their answers. Ask: *Would you do any of the volunteer work mentioned?*

4 Ask volunteers to read the sentences to check understanding. Have them circle the correct option. Check the answers orally with the class. Have them write sentences that are true for them using the expressions.

5 8.04 Play the audio for students to listen to the expressions. Have them repeat and draw their attention to the pronunciation.

LISTENING AND VOCABULARY

1 8.03 **Look at the image. Check (✓) the sentence you think describes the situation better. Then listen and check.**

1 ✓ A college student is asking people some questions for a project.
2 ◯ A reporter is interviewing people about the traffic in the city.

2 8.03 **Listen again. Check (✓) the correct people in the chart.**

Who ...	Girl	Boy	Woman
1 has done volunteer work?	✓	✓	
2 worries about poor people?	✓		
3 has/had the influence of family members?	✓	✓	
4 works/worked with older people?	✓	✓	
5 lost a family member last year?		✓	
6 definitely likes to read?		✓	✓

3 8.03 **Listen once more. Write the correct sentences.**

1 The girl started doing volunteer work when she was 12.
The girl started doing volunteer work when she was 14.

2 People go to the food bank because they don't know how to cook.
People go to the food bank because they don't have enough money for food.

3 The boy wrote letters for the residents at the retirement home.
The boy read books to the residents at the retirement home.

4 The boy's grandmother had dementia.
The boy's great-grandmother had dementia.

5 The woman does volunteer work at a book club.
The woman doesn't do volunteer work at a book club. / The woman belongs to a book club.

4 **Read the sentences from the interview and circle the correct options.**

1 I **work** (for) / *to* the local food bank.
2 They **fight** (for) / *with* everyone's right to education.
3 They really **care** (about) / *to* other people.
4 It's terrible to **suffer** *at* / (from) dementia.
5 It was difficult for me to **deal** *for* / (with) that.
6 I **belong** (to) / *with* a book club.

5 8.04 **Listen, check, and repeat the words in bold and the correct options in Exercise 4.**

90

WORKBOOK p.141

Homework

Workbook page 141, Exercises 3 and 4

1 Draw students' attention to the headings in the chart. Have them compare the first two questions from each column and ask them to notice the differences between the structure of the questions and elicit what the answers would be. Encourage students to ask more questions to understand the different structure: *Who does the girl work for?* (The food bank.) *Who works for the food bank?* (The girl.) Have students do this with the other examples in the chart. Play Track 8.03 again, if necessary, and have them complete the sentences with the missing words.

2 Students can use the grammar chart in Exercise 1 for help. Read answers a–f with students to check understanding. Have them analyze the answers and infer whether the questions will be subject or object questions. Have them order the questions and then match them to the answers. Check answers with the class.

USE IT!

3 Have students observe the images and the question prompts. Tell them they will be writing quiz questions for their friends. Students work individually and make the questions. Have them make two other questions on any topic they wish.

4 In pairs, have students take turns answering the questions. Have them check who was able to answer correctly.

LANGUAGE IN CONTEXT

1 Complete the subject questions from the interview in the chart. Use the words below.

• happened • inspired • made

Subject Questions	Object Questions
Who **works** for a food bank?	What organization **does** the girl **work** for?
What organization **gives** food to people?	What **does** the food bank **give** to people?
Who **belongs** to a book club?	What club **do** you **belong** to?
Who [1] inspired you?	How **did** your parents **inspire** you?
What [2] happened ?	When **did** that **happen**?
What [3] made you decide to do that?	What decision **did** you **make**?

2 Put the words in the correct order to make questions about the interview. Then match the questions with the answers.

1 Saturdays / the girl / on / where / go / does?
Where does the girl go on Saturdays? d
2 at / works / who / food bank / the ?
Who works at the food bank? b
3 gets / from / who / the food bank / help ?
Who gets help from the food bank? f
4 in / retirement home / lived / a / who ?
Who lived in a retirement home? e
5 the boy / what / do at the home / did ?
What did the boy do at the home? a
6 ago / happened / year / a / what ?
What happened a year ago? c

a He read to the residents.
b Volunteers.
c The boy's great-grandmother died.
d To the local food bank.
e The boy's great-grandmother.
f People who can't afford food.

USE IT!

3 Write six quiz questions with the prompts in your notebook.

1 Who painted the Mona Lisa?

1 Who / paint / the *Mona Lisa*?
2 Who / Juliet / fall in love with in Shakespeare's play?
3 What / destroy / Pompeii in 79 AD?
4 What colors / appear / on the South African flag?
5 When / the coronavirus pandemic / start / in China?
6 Which young girl / win / the Nobel Peace Prize in 2014?

2 Who did Juliet fall in love with in Shakespeare's play?
3 What destroyed Pompeii in 79 AD?
4 What colors appear on the South African flag?
5 When did the coronavirus pandemic start in China?
6 Which young girl won the Nobel Peace Prize in 2014?

4 Work in pairs. Take turns asking and answering the questions in Exercise 3. How many can you answer correctly? 1 Leonardo da Vinci 2 Romeo 3 (the eruption of) Vesuvius 4 red, white, green, yellow, black, blue 5 in 2019 6 Malala Yousafzai

WORKBOOK p.140 and 142 PRACTICE EXTRA

Grammar Game

Play "Tic-Tac-Toe" with your students. Draw a 3x3-square grid on the board and have students copy it into their notebooks. Encourage students to look back at the Language in Context sections in the unit when they fill their grid. They should complete it with a combination of these prompts: *verb + subject questions, verb + object questions, verb + simple past, or verb + present perfect*. They can use each prompt more than once. Model an example for students on the board. Put students into pairs to play. Model the game with a student. Student A chooses a square and makes a sentence using the prompt from that square, e.g.: *write + subject question* becomes *Who wrote this book?* If they make a correct sentence or question, they can draw an O or an X in that square. The first student to get three O's or X's in a line, horizontally, vertically, or diagonally wins.

Homework

Workbook page 142, Exercises 3 and 4

Practice Extra

Unit 8

Extension

Encourage students to visit any virtual museum they wish by typing "virtual museum" in their favorite search engine. Have them find some interesting facts about any topic they wish and make some subject questions or object questions for their partner to answer. Their partner must look for the answer on the Internet. Have them take turns asking and answering each other's questions. Give them ten minutes to form the questions and then another ten minutes to answer them.

Across the Curriculum
Lesson Aim: I can understand a text about the impact of human activities on nature.

8.2 Mindfulness and Meditation

The video on page 93 and accompanying exercises below can be used as a lead-in to the topic of the Across the Curriculum text, or after the reading activities to complete the unit.

Summary
The video is about meditation and mindfulness and how it can help you on a daily basis.

In Class
Tell students they are going to watch a video about meditation and mindfulness which have both been around for a very long time. Scientists have been studying meditation effects on the brain, and we know that it has many benefits. Have students close their eyes. Set a timer for one minute and have students sit in silence, with their eyes closed and have them focus on their breathing. Ask them to count how many times they breathe in and how many times they breathe out during this one minute. Having finished, ask them if they managed to do it, and if it was easy or difficult.

Exercise 1
Ask students to watch the video to answer the questions:

1 *How many people around the world meditate?* Check the answer with the class.
Up to 500 million people.

2 *What do you have to do to practice mindfulness or meditation?*
You sit still, close your eyes, relax your body, and pay attention to your breathing.

Exercise 2
Play the video again, write the following questions on the board and have students answer them. Then, ask them to watch the video again and make up two more questions to ask their partners.

1 Zen Buddhism developed in the ______ century.
( ) 10th (✗) 12th
( ) 20th

2 Which are some of the effects of meditation on the brain?
Your attention and memory get better. It helps to reduce stress, and to have better relationships with other people. It can help to lower your blood pressure.

ACROSS THE CURRICULUM

GEOGRAPHY

Where Do the HAPPIEST Teenagers in the World Live?

The answer is they probably live in the Netherlands, a country in Europe that is famous for its tulips and windmills, and smaller than most states in Brazil. With 17 million people, the country has succeeded in giving its teen inhabitants an optimistic view of life that contrasts with other rich countries, such as the UK and the United States.

What is the secret of Dutch teens' happiness? As for any complex question, there are several answers.

The Netherlands is a wealthy country that takes care of its young people. According to a report from UNICEF, 95% of Dutch children are happy with their lives.

The Netherlands Institute of Social Research states that Dutch teens in general have positive relationships at home, at school, and with friends. Parents encourage their children to be independent and teachers are not authoritarian. Teenagers feel they can trust adults.

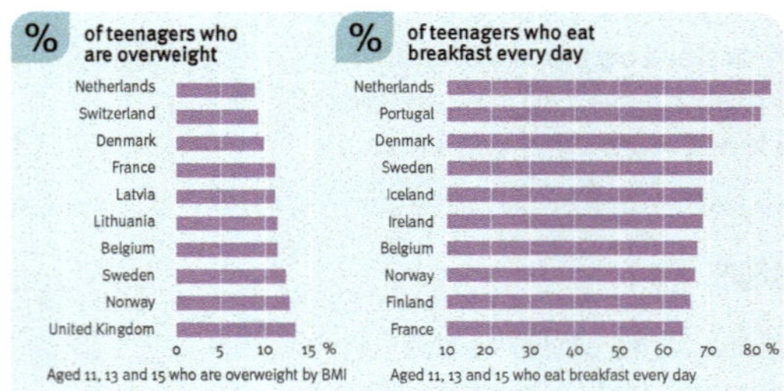

Dutch teens are generally healthy. Over 80% of them have breakfast every day and only 8% of the teen population are overweight. Most students ride their bikes to school every day (in fact, cycling is a normal form of transportation for people of all ages in the Netherlands).

There is some bullying in Dutch schools, but according to studies, it doesn't happen as often as in other countries. 86% of Dutch teenagers say their classmates are helpful and kind.

Although they have experienced more pressure from homework and exams in recent years, Dutch teens are still happy at school. One of the reasons is the school system, which allows high school students to change study programs or even repeat a year if they are not happy with their academic progress.

92

3 People in western countries like the USA became interested in ideas like meditation in the *1960s*.

4 Complete the sentence with the correct words.
Mindfulness and ________ date back to ________, a faith that people in some ________ countries have practiced for thousands of years.
( ) Buddhism, Asian, meditation
(✗) meditation, Buddhism , Asian
( ) Asian, Buddhism, meditation

At Home
Exercise 3
Ask: *Are there situations that you find stressful? What do you do? How do you feel?* Ask students to list the situations when they feel stressed and their feelings. Encourage them to download a meditation app and use it for a week when they feel stressed. Ask students to share their experiences if they were able to do this small meditation trial. Encourage them to do a quick meditation every morning when they wake up and before they go to sleep.

Background Information

A UNICEF survey shows that the Netherlands has the happiest teenagers in the world. The article gives some of the main reasons why this is may be the case.

8.05 Audioscript pT145

1 Have students look at the images on page 92. Ask: *What country are these images from? What makes you say that? Have you ever been there? List three things you know about this country.* Have students read objectives 1 and 2 and check the correct answer. Check as a class.

2 8.05 Have students read the sentences and alternatives before reading the text so they have a clear goal of what they are looking for. Ask them to read the text silently and check if they have any questions about the vocabulary. Have them check the correct alternatives. Have them listen to the audio and read again as they check their answers.

3 Have students read the numbers out loud. Have a volunteer read the sentences a–d. Invite students to read the text again to complete the sentences individually. Have them check in pairs. Have them do this survey amongst their class and compare the percentages with the Dutch survey.

Words in Context

4 Go through items 1–4 and ask students to find the words in the text. Students match the words to their definitions in pairs. Check answers with the class and encourage students to make a sentence with each word.

THINK!

Read the article on page 92 with students again. Ask: *Do you believe we can measure a country's happiness?* Have students research which country is considered the happiest, not only related to teenagers. Ask students to list what facts they would take into consideration to rank a country's happiness. Ask: *How about in Brazil? In what place would it come in the survey?* Have them justify their answer. Have them use the ideas mentioned in their text book.

1 Look at the title of the article and the images. Check (✓) the article's main objective.

1 ◯ to give different opinions about happiness among Dutch teenagers
2 ✓ to give information about happiness among Dutch teenagers

2 8.05 Read and listen to the article. Check (✓) the correct answers.

1 The Netherlands is … Brazil.
a ◯ bigger than b ✓ smaller than c ◯ the same size as
2 In general, Dutch teenagers are … teenagers in the UK and in the US.
a ✓ happier than b ◯ unhappier than c ◯ as happy as
3 Research shows that Dutch parents want their children to be … .
a ◯ optimistic b ✓ independent c ◯ rich
4 Dutch teenagers have a lifestyle that is good for their … .
a ◯ friends b ◯ family c ✓ health
5 Most teenagers in the Netherlands have a … image of their classmates.
a ✓ positive b ◯ negative c ◯ neutral
6 When Dutch students choose their study program at school, they … change it later.
a ✓ can b ◯ can't c ◯ must

3 Read the article again. Match the numbers below with the information a–e.

• 17 • 85 • 86 • 95

a percentage of Dutch teens who like the people they study with 86
b percentage of teens in the Netherlands who always have a meal at the start of the day 85
c percentage of children in the Netherlands that say they have a happy life 95
d population of the Netherlands in millions 17

WORDS IN CONTEXT

4 Match the words (1–4) with their definitions (a–d).

1 windmill b
2 wealthy d
3 state a
4 pressure c

a officially say or write
b a structure with parts that turn with the movement of the air
c sense of stressful urgency
d having a lot of money

WEBQUEST

Learn more! Check (✓) *T* (true) or *F* (false).
There are more bicycles than people in the Netherlands.
✓ True ◯ False

THINK!

How happy do you think teenagers are in your country? Think about teenagers' attitudes to family, school, and friends.

VIDEO

8.2

1 How many people around the world meditate?
2 What do you have to do to practice mindfulness or meditation?

WEBQUEST

If possible, bring in an image or project an image from the Internet of a bicycle. Ask your students if they like riding bikes and if they use them as a means of transportation or simply as a way to get some exercise. Have them read the statement in their books and ask them if it is true or false. Ask them to check on the Internet and bring back some answers. Remind students to check two or three websites to confirm their ideas. Have them discuss whether bicycles are a good means of transportation and the pros and cons of riding their bikes to school.

Unit 8
What's Important to Me?

Writing
Lesson Aim: I can write up an interview with a classmate.

8.06 Audioscript pT145

1 8.06 Draw students' attention to the website. Ask them to give examples of occasions they would use this sort of genre. Have them skim-read the interview and ask: *What is it about?* Have a volunteer read the words from Exercise 1 and check the topics mentioned in the text. Play the audio for them to check their answers.

2 Have students look back at the list of facts they listed in the *Think!* exercise on page 93. Have them use the list in order to write four questions about what makes their classmates happy.

LOOK!

Draw attention to the *Look!* box and read the information aloud. Ask students to notice the introduction to the interview they read. Have them read it silently. Ask them what kind of facts were used in the introduction. Ask them to list them in their notebooks.

3 Have students work in pairs in order to ask and answer the questions they wrote in Exercise 2. Make sure they take notes as they will use them for their final task.

4 Put students into pairs. Encourage students to follow the steps and use the interview in Exercise 1 as a model. Give students time to write up their questions and look at their notes to write the first version of their interview.

5 When they peer correct, ensure students focus on the items in the checklist. Monitor and help as necessary. Make sure they are respectful and clear when giving their feedback. Have them write the final version of their poster after they receive their classmate's feedback.

WRITING

1 8.06 **Read and listen to an interview with a Dutch teenager. Check (✓) the topics mentioned in the interview.**

1 ◯ hobbies 2 ✓ friends 3 ✓ school 4 ✓ family

INTERVIEWS

Kenno Appelhof is 15 years old. He has friends, goes to school, and argues with his parents sometimes, as most teenagers do. He also lives in the Netherlands, one of the countries where teenagers are the happiest in the world.

WSM Kenno, what makes you happy?

Kenno Oh, so many things. My dog Buddy makes me happy, my friends make me laugh and are an important part of my life.

WSM Who gives you help if you need it?

Kenno My family and close friends. They're people that I can depend on.

WSM How do you like your school?

Kenno I love going to school and I know getting a good education is important for my future.

Most of my friends are from school, so that's where I see them every day.

WSM What's the most important thing in your life?

Kenno I love school and spending time with my friends, but the most important thing in my life is my family. They really support me and care about my happiness. It's great to know there are people you can always trust.

2 **You're going to interview a classmate about what makes him/her happy and the important things in his/her life. Write four questions for your interview.**

1 Students' own answers
2 ......
3 ......
4 ......

3 **Work in pairs. Take turns asking your partner your questions from Exercise 2. Take notes on his/her answers.**

4 **Write up the interview you did with your classmate.**

1 Find or draw an image of the classmate you interviewed.
2 Write a short introduction about your classmate.
3 Write your questions and use your notes to write up your classmate's answers.
4 Write the first version of your interview. Use vocabulary from Unit 8.

5 **Switch your write-up of the interview with your classmate and check each other's work. Use the checklist below.**

◯ image of the person interviewed
◯ introduction about the person interviewed
◯ subject and object questions
◯ correct information in the answers

LOOK!

When we write up an interview, we organize it into questions and answers. We usually include a short introduction about the person interviewed.

YOUR DIGITAL PORTFOLIO

Edit your interview, then publish it. Upload it to the class portfolio for everyone to see!

Your Digital Portfolio

Give students a date for uploading their work and make sure they all look at one another's work.

Practice Extra

Unit 8

Lesson Aim: I can review what I have learned and reflect on my progress.

Tell students that the exercises on these pages review the vocabulary and language they have learned in Units 7 and 8. Point out that they can also check their progress and reflect on what they can do.

Vocabulary

1 Have students look back at Unit 7 and remind them of how we can transform some verbs into nouns and vice versa. Have a volunteer read sentences 1–6. Individually, have students correct the sentences, if necessary. Check answers with the class.

2 Invite students to read the questions and answers to check comprehension and context. Remind them of the adjectives + prepositions expressions and have them use the correct preposition to complete the sentences. Have students check in pairs.

3 Draw students' attention to the words *do*, *have*, and *make*. Ask volunteers to make sentences using each one of them. If necessary, have them look back at the examples on page 86. Have students read the text silently to check comprehension and context. Have students complete the sentences individually. Then have volunteers take turns reading the sentences of the text aloud to check.

4 Have volunteers read sentences 1–6. Remind them of the verb + preposition expressions. Have them circle the correct options. Check in pairs and have each pair come up with two sentences using two of the expressions of their choice.

REVIEW
UNITS 7 AND 8

VOCABULARY

1 Look at the underlined words and write *C* (correct) or *I* (incorrect). Write the correct words if necessary.

1 Mozambique was a Portuguese possession in Africa until the country achievement independence in 1975. I achieved
2 The economic development of some countries in Africa depends on tourism. C
3 The discover of diamonds in the national park has attracted a lot of attention. I discovery
4 Let's organize interviews with the volunteers for the animal shelter. C
5 We're worried about the survive of the wild animals in the forest. I survival
6 If they construction a road across the village, people will lose their houses. I construct

2 Complete the mini dialogues with the prepositions below.

• at • ~~in~~ • for • of (x 3)

1 A Are you interested in joining the drama club?
B Well, I'd love to, but I don't think I'm good at acting.
2 A Hey, you've been in this room since 3 p.m. Aren't you tired of studying?
B I sure am, but I'm afraid of not doing well in the history test tomorrow.
3 A That city is famous for the beautiful sculptures in its parks.
B Yes, and the people who live there are very proud of them.

3 Complete the text with *do*, *have*, or *make*.

Volunteering for young people

by Clara Santos

People who [1] do volunteer work [2] have the opportunity to [3] make a difference in the world. There are a lot of things you can do.
I volunteer for an organization that helps people who can't leave home – I [4] do their shopping every week, for example. My brother and sister [5] do physical activities with the kids in our neighborhood.
Volunteers don't have a salary or [6] make money from their work, but volunteering is a serious thing. Be sure you [7] make time for the tasks you promise to do because other people are depending on you.

4 Circle the correct options.

1 My older sister has suffered (from) / *with* insomnia for some time.
2 Do you belong *for* / (to) any sports clubs at your school?
3 I can't stand selfish people who don't care (about) / *with* others.
4 Lucy is a part-time babysitter. She works (for) / *from* a family with six children!
5 Can the school counselor help students deal *to* / (with) emotional problems?
6 Many women around the world fight (for) / *to* equal pay for men and women.

95

Lesson Aim: I can review what I have learned and reflect on my progress.

Language in Context

5 Remind students how to form present perfect sentences with the words *yet, already*, and *just*. Invite them to refer back to the chart on page 79 for reference. Draw three columns on the board and write *yet, already*, and *just* at the top of them. Have students draw these columns in their notebooks. Invite students to write sentences using the present perfect. Have them share their sentences. Draw students' attention to the images and have them circle the correct options. Have them justify their answers. Check answers with the class.

6 Give two examples of your own using *since* and *for*. Write them on the board. Ask students to justify your choice of words (*since* or *for*) in each of the sentences. Ask students to come up with their own examples in pairs. Go through the example in the book with the class, then have students write out the sentences individually, using the prompts in parentheses. Have them check in pairs.

7 Remind students of the difference between the present perfect and the simple past. Ask them to look back at the chart on page 89 and make up sentences using both tenses. Have students read through the prompts and draw their attention to the words that might give them a clue to which tense to use. Individually, have students write the questions. Have students ask and answer their questions in pairs. Monitor their activity by walking around the class.

8 Tell students to look at the underlined words. Ask: *Why are these words underlined?* (so students know whether they should make subject questions or object questions). Have them look back at page 91, if necessary. Have students write the questions and have them check in pairs.

LANGUAGE IN CONTEXT

5 Look at the images. Circle the sentence that describes each image.

1 

a The game has already started.
ⓑ The game hasn't started yet.

2 

ⓐ He has already finished breakfast.
b He hasn't finished breakfast yet.

3 

ⓐ They have just left school.
b They haven't left school yet.

6 Write present perfect sentences with the verbs in parentheses and *since* or *for*.

1 I began to study classical music in 2020. (study – since)
I have studied classical music since 2020.
2 We met Sayuri in July. It's December now. (know – for)
I have known Sayuri for six months.
3 My sister has a vlog. She started it in January. (have – since)
My sister has had a vlog since January.
4 The last time Luiza saw her grandparents was two weeks ago. (not see – for)
Luiza has not seen her grandparents for two weeks.
5 Mr. Harris is a math teacher. He began working as a teacher in 2019. (be – since)
Mr. Harris has been a math teacher since 2019.

7 Write questions with the prompts in the present perfect or the simple past.

1 you / ever / travel / to another country?
Have you ever traveled to another country?
2 you / go / to the movies last weekend?
Did you go to the movies last weekend?
3 your English class / have / a test yesterday?
Did your English class have a test yesterday?
4 your classmates / already / eat / their lunch?
Have your classmates already eaten their lunch?

8 Write questions for the answers. Pay attention to the underlined words/phrases.

1 I talked with Cathy last night.
Who did you talk with last night?
2 A car accident happened in front of our school.
What happened in front of our school?
3 K-pop bands made me decide to study Korean.
What made you decide to study Korean?
4 Lucas plays five musical instruments.
How many musical instruments does Lucas play?

CHECK YOUR PROGRESS

I CAN...

- talk about achievements and use adjectives with prepositions 🙂 ○ 🙁 ○
- use the present perfect with *already, just, yet, since*, and *for* 🙂 ○ 🙁 ○
- use expressions with *do, have*, and *make*, and verbs with prepositions 🙂 ○ 🙁 ○
- understand the difference between the present perfect and the simple past, and ask subject and object questions. 🙂 ○ 🙁 ○

LEARN TO LEARN

Listing collocations

Creating diagrams helps you see collocations (words/phrases that we often use with other words/phrases). Create diagrams of collocations in your notebook and use different colors (for example, blue for verbs and green for nouns). Also write examples using the collocations.

96

Check Your Progress

This section gives students an opportunity to reflect on what they have learned. Read each statement with the class. Elicit examples and/or information students remember. Alternatively, students could go through the statements in pairs or groups. If necessary, have them go back to the relevant unit to review each topic. Students then do the task in the Check Your Progress box individually. When they finish, ask: *What can you practice more? What is easy/difficult/interesting?* Invite students to give feedback.

Learn to Learn

Throughout the course, students do a variety of *learn to learn* activities, which offer them techniques for retaining vocabulary. Point out the chart to the students. Ask: *Do you use diagrams and mind maps to study?* Tell them that visual learning is a good strategy to memorize and learn new vocabulary and language. Encourage them to look back at the last two units and make diagrams with the collocations they learn during these units. Encourage them to use different colors to highlight the collocations.

Lesson Aim: I can understand a text about young inventors.

R.01 Audioscript pT145

1 Ask students: *Do you know any young inventors? Do you have a friend who has invented something awesome?* Having listened to your students' responses, invite them to look at the title and images in the article and ask: *What can you see? What is happening in the images? What do you think the text will be about?* In pairs, have them read the questions and answer them, without reading the text. Check answers with the class.

2 R.01 Draw two columns on the board, the first one titled *Ruth* and the second titled *Hannah*. Ask students to do the same in their notebooks. Invite students to read the text and have them take notes on the differences between the two teenagers and facts about their lives, according to the text. Play the recording and have them check their answers to Exercise 1 and their notes in the columns.

3 Have a volunteer read through questions 1–6 to check understanding. Ask students to answer the questions individually and then check in pairs. Ask them if they know anything else about Ethiopia. Have them research a little more about the country and write the facts they found out together with the facts from the text from Exercise 2.

4 Read through the questions with the students to check comprehension. In pairs, have students discuss their ideas and imagine how different Hannah's life would have been if she had not begun writing to Ruth. Have them answer the questions and check their answers with the class. Encourage them to dig deeper into the third question and justify their answers.

THINK!

Ask students if they have ever thought of inventing something to make the world a better place. Have them share their ideas. Have them answer the question in the *Think!* box.

READING 1

ACROSS THE CURRICULUM / SCIENCE

A TEENAGE INVENTOR

1 Look at the title and the images. Discuss the questions with a partner.

1 Make a list of the things you did before 9 a.m. this morning. How many of those activities used electricity?
2 What do you think the teenager invented?

2 R.01 Read and listen to the article. Were your ideas in Exercise 1 correct?

An Inspirational Teenage Inventor

Hannah Herbst was nine years old when she started writing to Ruth, her penpal in Ethiopia. After four years of writing to each other, Hannah learned many things from Ruth. One of the things that surprised Hannah the most was that many people in Ethiopia lived with limited access to electricity and running water. Hannah, from the US, had access to electricity and water every day. It made her sad to hear that many people were living in this situation. She decided she wanted to invent something to help solve the problem of energy poverty, even though she didn't know much about engineering and she didn't have a strong interest in math or science.

When Hannah was thirteen years old she started designing a prototype called BEACON – *Bringing Electricity Access to Countries through Ocean Energy*. Inspired by the ocean where she lived in Florida, she had the idea to create electricity using the energy of the ocean currents and store it in a battery.

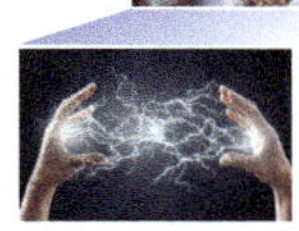

Hannah didn't design the prototype alone, she had different mentors who helped her. The mentors taught her that often the best solutions are the simplest ones. Before making a final design, her mentors encouraged her to change the prototype and develop her ideas. Her mentors also encouraged her to share her ideas in competitions. That's when she entered the competition called the 3M Young Scientist Challenge, and won the title of America's Top Young Scientist in 2015. The invention created many opportunities for Hannah, such as presenting the idea to the US President at the White House.

Hannah graduated from Atlantic University in 2020 where she studied Information Systems and Business Analytics. She loves to inspire students to study math and science and try to come up with inventions to solve the world's difficult problems.

3 Read the article again and answer the questions.

1 Who did Hannah write to regularly when she was young?
2 What problem did Hannah want to solve? Why?
3 What challenges did Hannah face?
4 What did her mentors teach her?
5 What source of energy did BEACON use?
6 What does Hannah do now?

4 Think about Hannah's journey to study computer engineering. Discuss the questions with a partner.

1 How were Hannah and Ruth's lives different as teenagers?
2 What things helped Hannah become a scientist?
3 Is it possible for everyone to have the same opportunities in life? Is that OK?

THINK!

Do you think young people can be good inventors? Why / Why not?

98

Extension

If there is time, ask students to research and list famous young inventors. Have them describe one or two of their inventions and share some of their work with the class. Have students discuss which inventions they believe have been the most important for the world. Have them justify their answers.

1 *An Ethiopian girl named Ruth.*
2 *Energy poverty. Because she learned that many people in the world have limited access to electricity and running water.*
3 *She didn't know much about engineering and she didn't have a strong interest in math or science.*
4 *Often the best solutions are the simplest ones. They encouraged her to present her ideas in competitions.*
5 *The ocean currents in Florida.*
6 *She graduated from university. She loves to inspire students to study math and science and to try to come up with inventions to solve the world's difficult problems.*

Lesson Aim: I can understand and give my opinion about a text about a green city.

R.02 Audioscript pT146

1 Have students look at the images. Ask: *Can you relate these images to your daily life?* Have them justify their answers. Write the name of the city on the board: *Ljubljana*. Ask students if they know where it is, and what they can tell you about this city. Have them research on the Internet, if possible. Then put students into pairs and have them answer the questions without reading the text.

2 **R.02** Ask students to read and listen to the article to identify whether their ideas from Exercise 1 were correct. Elicit answers to Exercise 1 from the whole class. Students can refer to the text for support. Have them tell you what else they discovered about the city. Have them build a mind map with basic information about the city, its problems, and their solutions.

3 Read sentences 1–5 to check comprehension. Draw students' attention to the fact that they have two tasks to do in this exercise. Have them find the relevant information in the text referring to each sentence and underline it in the text while writing *T* (true) or *F* (false). To check answers, invite volunteers to read out a sentence, say whether it is true or false, and have them justify their answer. Then, have students read the sentences in pairs and decide whether it is a fact or an opinion. Have them circle the facts and underline the opinions, justifying their answers.

4 Draw students' attention to the words in bold in the article. Have them make up sentences using the words to check comprehension. Individually, have students complete the sentences. If they are not sure of an answer, they can leave it until the end and go back to it. Students check their work in pairs.

READING 2

AROUND THE WORLD

LJUBLJANA: GREEN CITY

1 Look at the images. Discuss the questions with a partner.

1 What problem and solution do the images show?
2 Why do you think Ljubljana is a "green" city?

2 R.02 Read and listen to the report about Ljubljana. Were your ideas in Exercise 1 correct?

1 The problem of waste and the solution of recycling.
2 People do a lot of recycling.

A Report on a Green City

Name of city: Ljubljana
Country: Slovenia
Population of city: Over 288,000
Language: Slovene (or Slovenian)
Interesting fact: Ljubljana's aim is zero-waste

Introduction Ljubljana, the capital of Slovenia, is the first European capital with the aim of "zero-waste". The city separates, collects and recycles 68% of its waste. It wants to get to 78% over the next few years, but that's not going to be easy.

Problem Before 2004, most of the waste in Ljubljana went to a **landfill** or incinerators. The people of Ljubljana now produce only 115 kg of non-recyclable trash per person per year. That's amazing, but 115 kg of trash is still a problem. Why? We now know that burning or **burying** our trash creates health problems. It's also a terrible waste of our natural resources to use things just once and then throw them away.

Solution So how did Ljubljana change in such a short time? The first step was to collect separated waste from **door to door**. People started to feel responsible for their waste and they began to separate it better. If you separate used glass, cardboard, plastic, and organic trash, you can recycle them. But when you throw different kinds of trash away together, you create waste.

Ljubljana has **recycling bins** downtown and there are two waste recycling centers where people can take their trash. They also try to encourage people to reuse things that people throw away. At one of the recycling centers, they check, clean, **fix**, and sell things at low prices. And there are even classes to teach people how to fix broken things.

Conclusion Ljubljana is a good example of a green city, because people recycle and reuse a lot of their trash. Creating cities that are zero waste is important because if we reuse and recycle trash, we can save money and protect the environment and people's health.

3 Read the text again. Write *T* (true) or *F* (false). Then circle the facts and underline the opinions.

1 (Ljubljana has a population of over a quarter of a million people.) *T*
2 It's difficult for a city to recycle 78% of its trash. *T*
3 Burning our trash is a good idea. *F*
4 You create waste by throwing different types of trash away together. *T*
5 People in Ljubljana take their trash to the recycling centers. *T*

4 Complete the sentences. Use the words/phrases in bold in the article.

1 The politician went from *door to door* explaining the idea of "zero waste".
2 They couldn't *fix* our old car, so we took it to the recycling center.
3 *Burying* trash in the ground causes environmental problems.
4 In the US, they send half of their trash to a *landfill*.
5 Images on the *recycling bins* show people what they can throw away in each container.

THINK!
What things do you reuse instead of throwing them away? Why?

EXTRA READINGS 99

THINK!

Put students into groups to discuss ideas. Ensure all group members take part in the discussion and give their opinions. Have them make a list of objects they reuse and which they throw away and ask them to justify their answers. Ask them whether they believe they should reuse more objects.

Extension

Have students think about their own city. Have them write a small introduction about their city, identify a problem, think of a solution, and write a small conclusion. Have them use the article as reference. Have students share their ideas. Display students' work on the wall, if possible, with images, or have them share their work digitally.

Lesson Aim: I can read and understand a text about different forms of communication.

R.03 Audioscript pT146

1. Write the word *communication* on the board. Elicit and write words connected to the topic on the board. Ask students if they believe they communicate differently than how their grandparents used to communicate. Write their ideas on the board. Have them then open their books and look at the infographic and the title. Tell them they do not need to read the whole text, just focus on the title and the images. In pairs, have them answer the questions.
2. R.03 Have students read and listen to the text to check their ideas from Exercise 1. Ask: *What would your life be like without your cell phone to communicate with your friends? What are the advantages and disadvantages of modern ways of communication?* Have them discuss in pairs and make a pros and cons list. Have them compare the communication forms of the past with those of today.
3. Read the questions to check comprehension. Then tell them to read the text again to answer the questions. Check answers with the class. Encourage students to think of another two *Wh*– questions they could ask about the text. Have them share their questions and encourage the other students to answer them.
4. Draw students' attention to the questions and have them answer them in pairs. Share students' answers as a class. List all the different messaging sites on the board. Have them compare them to the communication forms from the article.

THINK!

Discuss the questions with the class. Have them refer to their answers from Exercise 2. Encourage students to be without their cell phone for half a day and ask them how they felt.

READING 3

ACROSS THE CURRICULUM / HISTORY

THE HISTORY OF COMMUNICATION

1 **Look at the title and the images. Discuss the questions with a partner.**

1. How did people send messages to each other before the invention of the telegraph?
2. Why was communication limited before the invention of the telegraph?

1 smoke signals, carrier pigeon, human messengers
2 Because it was dependent on geographical location.

2 R.03 **Read and listen to the infographic. Were your ideas in Exercise 1 correct?**

HOW PEOPLE COMMUNICATED IN THE PAST

The way we communicate with each other now is very different from the early forms of communication. Sending a simple message could take many days or even weeks in the past.

Smoke Signals

Smoke signals are the oldest form of visual communication. The Chinese used them first in 200 BCE to send messages along the Great Wall of China. In 150 BCE, the Greeks also used smoke signals to represent the alphabet so they could send messages easily to each other. Later, many countries around the world used smoke from the top of a hill to signify danger. Simple but effective!

Carrier Pigeon

The Egyptians used pigeons for long-distance communication from the 12th century AD. The pigeons carried messages from Egypt to cities that were hundreds of kilometers away. Then the Romans and Greeks used pigeons, and later, many European countries used pigeons during World War I and World War II to send messages that helped save many people's lives.

Human Messengers

In the Middle Ages and before, cities, countries, companies, and rich people had their own human messengers to send important messages as quickly as possible from one place to another. Some messengers travelled by horse and boat and spent many days travelling across countries and seas in order to deliver a message safely, while messengers in some mountainous regions had to walk or run. Messengers were usually men who were fit and healthy. Sometimes it was a dangerous job and some messengers even worked as spies.

The Telegraph

Early forms of communication were dependent on geographical location. That all changed with the invention of the telegraph. The telegraph was a machine that sent electric signals along wires from one place to another and the signals translated into a message. In 1844, Samuel Morse sent the first telegraph message in Morse code, long or short clicks, each combination of sounds representing letters in the alphabet.

Suddenly, humans could send messages over hundreds of kilometres almost instantly. This was the start of telephones and even the Internet!

3 **Read the text again and answer the questions.**

1. What did a smoke signal represent in many cultures?
   It signified danger.
2. When did carrier pigeons help save many people's lives?
   During World War I and World War II.
3. How did human messengers travel from one place to another?
   By horse, boat, walking, or running.
4. What secret job did some human messengers do?
   They worked as spies.

4 **Find out about your favorite messaging site and tell a partner about it. Think about these questions:**

- What type of site is it?
- When did it start?
- Who started it?
- How is it different from communication in the past?
- Why is it your favorite social media platform?

THINK!

How would life be different without a phone or the Internet? How would you communicate?

100

Extension

Put students into groups and have them draw a timeline of how different communication forms have progressed over time. Encourage them to research a little about each one (when it started, when it stopped being used, its features, etc.). If possible, have them look for images. Have them present their work to the class.

R.04 Audioscript pT146

1 Draw students' attention to the images and to the image that is part of the title banner in the blog. Have students discuss the questions in pairs, then feed back to the class.

2 R.04 Divide the class into six different groups. Have each group read one of the paragraphs. Then have six students who read different paragraphs sit together to exchange facts about what they read. Encourage students to take notes. Have students check if their ideas from Exercise 1 were correct. Then have them listen to the blog post. Ask them to take down more notes of some interesting facts about Yoruba culture. Ask them to imagine life in a traditional culture like this one. Have them make up questions, e.g.: *How does their art get out into the world?* Encourage them to ask any questions that come to their minds. Have them share their questions.

3 Have students find evidence for the example answer in the text. Read questions 2–6 to check comprehension. Then tell students to read the text again to answer them. Have them underline the evidence in the text for their answers. Check in pairs.

4 Draw students' attention to the words in bold in the blog. Read sentences 1–5 with students. Students complete the sentences individually and then check their work in pairs. Have them make up sentences using the words to check comprehension.

THINK!

Put students in small groups to discuss the questions. Have them discuss the concept of what makes art beautiful. Ask: *Does everyone like the same sort of art?* Give them a few minutes to brainstorm different kinds of art and note down their answers. Take feedback from the whole class. Finally, say: *Share a piece of art you think is beautiful.* Give them time to search the Internet. Have them look through virtual museums and art galleries.

READING 4

AROUND THE WORLD

THE YORUBA PEOPLE

1 **Look at the images and discuss the questions.**

1 What are these people doing?
2 What types of artwork can you see?

2 R.04 **Read and listen to the blog post about the Yoruba people and their art. Were your ideas in Exercise 1 correct?** 1 dancing, celebrating
2 sculptures, masks, costumes

Home | Destinations | About | Contact

THE YORUBA: GREAT ARTISTS

The Yoruba are one of the largest ethnic and cultural groups in western Africa and the Yoruba people have lived in urban societies since the 5th century AD. Ile-Ife in Nigeria was the ancient capital city of the Yoruba. Originally, the Yoruba worked as farmers, **traders**, and artists. Nowadays, the Yoruba live in a special cultural region called Yorubaland in the different countries of Nigeria, Benin, and Togo.

The Yoruba have a long tradition in art and many Yoruba people are amazing artists. Their wooden sculptures and terracotta **figures** show animals and people from all levels of society. Yoruba art also includes **pottery**, textiles, and metalwork.

In the Yoruba culture, the head is seen as the center of **power** and many ancient head sculptures made of bronze and teracotta still survive today. The heads are naturalistic in style and have a serene expression. These sculptures may represent kings and queens.

Most Yoruba art has a meaning or purpose. Some items are connected to their **beliefs**, while others are for celebrations. The Yoruba wear different traditional masks and costumes during festivals and ceremonies that can last for days. These masks and costumes are an important part of Yoruba culture. In the Egungun ceremony, the Yoruba make special Egungun masks and costumes, and perform traditional dances to honor their ancestors.

Egungun masks, costumes, and dancing

Traditionally, women and men in Yoruba culture are involved in different artistic trades. The women often make the pots used for cooking and eating, and more unique pots for special occasions, such as ritual bowls. The men are responsible for leather and beadwork. They use animal skins to make things like bags and sandals, and they decorate clothes and crowns for important people with bead designs of human faces, birds, and flowers.

Yoruba art and artists have influenced many artists around the world, and you can see many examples of ancient Yoruba art in many museums.

3 **Read the text again and answer the questions.**

1 Which part of Africa do Yoruba people come from?
They come from western Africa.
2 What is Yorubaland and where is it?
It's a special cultural region in Nigeria, Benin, and Togo.
3 What are typical materials used in Yoruba art?
wood, terracotta, textiles, metals such as bronze, leather (from animal skins), beads
4 Why do the Yoruba make art?
Some items are connected to their beliefs while others are for celebrations.
5 What is typical in many festivals and ceremonies?
The wearing of masks and costumes.
6 Who does artwork in Yoruba culture?
Men and women, with the women often making pots and the men making items from leather and beads.

4 **Complete the sentences with the words in bold in the article.**

1 It's important to respect their beliefs although we might not share them.
2 Her parents were market traders, selling fruit and vegetables.
3 His hobby is pottery. He makes a lot of beautiful bowls and plates.
4 There were two figures in the painting, a man and a woman.
5 Amazing artwork has the power to inspire people.

THINK!

Do you think it's important for everyday objects to be beautiful? Why / Why not?

Extension

Have students write a letter to a person from the Yoruba culture, asking the questions they made up in Exercise 2. If possible, have them research the answers by looking them up on Internet. Have them share their findings.

PUZZLES AND GAMES SB P102

1

b get a job, 4
c get married, 1
d have children, 6
e take an exam, 3
f leave home, 5

2

2 leave home 3 take an exam
4 get married 5 have children
6 take a course

3

E	E	Q	I	Y	B	K	L
K	N	K	A	A	U	G	O
A	J	L	A	W	I	E	S
T	P	W	A	M	L	E	D
W	R	T	Y	A	D	K	O
O	C	E	K	A	B	A	U
H	R	W	B	P	G	T	U

1 bake 2 play 3 do 4 watch 5 go

4

a should go to sleep earlier.
b They should take a walk or do exercise.
c He should do yoga.
d She shouldn't eat junk food.
e She shouldn't skip breakfast before school.
f He should join a gym.

The image matches sentence e.

PUZZLES AND GAMES SB P103

1

2 promise
3 value
4 influence
5 logo
6 product

2

2 You / don't / have / go / grocery store: You don't have to go to a grocery store. a
3 all / passengers / must / have / ticket: All passengers must have a ticket. d
4 He / doesn't / have / study / technology: He doesn't have to study technology. e
5 She / has / design / new / logo: She has to design a new logo. c

3

1 recycle
2 reuse
3 reduce

Do you protect the environment?

4

1 produces
2 makes, reduce
3 reduce, pollute
4 reduce, is
5 save, take

reuse

PUZZLES AND GAMES SB P104

1

2 weird
3 brilliant
4 freezing
5 silly

crazy

2

1 If you changed your name, what name would you choose?
2 If you changed one thing on Earth, what would it be?
3 If you had a special talent, what would you do with it?
4 If you were a famous musician, what instrument would you play?

3

a	e	p	l	o	y	e	i	t
h	s	j	h	y	m	y	d	v
r	i	b	r	p	a	s	v	x
g	e	d	k	g	e	c	l	a
p	g	t	h	k	e	k	o	p
u	q	a	v	c	g	n	l	u
e	r	f	o	r	m	t	o	i
j	z	j	o	n	n	u	w	t
e	a	n	z	y	m	j	s	c

2 reggae
3 jazz
4 rock
5 heavy metal
6 country music

4

Band	Cuban Band	British Boy Band	Canadian All-Girl Orchestra	South Korean Band
Location of Biggest Concert	Washington		Barcelona	Rio de Janeiro
Type of Music	R & B	techno	classical	pop
Size of Band	5	4	32	7

The band that have played in Washington: Cuban band

PUZZLES AND GAMES SB P105

1

2 survive, survival
3 produce, production
4 develop, development
5 organize, organization
6 discover, discovery

2

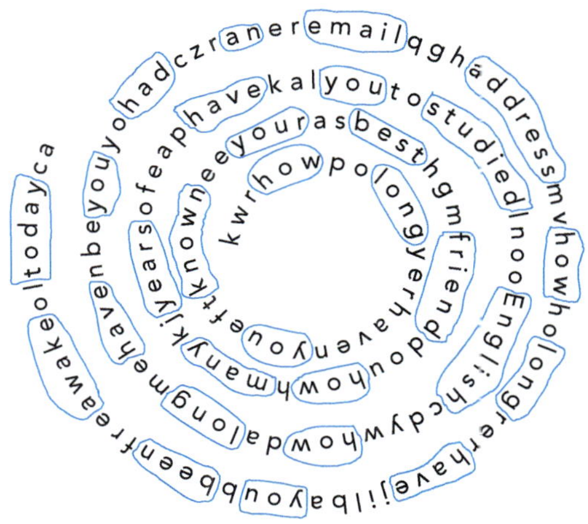

1 How long have you known your best friend?
2 How many years have you studied English?
3 How long have you had an email address?
4 How long have you been awake today?

Student's own answers

3

2 had trouble
3 do physical activities
4 make a difference
5 make decisions
6 had an opportunity, did well
7 have time

4

2 Their families have helped them a lot.
3 They have already had an opportunity to meet some interesting people.

Decisions!

Lesson Aim: I can create an infographic about my school's carbon footprint.

1 Write the following question on the board and elicit answers: *What is a carbon footprint?* Listen to students' answers. Have them do some quick research on the Internet if they cannot answer the question. Then ask: *Do you believe you can reduce your carbon footprint? Is it easy? Can we do this overnight?* In pairs, have students make a list of things they believe they can do to reduce their carbon footprint in their households, e.g.: *By making small changes to our actions such as eating less meat, taking fewer connecting flights, line drying clothes, riding a bike to school,* etc. Have them share their lists. Invite students to look at the infographic on page 107. In pairs, have students read sentences 1–2, skim the infographic, and check the correct alternative. Have them check in pairs.

2 Have students analyze the infographic and read the question. Draw their attention to the design and ask students when infographics are the best genre to use. Encourage them to think of ideas of different types of infographics (informational, statistical, comparison, timeline, etc.). Have them share their thoughts in small groups.

3 Read through the instructions and the alternatives below. Ask them what a persuasive text is. Have them work in pairs and analyze the infographic in detail in order to check the alternatives. Encourage them to add any other feature of a persuasive text. Have them check first in pairs and then as a whole class.

4 Have a volunteer read through questions 1–5 to check understanding. Have students answer the questions individually. Check answers in pairs and encourage students to show their partners where they found the answers. Then, check the answers as a whole class.

PROJECT
WRITING A PERSUASIVE TEXT

CREATE AN INFOGRAPHIC ABOUT YOUR SCHOOL'S CARBON FOOTPRINT.

1 Look at the infographic on page 107. What's the infographic about? Check (✓) the correct answer.

1 ☑ what people should do to reduce their school's carbon footprint
2 ◯ what people should do to calculate their school's carbon footprint

2 Look at the design of the infographic. What do you notice about it? Discuss your ideas with a partner.

3 Look at the writing techniques below. Check (✓) the techniques which are features of a persuasive text. Then find and circle examples of these techniques in the infographic.

1 ☑ repeat key words
2 ◯ explain a process
3 ☑ use powerful verbs
4 ☑ include strong adjectives
5 ◯ create suspense
6 ☑ use emotive words
7 ☑ use rhetorical questions

4 Read the infographic and answer the questions.

1 How much of UK carbon emissions are schools responsible for?
2%

2 What takes about half of a school's energy consumption and what takes about a quarter?
Heating takes about half and lighting takes about a quarter.

3 What should people do if they're not using equipment?
Switch it off.

4 How can people reduce pollution outside the school?
By walking or cycling to and from school.

5 Why is it important to use eco-friendly companies to supply products and services for schools?
Because eco-friendly companies don't create as many emissions as non-eco-friendly companies.

PROJECT TASK

1 PLAN

1 Find out about your school's carbon footprint. Search for and use an online "school carbon footprint calculator."
2 Think about the design of your infographic. Look for images and information to use.
3 Write a first version of your text. Remember to include information about your school, the main areas that have an impact on the school's carbon footprint, and suggestions of ways to reduce it.
4 Finalize your text. Remember to include the features of a persuasive text from Exercise 2.
5 Design and create a final version of your infographic with the text and images.
6 Check grammar, spelling, and punctuation, and practice pronunciation of any difficult words.

THINK!

Is reducing your carbon footprint a priority in your community? Why / Why not?

2 YOUR DIGITAL PORTFOLIO

Upload your infographic to the class portfolio for everyone to see! Present your infographic to the class.

3 REFLECT

Which features of a persuasive text did you include in your infographic? How do they make your text more persuasive?

106

THINK!

Put students into groups to discuss the question. Have them share their thoughts about how concerned people are about carbon footprints in their community and in their households. Ask: *How engaged are you in reducing your carbon footprint?*

Project Task

1 Plan

Go through the steps below with the class and monitor their work by giving general correction and feedback.

1. Tell students to search for a school carbon footprint calculator on the Internet. Have them follow the steps of the page to calculate their school's carbon footprint.
2. Encourage students to look at different designs of infographics and have them discuss how they are going to build their own. Have them think about the features they believe are the most important. Impactful images are important to serve the purpose of their infographic. Remind them they can create a digital infographic or a printed version.
3. Have students write the first version of their infographic with the information they believe is the most important to persuade people that we must take action now. Make sure they have all the necessary information. Encourage students to use their creativity to portray all this information.
4. When students have created the text for the infographic, have them analyze it to make sure they have included persuasive elements to the text. Have them look back at Exercise 3 for this.
5. Have them create the final version, including images, icons, text, etc. If possible, hand out poster paper, pens, and other necessary materials for students to make their infographic colorful and appealing.
6. Have students check their texts. If they are working in class, you can put them into pairs for peer correction. Encourage them to refer to the units in their Student's Book to check grammar, spelling, and punctuation. Have students create a clean version of their infographic using their corrected texts and final images. Monitor and help as necessary.

2 Your Digital Portfolio

Remind students to upload their infographics to the class portfolio. If they made a printed infographic, they should take a photo of it and upload it to the virtual class space. Alternatively, you could have a display in the classroom with students' work on the walls. If possible, a low time in class for every student to present their infographic.

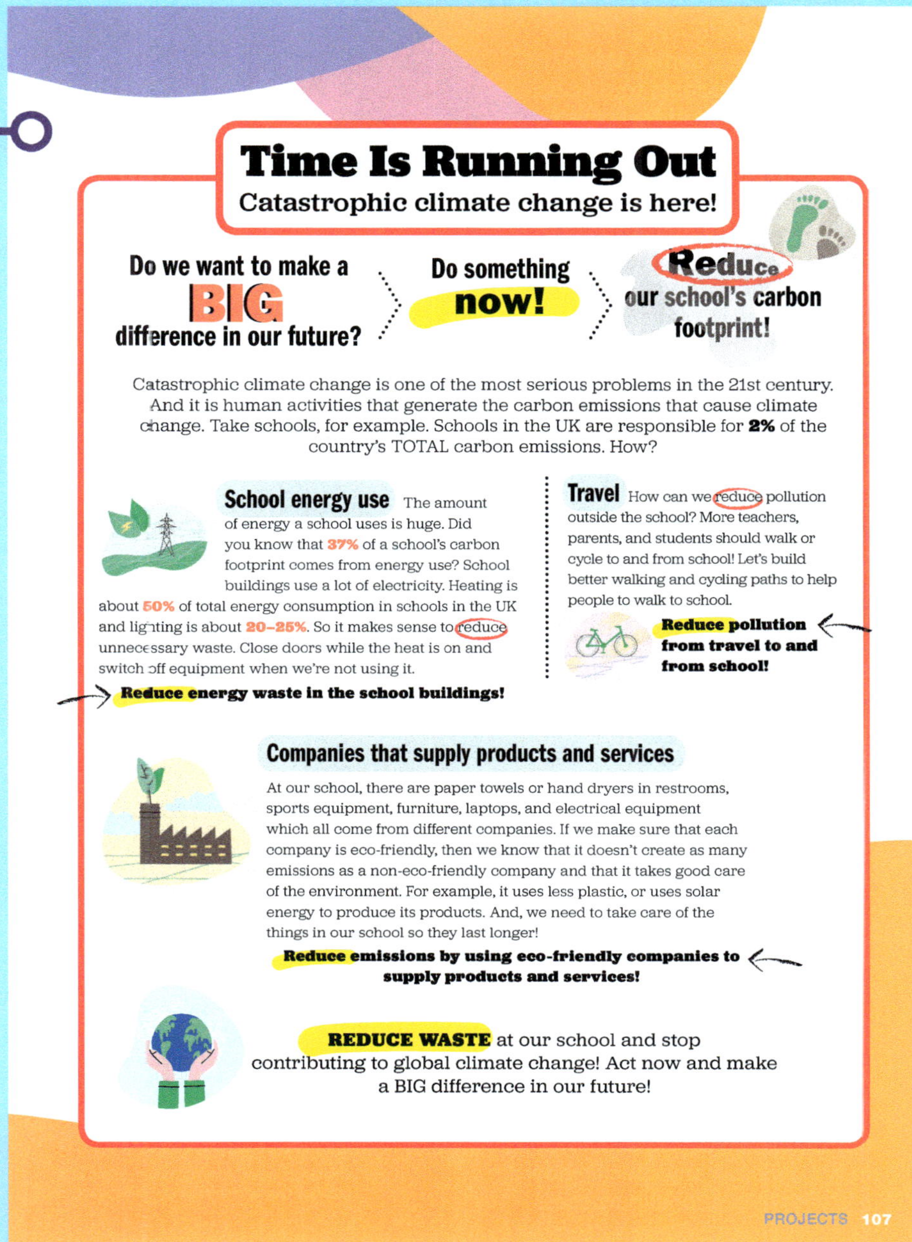

Time Is Running Out

Catastrophic climate change is here!

Do we want to make a BIG difference in our future? Do something now! Reduce our school's carbon footprint!

Catastrophic climate change is one of the most serious problems in the 21st century. And it is human activities that generate the carbon emissions that cause climate change. Take schools, for example. Schools in the UK are responsible for **2%** of the country's TOTAL carbon emissions. How?

School energy use The amount of energy a school uses is huge. Did you know that **37%** of a school's carbon footprint comes from energy use? School buildings use a lot of electricity. Heating is about **50%** of total energy consumption in schools in the UK and lighting is about **20–25%**. So it makes sense to reduce unnecessary waste. Close doors while the heat is on and switch off equipment when we're not using it.

Reduce energy waste in the school buildings!

Travel How can we reduce pollution outside the school? More teachers, parents, and students should walk or cycle to and from school! Let's build better walking and cycling paths to help people to walk to school.

Reduce pollution from travel to and from school!

Companies that supply products and services

At our school, there are paper towels or hand dryers in restrooms, sports equipment, furniture, laptops, and electrical equipment which all come from different companies. If we make sure that each company is eco-friendly, then we know that it doesn't create as many emissions as a non-eco-friendly company and that it takes good care of the environment. For example, it uses less plastic, or uses solar energy to produce its products. And, we need to take care of the things in our school so they last longer!

Reduce emissions by using eco-friendly companies to supply products and services!

REDUCE WASTE at our school and stop contributing to global climate change! Act now and make a BIG difference in our future!

PROJECTS 107

3 Reflect

Put students into groups to discuss their infographics. Encourage them to give feedback and say something they like about each person's work. Encourage them to analyze the persuasive elements. Then have each group vote on their favorite one. Groups share their results with the class and give their reasons referring to design and text. Finally, have students vote for one of the short-listed options to choose the favorite infographic in the class.

Cambridge Life Competencies Framework

I can …

- create a persuasive poster or webpage using creative ideas. **(Creative Thinking)**
- develop a clear description with a logical sequence of points. **(Communication)**
- make informed choices about my carbon footprint. **(Social Responsibility)**
- get involved in collective action in the school/community. **(Social Responsibility)**
- identify evidence and its reliability. **(Critical Thinking)**

Lesson Aim: I can design a board game or card game for a specific purpose.

1 Begin by asking: *What is your favorite board game? Why?* Encourage students to discuss their favorites and have them justify their answers. Having discussed this, have students look at the board game on page 109. Ask: *What can you see? What is the main goal of this board game? Who is the board game for?* Elicit answers and have the class write their answers in the space provided.

2 Read through the headings in the chart with the students. Have them read the introduction and description of the board game on page 109 in detail and have them underline where they can find the necessary information. Have them complete the chart. Invite students to read the answers aloud to check.

3 Ask a volunteer to read questions 1–6 to check comprehension. Have students read the description of the board game again in order to answer the questions. Have them do this individually. Check answers with the class.

THINK!

Have students read through the questions and think about them individually, then have them share their thoughts in pairs. Finally, open up the discussion to the class. Ask them if they know any specific board games with educational purposes. Encourage them to make a list of all the benefits of playing games and share them with the class.

PROJECT
DESIGNING A BOARD GAME OR CARD GAME

GIVE A PRESENTATION ABOUT YOUR BOARD GAME OR CARD GAME.

1 Look at the title and contents of the board game on page 109 and answer the questions.

1 Who's the game for?
teenagers

2 What do you need to play this game?
board, 24 Dilemma cards, 4 counters, dice

2 Read the introduction to the description of the game and complete the chart.

Name of Game	Dilemma Teens
Aim of Game	solve the teen dilemmas
How to Win	be the first player to reach HOME SWEET HOME.

3 Read the whole description and answer the questions.

1 How many players can play the game? 2–4
2 Where do players put their counters to start the game? On the Big Wide World square.
3 Who starts the game? The oldest player.
4 If a player falls on a Dilemma square who takes a Dilemma card? Player B (or one of the other players).
5 What happens if the player suggests the correct solution to the dilemma? He/She moves to the next square.
6 What happens on an Oops! square? He/She has to follow the instructions on the square.

PROJECT TASK

1 PLAN

1 Choose a type of game to design: a board game or a card game, and decide who the game is for.
2 Decide what you need in order to play the game, the aim of the game, how to win, how to play the game, and what the game will look like. Look for images or draw your own.
3 Write a first version of the description of your game. Remember to include the name, an introduction to your game explaining who the game is for, the aim of the game and how to win, the contents, and clear instructions on how to play the game.
4 Design and create a final version of the description of your game, and include images to make the game look attractive.
5 Check grammar, spelling, punctuation, and practice pronunciation of any difficult words.

THINK!

Why do think people play board or card games? What can you learn from playing these games?

2 YOUR DIGITAL PORTFOLIO

Upload your game to the class portfolio for everyone to see! Present your game to the class.

3 REFLECT

Which is your favorite game? Why?

108

Lesson Aim: I can design a board game or card game for a specific purpose.

Project Task

1 Plan

Go through the steps with the class and check understanding. Allow students to decide whether they would like to do this project as a group or individually.

1. Tell students to decide on the type of game they will create. Encourage them to research different board games or card games on the Internet for inspiration.
2. Tell students to think the whole game through: goals, how people will win, design, rules, bits and pieces that will be part of the game, etc. Encourage students to design it on paper beforehand.
3. Have students write a step-by-step guide of how the game will work, using the board game on page 109 to guide them. Encourage students to talk to each other to share ideas and designs.
4. Have students decide on the final version. Have them do a test drive of the game together. If possible, hand out poster paper, pens, and other necessary materials for students to make their board games or card games colorful and appealing. Alternatively, students may want to make a digital board game.
5. Students can edit and correct their information on their own at home. Have them test the game with their family and friends if they understand English. Encourage them to refer to the units in their books to check grammar, spelling, and punctuation. Finally, have students create a clean version of their game using their corrected texts and final images.

   If students are making a digital game, they can upload their texts and images to the positions they want them.

2 Your Digital Portfolio

Remind students to upload their games to their class portfolio. If they made a printed game, they should take a photo of it and upload it to the virtual class space. Encourage students to play each other's games and give feedback. If possible, allow time in class for every student to present their games and allow all to play them.

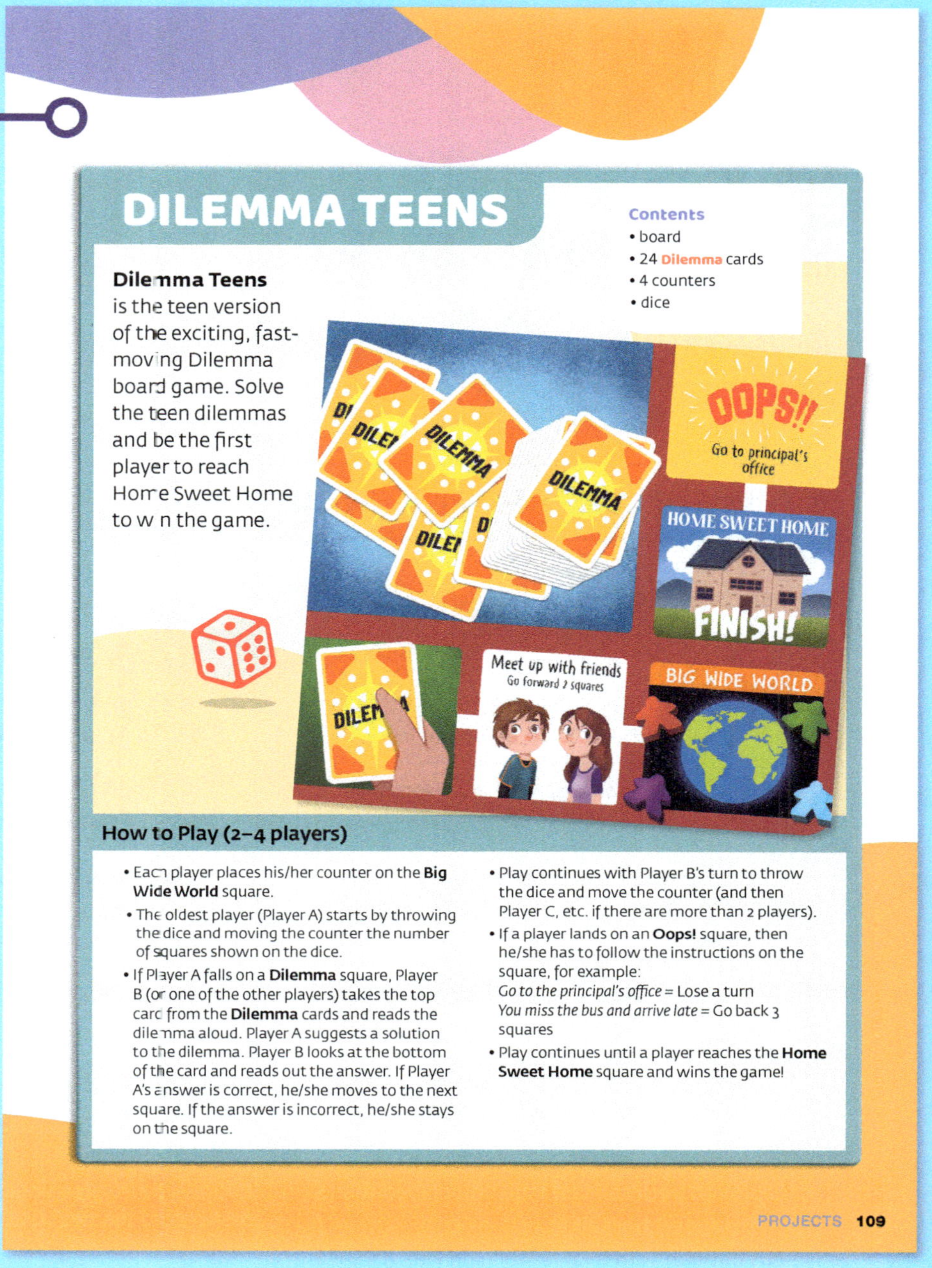

DILEMMA TEENS

Contents
- board
- 24 Dilemma cards
- 4 counters
- dice

Dilemma Teens is the teen version of the exciting, fast-moving Dilemma board game. Solve the teen dilemmas and be the first player to reach Home Sweet Home to win the game.

How to Play (2–4 players)

- Each player places his/her counter on the **Big Wide World** square.
- The oldest player (Player A) starts by throwing the dice and moving the counter the number of squares shown on the dice.
- If Player A falls on a **Dilemma** square, Player B (or one of the other players) takes the top card from the **Dilemma** cards and reads the dilemma aloud. Player A suggests a solution to the dilemma. Player B looks at the bottom of the card and reads out the answer. If Player A's answer is correct, he/she moves to the next square. If the answer is incorrect, he/she stays on the square.
- Play continues with Player B's turn to throw the dice and move the counter (and then Player C, etc. if there are more than 2 players).
- If a player lands on an **Oops!** square, then he/she has to follow the instructions on the square, for example:
  Go to the principal's office = Lose a turn
  You miss the bus and arrive late = Go back 3 squares
- Play continues until a player reaches the **Home Sweet Home** square and wins the game!

PROJECTS **109**

3 Reflect

Put students into groups to discuss the games. Encourage them to give feedback and say something they like about each person's game. Then have each group vote on their favorite game. Groups share their result with the class and give their reasons. Write the groups' chosen games on the board. Finally, have students vote for one of the short-listed options to choose the favorite game in the class.

Cambridge Life Competencies Framework

I can …

- actively participate in activities that require creative thinking with others. **(Creative Thinking)**
- make an assignment original by adding new angles. **(Creative Thinking)**
- develop a clear description or narrative with a logical sequence of points. **(Communication)**
- deal appropriately with praise, setbacks, and criticism. **(Emotional Development)**
- state opposing opinions in a respectful way. **(Emotional Development)**

1 MY LIFE PLAN

LANGUAGE REFERENCE

Will and *Be going to*

	Will for Predictions	*Be going to* for Intentions
Affirmative (+)	I think I**'ll live** abroad when I'm older. Perhaps she**'ll be** an engineer.	**I'm going to learn** to drive. They**'re going to get** married.
Negative (–)	He **won't get** the grades he needs. She probably **won't go** to university.	**I'm not going to study** French. We**'re not going to take** the same course.
Questions (?)	**Will** Rosa **take** the exam? **Will** they **go** to the same college?	**Are** you **going to leave** home? **Is** he **going to work** in São Paulo? When **are** we **going to visit** them?

We often use *will* with *I believe*, *I (don't) think*, *I'm sure*, *maybe*, *perhaps*, *probably*.

Reflexive Pronouns

Singular	Plural
I often **talk to myself** when I'm working. You **enjoyed yourself** last time you played tennis. She **introduced herself** to us. He **cut himself** with a knife while he was cooking. My phone **turns itself** off when it's too hot.	We **test ourselves** at the end of each class. OK everyone, **give yourselves** ten minutes to rest before the next game. Art is a natural way for children to **express themselves**.

***By* + *myself*, *yourself*, etc. means *alone*, *on one's own*.**

Life Stages

finish school
get a job
get married
go to college
graduate
have children
leave home
retire
take a course
take an exam

Studying

get a good grade
make progress
practice
prepare
review
take a break

VOCABULARY

1 Label the images with the words/phrases below.

• ~~get a job~~ • get married • graduate • have children • leave home • take an exam

1

get a job

2

leave home

3

graduate

4

take an exam

5

get married

6

have children

2 Match 1–6 with a–f.

1 My sister says she's not going to have b
2 He's very interested in languages and he wants to take e
3 A month after Amy left college, she got a
4 At 65 my grandad decided to d
5 In my country, most children finish c
6 After school, my older brother went f

a a really good job.
b children.
c school at 18.
d retire.
e a course in Italian.
f to college to study music.

3 Put the letters in the correct order and complete the sentences.

1 Did Carlo get a good grade (ragde) in his French test?
2 My reading and writing is OK, but I need to practice (capritec) my speaking skills more.
3 My English course is going really well. I'm definitely making progress (rogperss).
4 We have to review (evrewi) some vocabulary for our class on Friday.
5 Remember to take a break (ekarb) every hour or so when you're studying.
6 Unfortunately, Evie didn't have enough time to prepare (erparpe) for her exam.

4 Complete the dialogue with the correct words/phrases for studying.

Mariana Your mom says you're studying Spanish, Isabel. How's it going?
Isabel OK, I think. My teacher says I'm making good [1] progress. I'm certainly better than I was last year!
Mariana That's great to hear!
Isabel But I find listening difficult. I need to [2] practice that more.
Mariana Mmm … I think listening is the hardest part of learning a language.
Isabel Anyway, I'd better go. I'm [3] preparing for a vocabulary test tomorrow and I really want to get [4] a good grade. I have a lot of words to [5] review.
Mariana Well good luck and go for a walk or something after an hour or two. Don't forget to [6] take a break!

GRAMMAR

1 Put the words in the correct order.

1 with / will / probably / disagree / us / he .
He will probably disagree with us.

2 going / to / I'm / try to / job in / get a / a café .
I'm going to try to get a job in a café.

3 next / grandma / your / retire / will / year ?
Will your grandma retire next year?

4 will / the / enjoy / sure / I'm / movie / you .
I'm sure you will enjoy the movie.

5 get / Margarita / are / and Carlos / to / married / going ?
Are Margarita and Carlos going to get married?

6 angry / think / I / parents / don't / will be / your / with you .
I don't think your parents will be angry with you.

7 a / not / have / going / we're / to / sleepover .
We're not going to have a sleepover.

8 won't / it / rainy / afternoon / be / this .
It won't be rainy this afternoon.

2 Cross out the six incorrect words and write the correct words below.

Hey Alicia, how are you doing? Are you feeling better now? Raquel and I are going to ~~having~~ a picnic in the park tomorrow. Can you come? We're meeting at 4 by the lake – it won't ~~being~~ so crowded then. I'm going to ~~bringing~~ food and Raquel ~~are~~ going to bring drinks. It will ~~being~~ hot so remember your hat! ~~I~~ going to invite Julia, too. Hope to see you tomorrow.
6:25

1 have
2 be
3 bring
4 is
5 be
6 I'm

3 Match 1–6 with a–f.

1 Painting and drawing helps me to express e
2 By the age of 13, he could take care of d
3 To practice your pronunciation, you can record a
4 My eight-year-old sister made this beautiful cake by c
5 The party was great. We really enjoyed f
6 By 2030, all new cars will be able to drive b

a yourself.
b themselves.
c herself.
d himself.
e myself.
f ourselves.

4 Complete the sentences with the correct simple past form of the verbs below and the correct reflexive pronoun.

• build • cut • ~~give~~ • look at • make • teach

1

After studying for three hours, he gave himself a break.

2

Abigail and Emma made themselves some breakfast.

3

He looked at himself in the mirror.

4

Joe accidentally cut himself.

5

Marcela taught herself to play the guitar.

6

They built themselves a new kitchen.

READING

1 Read the text quickly and check (✓) the correct answers.

1 Why does Laura email her grandfather?
- ○ to ask him for a job
- ✓ to tell him what she's going to do next year
- ○ to ask if she can stay with him

2 What are Laura's plans?
- ○ to work
- ○ to travel
- ✓ to work and then travel

To: Felipe Oliveira

Hi Grandpa

Thanks for your message on Sunday. I took my last exam yesterday (geography) so I was studying all week. I *think* my exams went OK. Computer science was fun (!), but math was difficult. I really hope I get good grades. I guess we'll see in August …

Anyway, you asked about my plans, so here they are! I'm going to take a break from studying before I go to college. I'd like to go traveling for a few months next year, but it will be expensive so I'm going to get a job here and earn some money first. I'm sure you remember my best friend Helena. She and another classmate, Ryan, work in a café on the weekends (see the photo) and I'm going to work there for 15 hours a week starting in July. It's not far from our house so I'll cycle there and back. I'll probably try to get some other work too, maybe at the mall in town. I hope I'll have enough money to go traveling next March.

And where will I go on my trip? Well, probably Italy so I can practice my Italian. Aunt Sofia and Uncle Luca said I can stay with them, which is exciting. I'd love to see my cousins again and I'd like to see Rome again too – Aunt Sofia took this amazing photo of the Colosseum the other evening! Can you believe I was only eight years old the last time we visited them?

Anyway, I'll finish this email now and go and make myself some breakfast. I hope you're well.

Speak soon!

Love,

Laura

2 Read the text and write *T* (true) or *F* (false) next to the statements.

1 Laura's grandfather emailed her last weekend. T
2 Laura's computer science exam was easier than her math exam. T
3 She's going to work in her best friend's café. F
4 She will take the bus to and from the café. F
5 She hopes to get two jobs. T
6 Laura's relations in Italy invited her to stay with them. T

3 Write answers to the questions.

1 Which exam did Laura enjoy?
She enjoyed the computer science exam.

2 When will Laura know the results of her exams?
She'll know the results of her exams in August.

3 What did Laura's grandfather ask her about in his last email?
He asked her about her plans.

4 Where will Laura look for a second job?
She'll look for a second job at the mall in town.

5 What three reasons does Laura give for going to Italy?
She wants to practice her Italian, see her cousins again, and see Rome again, too.

2 WHAT MAKES US HAPPY?

LANGUAGE REFERENCE

Should/Shouldn't for Advice

Affirmative (+)	Negative (–)	Questions (?)
You **should take** a break.	You **shouldn't eat** so much sugar.	**Should** I **call** him?
He **should eat** more fruit and vegetables.	She **shouldn't sit** down all day.	**Should** he **go** for a run?
I think they **should do** more exercise.	They **shouldn't drink** all that cola.	**Should** we **leave** now?

Tag Questions

Affirmative (+) Sentence	Negative (–) Tag
I'm early,	**aren't I?**
You eat fish,	**don't you?**
He told you,	**didn't he?**
She's Spanish,	**isn't she?**
It was crowded,	**wasn't it?**
We can leave now,	**can't we?**
They're having a sleepover,	**aren't they?**
Negative (–) Sentence	**Affirmative (+) Tag**
I was anxious,	**wasn't I?**
You weren't late,	**were you?**
Paolo isn't angry,	**is he?**
She isn't doing yoga,	**is she?**
She didn't retire,	**did she?**
You can't buy tickets now,	**can you?**
They don't play in a band,	**do they?**

The negative tag for *I am* (*I'm*) is *aren't I?*.

More Free-time Activities

bake cookies
build models
do gymnastics
do yoga
go skateboarding
make jewelry
play board games
take a walk
take singing lessons
watch the sunset

Health and Fitness

go for a run
make friends
prevent diseases
reduce stress
stay in shape
work out

VOCABULARY

1 Complete the sentences with the correct form of the verbs below. Then match images a–f with sentences 1–6.

• build • ~~do~~ • do • go • play • watch

1 Do you ___do___ yoga at school? ___f___
2 We ___went___ skateboarding last weekend. ___b___
3 Shall we climb the hill and ___watch___ the sunset? ___d___
4 They ___did___ gymnastics when they were younger. ___c___
5 Two of the students were ___building___ a model. ___a___
6 I love ___playing___ board games with my family. ___e___

2 Match 1–6 with a–f.

1 My sister makes ___c___
2 How often does Martina go ___e___
3 Serena and I baked ___f___
4 Do you still take ___d___
5 Would you like to play ___b___
6 Danny and I took ___a___

a a walk by the river.
b a board game?
c her own jewelry.
d singing lessons?
e skateboarding?
f some cookies yesterday.

3 Put the letters in the correct order and complete the sentences.

1 I work ___out___ (uto) at the gym three times a week.
2 He stays in ___shape___ (haspe) by swimming and running.
3 My mom goes for a ___run___ (urn) before work in the mornings.
4 Yoga is really good for ___reducing___ (icegrudn) stress.
5 Regular exercise can help ___prevent___ (rtenpev) some diseases.
6 Joining a soccer team helped Camila to ___make___ (aekm) friends.

4 Complete the text with correct form of the verbs in Exercise 3.

There are so many benefits to exercise. It can [1] ___reduce___ stress, it helps you to [2] ___stay___ in shape and doctors say it can even [3] ___prevent___ diseases. There are so many different exercise options, too, and some of them are free. For example, you can take a walk or [4] ___go___ for a run without spending any money, or you can [5] ___work___ out in your own living room. Joining a running club or a gym can also help you to [6] ___make___ friends. So choose your exercise and get started!

COMMENT SHARE LIKE

GRAMMAR

1 Complete the sentences with *should* or *shouldn't* and the verbs below.

• drink • eat • practice • spend • use • ~~walk~~

1 My dad should walk more and drive less.
2 You should practice your English every day.
3 Theo shouldn't use his phone so much.
4 People shouldn't eat so much junk food.
5 We shouldn't spend so much time at our computers.
6 Marta should drink more water.

2 Read about Daniel. Then use the phrases to write sentences with *should* or *shouldn't* giving him advice.

Daniel is often tired in class and can't concentrate on his work. He wants to be healthier and more active, but he always plays video games in the evening and goes to bed late. In the mornings, he finds it difficult to get up, and he doesn't have time for breakfast. He lives quite near his school, but because he's always late, he takes the bus.

1 go to bed earlier
He should go to bed earlier.
2 play video games late in the evening
He shouldn't play video games late in the evening.
3 get up an hour before school starts
He should get up an hour before school starts.
4 eat a healthy breakfast before he goes to school
He should eat a healthy breakfast before he goes to school.
5 take the bus to school
He shouldn't take the bus to school.
6 walk to school
He should walk to school.

3 Circle the correct options.

1 You didn't see Eduardo, *do* / *did* you? (circled: did)
2 They got married, *weren't* / *didn't* they? (circled: didn't)
3 It was exciting, *wasn't* / *was* it? (circled: wasn't)
4 They're staying with their cousins, *don't* / *aren't* they? (circled: aren't)
5 Brenda can speak Italian, *can't* / *doesn't* she? (circled: can't)
6 The restaurant isn't expensive, *isn't* / *is* it? (circled: is)

4 Complete the dialogue with the correct tag questions.

A You weren't at Enzo's party, [1] were you?
B Yes, I was!
A Of course you were, sorry! You didn't see Samuel there, [2] did you?
B No, I didn't.
A We're meeting Samuel at two o'clock, [3] aren't we?
B Yes, in the café.
A But we're not eating there [4] are we?
B No, that's right.
A You eat fish, [5] don't you?
B Yes, I love fish.
A But you don't eat meat, [6] do you?
B No, that's right.

READING

1 Read the text quickly and check (✓) the correct answers.

1 Why is Ana worried?
- ○ her friend isn't getting good grades at school
- ✓ her friend is working too hard

2 What's Ana going to do?
- ✓ visit her friend and do some activities together
- ○ help her friend with her work

MARCIA

Hey, Marcia, you weren't at Paolo's party, were you? Are you OK? 11:20 pm

Hey, Ana! Good to hear from you. Yeah, I'm fine, thanks. I was just busy that evening. Did you have fun? 11:20 pm

Yeah, it was a really good party, but Patricia and I were sad you weren't there. You usually like going to parties, don't you? 11:20 pm

Yes, I do, but I was studying that evening. I had a French test on Monday so I was reviewing some vocabulary. To be honest, I didn't really want to go. I wasn't feeling very sociable – I was anxious about the test. And next week I have another test … 11:22 pm

But you always get good grades. Do you remember the last French test? You got over 90%, didn't you? I think you study too hard. I hope you're remembering to take a break – do some yoga or take a walk or something. 11:23 pm

No, I'm too busy. 11:23 pm

Marcia, I'm serious now – I'm worried about you! It's not healthy to study all the time, is it? Even our teachers tell us we shouldn't work all the time! I really think you should give yourself a break. Listen, I've got a plan! I'm going to come round this weekend and we're going to bake some of those amazing chocolate cookies and play some board games. How does that sound? 11:24 pm

That sounds great. It'll be really nice to see you, Ana. You're a good friend! 11:25 pm

2 Read the text and circle the correct options.

1 Ana wants to know why Marcia wasn't at *school* / *a party*. (circled: *a party*)
2 Marcia was *ill* / *studying* last Saturday evening. (circled: *studying*)
3 Ana *enjoyed* / *didn't enjoy* Paolo's party. (circled: *enjoyed*)
4 Ana thinks Marcia should study *more* / *less*. (circled: *less*)
5 Ana wants to visit Marcia and *play board games* / *do yoga* together. (circled: *play board games*)
6 Marcia says she *is too busy* / *would like* to see Ana. (circled: *would like*)

3 Write answers to the questions.

1 Who missed Marcia at Paolo's party as well as Ana?
Patricia missed Marcia at Paolo's party as well as Ana.

2 What did Marcia do on Monday?
She had a French test.

3 How was Marcia feeling on Saturday night?
She was feeling anxious.

4 What grade did Marcia get in her last French test?
She got over 90%.

5 What two things are Marcia and Ana going to do on the weekend?
They're going to bake chocolate cookies and play board games.

3 CONSUMER WORLD

LANGUAGE REFERENCE

Have to and *Must*

Have to		
Affirmative: Obligation		
I/You/We/They	**have to**	get a visa.
He/She	**has to**	
Negative: No Obligation		
I/You/We/They	**don't have to**	take the bus.
He/She	**doesn't have to**	

Must		
Affirmative: Obligation		
I/You/We/They/He/She	**must**	tell the teacher.
Negative: Prohibition		
I/You/We/They/He/She	**must not**	be late.

We use *must not* to say something is the wrong thing to do.

Have to: Questions and Short Answers

Do I **have to wear** my uniform? **Do** you **have to pay** for medicine? **Do** we **have to take** our shoes off? **Do** they **have to show** their passports?	Yes, I/you/we/they **do**. / No, I/you/we/they **don't**.
Does he **have to go** to the principal's office? **Does** she **have to sign** this?	Yes, he/she **does**. / No, he/she **doesn't**.
How many exams **does** he **have to take**? Why **do** they **have to leave** tomorrow?	

We use *There <u>was</u>* for singular nouns and *There <u>were</u>* for plural nouns.

Advertising

advertise
advertisement
attract
headline
influence
logo
persuade
product
promise
value

Money

cost
invest
label
on sale
own
sell

VOCABULARY

1 Circle eight more advertising words.

proadvertisefomlogomumpersuadezoheadlinepretinfluencewsproductklasvaluebreypromiseattract

1 advertise
2 logo
3 persuade
4 headline
5 influence
6 product
7 value
8 promise
9 attract

2 Match 1–6 with a–f.

1 advertisement e
2 attract f
3 headline a
4 logo b
5 product d
6 promise c

a line of words in large letters at the top of an advertisement or a story in a newspaper, etc.
b image or symbol that a company uses to sell things
c tell someone that you will certainly do something
d thing that a company makes and sells
e picture, short film, etc. that tries to make people buy something
f make people interested in something

3 Put the letters in the correct order and complete the sentences.

1 I usually wait till clothes are on sale (no esal) before I buy them.
2 The government needs to invest (venits) more money in transportation.
3 Excuse me, how much does this jacket cost (soct)?
4 We went to a store that sells clothes by her favorite label (balle).
5 I never wear those blue sneakers. I think I'll sell (lesl) them.
6 How many hats do you own (won), Leticia?

4 Complete the dialogue with the correct form of the words/phrases below.

• cost • invest • ~~label~~ • on sale • own • sell

Sophie Hey, look at these jeans! I really love this [1] label. They make the best jeans.
Aline Yeah, they're really cool. Are you going to buy them?
Sophie I can't afford them. They [2] cost far too much!
Aline No, they're [3] on sale. Look – they're half price!
Sophie Wow, that's a bargain! I can't buy them though. I already [4] own five pairs of jeans and my mom thinks that's four too many. She doesn't understand why I like nice clothes. She never spends money on things like that. She just [5] invests her money so she can earn more money.
Aline You have five pairs of jeans, did you say?
Sophie Yeah, although I don't wear all of them.
Aline Well, maybe you could [6] sell the jeans that you don't wear, and then you can buy these?
Sophie That's a good idea, Aline – thanks!

GRAMMAR

1 Complete the dialogue with the words below.

• don't • has • have (x 2) • must • ~~to~~

Bruna Do you have any rules in your house?
Joseph Yes, one or two. We have [1] *to* do some work around the house to get our pocket money. So, my brother [2] *has* to clean the bathroom once a week and I [3] *have* to wash my mom's car. What about you?
Bruna Well, one important rule is that we [4] *have* to eat in the kitchen. We [5] *must* not eat in our bedrooms or in the living room.
Joseph That's the same in my house.
Bruna But we're lucky. We [6] *don't* have to do any jobs to get our pocket money.
Joseph You are lucky!

2 Circle the correct options.

1 Remember, you (*must not*) / *don't have to* be late for your exam!
2 You *must not* / (*don't have to*) bring any food to the picnic. We're taking enough for all of us.
3 We must get to Gabriel's house by six o'clock so we really (*must not*) / *don't have to* miss the bus.
4 Luke can come to the party with me if he likes but he *must not* / (*doesn't have to*).
5 Beatriz will need her passport with her so tell her she (*must not*) / *doesn't have to* forget it.
6 You *must not* / (*don't have to*) pay for the concert – it's free!

3 Complete the mini dialogues with the correct form of *do* or *have*.

1 A *Do* you sometimes *have* to cook for your family?
B No, I *don't*.
2 A *Do* they *have* to pay for their school books?
B Yes, they *do*.
3 A *Does* she *have* to save any of her pocket money?
B No, she *doesn't*.
4 A *Does* he *have* to get a good grade?
B Yes, he *does*.

4 Write questions and answers with the prompts and *have to*.

1 Claudia / get up / early?
no / she
Does Claudia have to get up early?
No, she doesn't.

2 you / take / a course?
yes / I
Do you have to take a course?
Yes, I do.

3 Rosa and Miguel / get / a visa?
no / they
Do Rosa and Miguel have to get a visa?
No, they don't.

4 he / drive / there?
yes / he
Does he have to drive there?
Yes, he does.

5 they / pay for / tickets?
no / they
Do they have to pay for tickets?
No, they don't.

6 we / speak English?
yes / we
Do we have to speak English?
Yes, we do.

READING

1 Read the text quickly and check (✓) the correct answers.

1 How do most young people born between approximately 1995 and 2005 feel about ads?
- ◯ They don't like any of them.
- ✓ They don't like digital advertisements.
- ◯ They don't like traditional advertisements.

2 What are companies doing about this?
- ◯ They're not investing in traditional ads to attract young people.
- ✓ They're investing in other ways of attracting young people.

Get the marketing news that matters each day.

GEN Z HATE YOUR ADS!

David Smith on February 10 at 6:32

A recent study of young people's attitudes towards advertisements revealed some interesting facts. Young people born between approximately 1995 and 2005, (often called Generation Z or, informally Gen Z), hate advertisements! However, to be more precise, they don't hate all ads. They hate a specific type of advertisement – the digital or online ad.

In the study, almost 70% of young people born between these dates said they preferred more traditional advertisements, for example on billboards at the side of the street or on buses. As one young person explained: "When I walk or cycle along a street, I can choose to look at the ads, but I don't have to. When I'm using my cell phone and companies are advertising all these products, I have to see them – I have no choice." Companies that make products for young people are listening to them and are now investing more in traditional advertisements.

The study shows that young people have clear ideas about the sort of ads they want to see. Most said that they didn't like advertisements in which the logo was very obvious, and they didn't like to see celebrities advertising products. They are more likely to listen to influencers. They liked advertisements that told interesting stories or were funny or creative. They also liked great music in their ads.

So why is this? Well, perhaps it's because this generation watches movies and series online where there are no advertisements. This is the norm for them. It's clear that in the future, companies will have to find different ways to attract young people to their products.

F

More

2 Read the text and complete each sentence with one word.

1 A recent study investigated young people's *attitudes* towards ads.
2 *Generation* Z refers to young people born between approximately 1995 and 2005.
3 Traditional advertisements on *billboards* at the side of the street or on buses are the type of ads that most young people prefer.
4 *Influencers* are more successful than celebrities in attracting young people to a product.
5 It is the *norm* for this group of young people to watch movies and series without ads.

3 Write answers to the questions.

1 What percentage of this group of young people prefer more traditional advertisements?
Over 70% of this group of young people prefer more traditional advertisements.

2 Why do these young people prefer traditional advertisements?
Because they don't have to but can choose to look at them.

3 What don't they like to be obvious in advertisements?
They don't like the logo to be obvious.

4 What do they like to hear in advertisements?
They like to hear great music.

5 How do young people usually watch movies and series?
They usually watch movies and series online.

4 WE CAN SAVE OUR PLANET

LANGUAGE REFERENCE

Zero Conditional and First Conditional

Zero Conditional	
***If* Clause (*If* + Simple Present)**	**Result Clause (Simple Present)**
If you **mix** red and yellow, **If** you **buy** recycled products,	you **get** orange. you **save** energy.
First Conditional	
***If* Clause (*If* + Simple Present)**	**Result Clause (*will/won't* + Infinitive)**
If the weather **improves**, **If** we all **drive** less, **If** she **fails** her exams,	we **will go** out. the air **will be** cleaner. she **won't go** to college.

The *if* clause can come first or second in zero and first conditional sentences. If the *if* clause comes second, we don't use a comma: *You get orange if you mix red and yellow*.

May and *Might* for Possibility

Affirmative (+)	I **may go** to the mall after class. We **might see** you at the weekend. Leonardo **might be** able to help us.
Negative (–)	They **may not come** to the party. She **might not have** enough money to go on vacation.

We don't usually use *may* and *might* in questions. We can form questions using *Is it possible that …?* or *Do you think …?*.

The Environment

cut down
destroy
pollute
protect
recycle
reduce
reuse
throw away
turn off
waste

Verbs and Phrases + Prepositions

agree with
depend on
pay attention to
succeed in
take care of
worry about

VOCABULARY

1 Look at the images and complete the sentences with the correct environment words.

1 

We make sure we never ...throw away... any food.

2 

You can ...recycle... bottles, paper, and plastic in town.

3 

Remember to ...turn off... the light when you leave a room.

4 

We must not ...cut down... so many trees.

5 

A lot of vehicles ...pollute... the air in all our cities.

6 

Governments aren't doing enough to ...protect... the planet.

2 Check (✓) the two words/phrases that complete each sentence.

1 We must recycle more of our …
a ✓ plastic. b ✓ glass. c ◯ rivers.
2 We are polluting our …
a ✓ air. b ◯ trash. c ✓ oceans.
3 We currently waste a lot of …
a ✓ energy. b ✓ water. c ◯ air.
4 Unfortunately, we are destroying …
a ◯ the air. b ✓ the planet. c ✓ the environment.
5 We must try to reduce …
a ✓ plastic use. b ✓ CO_2 emissions. c ◯ water.
6 At the end of the day, make sure you turn off any …
a ✓ computers. b ✓ lights. c ◯ energy.
7 You can reuse …
a ✓ bags. b ◯ air. c ✓ plastic bottles.

3 Complete the dialogue with the correct words.

A Do you worry [1] ...about... the environment?
B Yes, I do. We should do more to take care [2] ...of... our planet. Our future depends [3] ...on... it.
A I agree [4] ...with... you. If we destroy it, there won't be a future for people. Politicians should pay attention [5] ...to... young people like you – I'm sure you'll succeed [6] ...in... making them listen.

4 Match 1–6 with a–f.

1 I'm not sure I agree ...d...
2 We need to pay attention ...a...
3 The campaign succeeded ...f...
4 We really must take more care ...e...
5 Most young people worry ...c...
6 We all depend ...b...

a to what scientists are saying.
b on nature for our existence.
c about climate change.
d with you.
e of our oceans.
f in reducing food waste.

GRAMMAR

1 Complete the zero conditional sentences using the correct form of the verbs below.

• add • break • get • ~~go~~ • turn off • use

1 If I ___go___ to bed late, I feel tired the next day.
2 The sauce tastes a lot better if you ___add___ a little salt to it.
3 If you drop a plate on this floor, it ___breaks___.
4 You save electricity if you ___turn off___ your computer at night.
5 If public transportation is reliable, people ___use___ their cars less.
6 I'm always very happy if I ___get___ good grades in my tests.

2 Complete the first conditional sentences using the verbs in parentheses.

1 Harry ___will make___ (make) more progress if he ___studies___ (study) harder.
2 If you ___do___ (do) more exercise, you ___will/'ll feel___ (feel) healthier.
3 If it ___rains___ (rain) this afternoon, we ___will/'ll drive___ (drive) to the bowling alley.
4 I ___will/'ll tell___ (tell) Luis about the party if I ___see___ (see) him at lunchtime.
5 If we ___take___ (take) our bikes on vacation, we ___won't need___ (not need) to use the car.
6 If she ___stays___ (stays) here any longer, she ___won't be___ (not be) in time for the talk.

3 Complete the sentences using *may* or *might* and the verbs in parentheses.

What are these people's plans for today?

1

Charlotte ___might go for a run___. (might / go)

2

Tom ___may take a walk___. (may / take)

3

She ___may bake (some) cookies___. (may / bake)

4

He ___might do (some) yoga___. (might / do)

5

They ___may play a board game / play board games___. (may / play)

6

He ___might go skateboarding___. (might / go)

4 Rewrite the sentences using the words in parentheses.

1 It's possible that he will agree with us. (may)
___He may agree with us.___
2 Perhaps she's not at home. (might)
___She might not be at home.___
3 Maybe we'll persuade Yolanda to come with us. (might)
___We might persuade Yolanda to come with us.___
4 There's a chance the sneakers are on sale. (may)
___The sneakers may be on sale.___
5 It's possible that we'll be able to stop climate change. (might)
___We might be able to stop climate change.___
6 Perhaps he won't have time to finish the model. (may)
___He may not have time to finish the model.___

READING

1 Read the text quickly and check (✓) the correct answers.

1 Why does Samuel Carvalho write blog posts?
- ○ to tell readers how to make vegetarian food
- ○ to tell people about environmentally friendly ways to travel
- ✓ to persuade readers to do things that protect the planet

2 What does Samuel suggest we should do?
- ○ continue doing activities that may destroy the planet
- ○ stop doing activities that may destroy the planet
- ✓ reduce activities that may destroy the planet

A Future With No Fun?

Posted on July 25th **by Samuel Carvalho**

We all depend on a healthy planet for our future. The problem is, our planet isn't healthy and we really have to do something about it before it's too late. You know the advice – you read it all the time:

- stop traveling by airplane and car
- stop buying new things and start reusing the things that you already own
- stop eating meat

But it's difficult, isn't it? We don't want to stop enjoying ourselves. There are beautiful parts of the world we want to visit, exciting new products we want to own, and interesting dishes we want to try (some with meat). We don't want to stop doing and having these things, so we pay no attention to the advice.

But there might be another way ... Maybe we don't have to stop completely, just reduce what we do, for example:

- fly once a year
- only buy two pieces of clothing in summer, two in winter, etc.
- eat vegetarian food half of the week

These are small changes that everyone can make and then we won't pollute the atmosphere as much and we'll waste a lot less. Perhaps, if we all make these small changes to our lives, we'll have a future on Earth.

ABOUT ME

My name is Samuel Carvalho and I want you to change the way you live in order to take care of our planet! (Actually, if you don't eat meat and never fly or buy anything new, don't change a thing! You can still read my posts, though!) 😉

2 Read the text and complete each sentence with one word.

1 Samuel wants his readers to take care of the planet.
2 The advice we all know tells us to stop buying new things.
3 It also tells us to stop eating meat.
4 Samuel says no one wants to stop enjoying themselves.
5 He says perhaps we should fly just once a year.
6 He says perhaps we should eat vegetarian food half of the week.

3 Write answers to the questions.

1 Which vehicles does Samuel mention?
He mentions airplanes and cars.
2 According to Samuel, what do we all want to visit?
We all want to visit beautiful parts of the world.
3 What do we all want to own?
We all want to own exciting new products.
4 How many pieces of clothing does Samuel suggest we buy?
Only two pieces of clothing in summer, two in winter, etc.
5 If we make these small changes, what two good things will happen?
We won't pollute the atmosphere as much and we'll waste a lot less.

5 MY ONLINE SELF

LANGUAGE REFERENCE

Second Conditional

If Clause (*If* + Simple Past)	Result Clause (*would/wouldn't* + Infinitive)
If I **had** more time,	I **would learn** another language.
If she **worked** harder,	she **would get** better grades.
If we **took** care of the environment,	we **wouldn't have** all these issues.
Questions (?)	
If you **had** a problem, **would** you tell your teacher?	
What **would** you **say** if Nicolas **invited** you to go on vacation with him?	

To talk about unreal conditions, we use *would/wouldn't* (not *will/won't*).

Indefinite Pronouns

Affirmative (+)	Negative (–)	Questions (?)
Someone posted a photo of him online.	I didn't see **anyone** I knew in town. **No one** told me he was ill.	Did **anyone** comment on your post?
Could you buy **something** to take to the party tonight?	I didn't see **anything** I wanted to buy.	Is there **anything** we can do to help?
They don't sell ice cream here – let's go **somewhere** else.	I can't find my phone **anywhere**. Young people have **nowhere** to go in the evenings round here.	Did you go **anywhere** nice this summer?

Strong Adjectives

brilliant
crazy
freezing
huge
shocking
silly
spectacular
ugly
useless
weird

The Internet

download
file
password
post
screenshot
search
tweet
upload

VOCABULARY

1 Find eight strong adjectives.

A	M	L	S	I	L	L	Y	C	I	P
V	D	P	I	K	J	R	T	U	F	M
I	S	S	E	F	C	R	U	Z	E	Q
U	H	U	G	E	S	A	G	G	N	U
K	O	E	S	U	S	E	L	E	S	S
L	C	C	D	U	I	L	Y	D	F	T
D	K	T	C	R	A	Z	Y	I	O	U
E	I	G	Y	T	B	E	R	J	A	S
D	N	F	R	E	E	Z	I	N	G	E
U	G	H	E	M	V	S	S	E	R	T
I	S	B	E	W	E	I	R	D	P	O

2 Replace the phrases in bold with the words below.

• brilliant • crazy • freezing • huge • spectacular • ~~weird~~

1 She was wearing a ~~**very strange**~~ *weird* hat.
2 Their father was a **very clever** *brilliant* engineer.
3 Outside it was **very cold and snowy** *freezing*.
4 They live in a **very big** *huge* house.
5 The fireworks at the end of the festival were **very exciting to look at** *spectacular*.
6 Some of his ideas are **very stupid** *crazy*.

3 Match 1–8 with a–h.

1 file *b*
2 search *f*
3 password *c*
4 tweet *g*
5 upload *h*
6 download *a*
7 post *d*
8 screenshot *e*

a copy or move a document from the Internet to your computer
b information that a computer stores as one unit with one name
c secret letters or numbers that you type into a computer so that you can use it
d put a message or image online so that people can see it
e image of something taken from a computer screen
f look for information on a computer, the Internet, etc.
g put a short comment on Twitter
h copy or move a document from your computer to the Internet

4 Circle the correct options.

1 I ***uploaded*** / *downloaded* / *tweeted* the photos to the website.
2 I can't remember my *screenshot* / ***password*** / *file* and I can't access my account!
3 Can you take a *file* / *password* / ***screenshot*** of the error message, please?
4 I *tweeted* / ***searched*** / *posted* the Internet for information on the subject.
5 You can ***download*** / *upload* / *tweet* the app from their website.
6 All my important *screenshots* / ***files*** / *passwords* are on this computer.

GRAMMAR

1 Circle the correct options.

1 If we *reused* / *reuse* more of our plastic, the oceans would be cleaner.
2 Would she feel better if she *would go* / *went* for a run every morning?
3 If you had a thousand dollars, what *would* / *will* you buy?
4 Olivia *would* / *will* get better grades if she paid attention to her spelling.
5 We wouldn't have all these problems if we *take* / *took* better care of our planet.
6 I think my grandad would get really bored if he *would retire* / *retired* now.

2 Complete the second conditional sentences with the correct form of the verbs in parentheses.

1 She would make (make) more progress if she took (take) a course.
2 I think Rafael would be healthier (be) healthier if he did (do) more exercise.
3 If I had (have) more time, I would play (play) in a band.
4 Most people would be (be) happier if they worked (work) less.
5 If we reduced (reduce) the amount of food we bought, we wouldn't waste (not waste) so much.
6 Noah would have (have) more money if he got (get) a job.

3 Complete the dialogues with the words below.

• ~~anyone~~ • anything • anywhere • someone • something • somewhere

A Did you meet your friends at the mall?
B No, I didn't meet [1] anyone . I was looking for [2] something for Ethan's birthday, but I couldn't find [3] anything I liked.
A Maybe the mall is the wrong place for Ethan. Perhaps you should go [4] somewhere else to look for a present.
B Well, at the moment I'm looking for my glasses. They're not in my bedroom, the living room, or the kitchen. I can't find them [5] anywhere !
A Maybe [6] someone moved them? You often leave them on the floor.

4 Match 1–6 with a–f.

1 She posted e
2 I never go f
3 I didn't tell c
4 He never does b
5 I'm sure I saw a
6 It's noisy here. Let's go d

a someone in the yard.
b anything to help.
c anyone about the problem.
d somewhere else.
e something about the president.
f anywhere without my phone.

READING

1 Read the text quickly and check (✓) the correct answers.

1 Which sentence is the best description of the article?
- ◯ Most young people are rejecting social media.
- ✓ Some young people are rejecting social media.
- ◯ All young people love using social media.

2 How many young people describe their experiences in the article?
- ◯ two ✓ three ◯ four

MEET THE YOUNG PEOPLE WHO REJECT SOCIAL MEDIA

We often hear about young people who live their lives through social media, but some young people are finding that they're happier without it.

Victor, a 16-year-old student from Brasília, rejected social media when he noticed that his classmates were busy texting and reading messages from each other, but not speaking. "People weren't even calling each other. Face-to-face communication just wasn't happening. I thought, this is silly. Social media isn't improving our lives – it's making them worse! I'm going to do things differently."

For 15-year-old Maria Pereira, things changed while she was in a café with some friends. "Three of us were enjoying ourselves, chatting while we ate lunch," she says, "but one of our friends was looking at her phone the whole time. Basically, she was posting online pictures of the food we were eating and then counting the number of likes she got. We were all talking to each other, but she wasn't paying attention to anything that anyone was saying. She wasn't even eating. It was crazy! I decided then that I would stop using social media."

Other young people are choosing to take a break from social media. 17-year-old Lucas stopped using social media three months ago so he could prepare for his exams: "If I had more time, I'd use social media, but right now, my studies are more important."

But although some young people feel they would be happier if social media didn't exist, this isn't true for people of all ages. Some studies suggest that older people are using social media more, for example, to communicate with family members who live far away. For these people, social media improves the quality of life.

2 Read the text and complete each sentence with one word.

1 Victor noticed that his friends weren't ___speaking___ to each other.
2 Maria decided to stop using social media one day when she was in a ___café___.
3 One of Maria's friends was ___posting___ pictures of her food online during lunch.
4 She wasn't paying ___attention___ to the conversation.
5 Lucas stopped using social media so he could study for his ___exams___.
6 Studies show that some ___older___ people are now using social media more.

3 Write answers to the questions.

1 Why weren't Victor's friends speaking to each other?
They were busy texting and reading messages from each other.

2 What was Maria's friend counting in the café?
She was counting the number of likes for her food photos.

3 What is more important to Lucas than social media?
His studies are more important to him than social media.

4 What are some older people using social media for?
Some older people are using social media for communicating with family members who live far away.

5 What does social media do to some older people's lives?
Social media improves the quality of some older people's lives.

6 THE WORLD OF MUSIC

LANGUAGE REFERENCE

Past Progressive: Affirmative and Negative

Affirmative (+)	Negative (–)
I'**ve lived** abroad.	I **haven't lived** abroad.
I **have lived** abroad.	I'**ve never lived** abroad.
You'**ve written** several books.	You **haven't written** any books.
You **have written** several books.	You'**ve never written** any books.
She'**s been** to a few concerts.	She **hasn't been** to any concerts.
She **has been** to a few concerts.	She'**s never been** to any concerts.
We'**ve seen** all of her movies.	We **haven't seen** her movies.
We **have seen** all of her movies.	We'**ve never seen** her movies.
They'**ve heard** a lot of jazz.	They **haven't heard** any jazz.
They **have heard** a lot of jazz.	They'**ve never heard** any jazz.

If we say when the action happened, we use the simple past, not the present perfect.

Present Perfect: Questions and Short Answers

***Yes/No* Questions (?)**	**Have** you **ever been** to the US? **Has** Alan **read** any of his books? **Have** they **finished** school?	Yes, I **have**. / No, I **haven't**. Yes, he **has**. /No, he **hasn't**. Yes, they **have**. / No, they **haven't**.
***Wh–* Questions (?)**	What **have** you **done** this week? How **has** the area **changed?** How many murals **have** they **painted**?	

Types of Music

classical music
country music
heavy metal
hip-hop
jazz
pop
R & B (rhythm and blues)
reggae
rock
techno

Musical Instruments

drums
flute
French horn
guitar
keyboard
saxophone
trumpet
violin

VOCABULARY

1 **Circle seven more types of music.**

bikclassicalzopreggaeslkihip-hopairockoiupcountryeiytjazzbipopaoR&Bwutechnopo

1 classical
2 reggae
3 hip-hop
4 rock
5 country
6 jazz
7 pop
8 R&B
9 techno

2 **Match 1–6 with a–f.**

1 jazz c
2 classical music d
3 country music a
4 heavy metal e
5 hip-hop b
6 techno f

a

b

c

d

e

f

3 **Label the images with the correct musical instruments.**

1

drums

2

trumpet

3

keyboard

4

violin

5

French horn

6

guitar

7

flute

8

saxophone

4 **Match 1–8 with a–h.**

1 trumpet g
2 guitar b
3 keyboard e
4 drums f
5 French horn d
6 violin c
7 saxophone a
8 flute h

a long metal instrument that you blow into while pressing small parts
b instrument with strings that you play with your fingers
c wooden instrument that you hold against your neck and play by moving a stick across strings
d metal instrument with a circular tube that you blow into
e electronic instrument similar to a piano
f round instruments that you hit with your hand or a stick
g metal instrument that you blow into with three buttons
h instrument that you hold to the side of your mouth and blow into

GRAMMAR

1 Check (✓) the correct sentences.

1 a ○ I never went skiing in my life.
  b ✓ I've never been skiing in my life.
2 a ○ I've learned to play the guitar when I was a child.
  b ✓ I learned to play the guitar when I was a child.
3 a ○ The tree in your yard is so tall now – it really grew!
  b ✓ The tree in your yard is so tall now – it's really grown!
4 a ✓ He changed his password yesterday.
  b ○ He's changed his password yesterday.
5 a ✓ We didn't have dinner at home last night.
  b ○ We haven't had dinner at home last night.

2 What have Juliana, Luis and Marcos done? What have they never done? Write sentences using the prompts.

1 
Juliana / go to / a heavy metal concert ✓
Juliana's been to a heavy metal concert.

2 
Juliana / go to / a classical music concert ✗
Juliana's never been to a classical music concert.

3 
Juliana / play / soccer ✗
Juliana's never played soccer.

4 
Juliana / play / tennis ✓
Juliana's played tennis.

5 
Luis and Marcos / eat / Japanese food ✗
Luis and Marcos have never eaten Japanese food.

6 
Luis and Marcos / eat / Italian food ✓
Luis and Marcos have eaten Italian food.

7 
Luis and Marcos / do gymnastics ✓
Luis and Marcos have done gymnastics.

8 
Luis and Marcos / do yoga ✗
Luis and Marcos have never done yoga.

3 Complete the mini dialogues with one word.

A [1] Have you ever baked cookies?
B No, I [2] haven't.

A [3] Have Logan and Antonio arrived?
B Yes, they [4] Have.

A [5] Has Mia been to the UK?
B No, she [6] hasn't.

4 Complete the dialogue with the correct form of the verbs below.

• be • ~~do~~ • do • go • study • take

A What have you [1] done today, Amelia?
B Well, I've [2] studied most of the day, actually – mainly geography and history. I [3] took a break at lunch – I went to the park and met Mason. What about you? Have you [4] been busy?
A Yes, I have. I've [5] done a lot of exercise. I [6] went for a run this morning and then I did some yoga. I did my math homework, too.

READING

1 Read the text quickly and check (✓) the correct answers.

1 What's unusual about the band that Katy finds out about?
- ◯ They practice a lot.
- ✓ Their instruments are made from trash.
- ◯ They play a lot of different music.

2 What type of music do they play?
- ◯ jazz
- ◯ rock
- ✓ jazz, rock, and reggae

THIS WEEK, ONE OF OUR YEAR 8 STUDENTS, KATY, MET NATALIA AND ETHAN FROM THE BAND RECYCLABEATS TO TALK ABOUT THEIR UNUSUAL MUSIC.

KATY Could you tell us about your band, Natalia?

NATALIA Sure. Basically, we play musical instruments that we've made from things people have thrown away. For example, this violin that I'm holding – Ethan and I made this from an oil can and a few other bits that we found.

KATY That's amazing! You played it for me just now and it sounds really good!

ETHAN Thank you!

KATY And how would you describe the music that you play?

ETHAN Well, generally, we like to play music that people can dance to, but it's a mixture of styles, really – some jazz, some rock, even reggae.

KATY Nice! And where have you played?

ETHAN We've played all over the country, actually. We've performed in towns and schools, at parties, and even at one or two festivals.

KATY Cool! When did you start recycling materials to make instruments?

ETHAN Well, I've made instruments from trash as long as I can remember. My mom was really into recycling – she hates wasting stuff – so when I was little, we made drums from empty cans and parts of balloons. They weren't the best drums I've ever played, but I was very happy with them. One summer, she even made me a guitar from an old box.

KATY Wow, she was very creative!

NATALIA But to be honest, the most important thing in a band is the people, not the instruments. We all love playing together and we make sure we practice a lot, so we make a great sound.

KATY I know you do – I've heard you! Ethan and Natalia, thank you so much for talking to me today!

2 Read the text and complete each sentence with one word.

1 The band use instruments made from things that people have *thrown* away.
2 They use a *violin* which was made from an old oil can.
3 Ethan describes their music as a *mixture* of different styles.
4 Ethan's *mom* made instruments for him when he was a child.
5 She made drums from empty cans and a guitar from an old *box*.
6 Natalia says the *people* in a band are more important than the instruments.

3 Write answers to the questions.

1 Where has the band played?
They've played in towns and schools, at parties, and at festivals.

2 What instrument did Natalia play for Katy?
Natalia played a violin for Katy.

3 What does Ethan's mother not like?
Ethan's mother doesn't like wasting stuff.

4 How does Katy describe Ethan's mother?
Katy describes Ethan's mother as very creative.

5 Why does Natalia think the band sound so good?
Because they love playing together and they practice a lot.

7 AFRICA: PAST, PRESENT, AND FUTURE

LANGUAGE REFERENCE

Present Perfect with *Already*, *Just*, and *Yet*

Already	*Just*	*Yet*
No food for me, thanks. **I've already eaten.** I offered to lend Sara the book, but she**'s already read** it. It's a new disease, but scientists **have already developed** a vaccine.	Jack is definitely here. **I've just seen** him. I'm calling to say we**'ve just arrived**. It was sunny this afternoon, but it **has just started** raining.	They **haven't organized** their vacation **yet**. She **hasn't taken** the exam **yet.** **Have** you **had** lunch **yet**? **Has** Jose **decided** if he's coming **yet**?

Use *already* and *just* after *have/has*.

Present Perfect with *Since* and *For*

Since	*For*
I**'ve lived** in Recife **since** 2020. We**'ve been** here **since** three o'clock. It**'s snowed since** we arrived. They**'ve had** their cat **since** William was four.	I**'ve lived** in Brazil **for** three years. He**'s studied** there **for** five years. She**'s known** Alexis **for** a long time.

Questions and Answers
How long has he **lived** abroad? He's lived abroad **for** five years. / He's lived abroad **since** he was 10.
How long have you **had** this bike? **For** two years. / **Since** last summer.

Achievements

achieve
achievement
construct
construction
develop
development
discover
discovery
organize
organization
produce
production
survive
survival

Adjectives + Prepositions

afraid of
famous for
good at
interested in
proud of
tired of

VOCABULARY

1 Complete the sentences with the words below. Use the correct form of the verbs.

• ~~achieve/achievement~~ • construct/construction • discover/discovery • produce/production

1 a To win a silver medal at the Olympics at the age of 17 was a fantastic achievement.
b After seven years of studying, she finally achieved her ambition to become a doctor.

2 a The discovery of oil during this decade changed the country's economy.
b I recently discovered that my grandma's grandfather was Italian.

3 a The construction of the mall took two years.
b They decided to construct a bridge across the river.

4 a In the past, they produced a lot of cheese in this region.
b We use water in the production of almost all products.

2 Put the letters in the correct order and complete the sentences.

1 These plants cannot survive (vivruse) in very cold weather.
2 She works for an organization (roganatioinz) that helps immigrants to find homes and work.
3 It sometimes takes years for a company to develop (vedelpo) a new product.
4 He owns a company that organizes (narogizes) music festivals.
5 They were responsible for the development (elopdevment) of a cure.

3 Complete the sentences with the correct words. Then match sentences 1–6 with the correct image (a–f).

1 My older sister is proud of her baking. e
2 Isaac is good at swimming. d
3 My cousin is afraid of the dark. f
4 Italy is famous for its art. c
5 Martha's interested in photography. a
6 He's tired of doing the same job. b

a

b

c

d

e

f

4 Rewrite the sentences using the phrases in Exercise 3.

1 The children were pleased with their mural.
The children were proud of their mural.

2 Victoria runs well.
Victoria is good at running.

3 My brother gets very anxious when he sees spiders.
My brother is afraid of spiders.

4 Switzerland has mountains that everyone knows about.
Switzerland is famous for its mountains.

5 I'm bored because I eat the same sandwiches every day.
I'm tired of eating the same sandwiches every day.

6 I always want to hear about the music industry.
I'm interested in the music industry.

GRAMMAR

1 Circle the correct options.

Hey, I've [1]*yet* / ***just*** seen your photo – thanks! Good to hear from you! 11:20 pm

Hi! Sorry, I've only [2]*already* / ***just*** got back from the US. We had an amazing time. 11:20 pm

Great! I want to hear all about it next Friday! Today's going to be busy. Pedro and I are throwing a surprise birthday party for a friend this evening, but we haven't organized everything [3]***yet*** / *already*. 11:21 pm

Oh no! 11:21 pm

Well, we've [4]*yet* / ***already*** bought everything, but we haven't cooked anything [5]*just* / ***yet***. 11:21 pm

What about the ? 11:22 pm

Oh yes, Pedro's [6]***already*** / *yet* bought the present! 11:22 pm

2 Write sentences using the prompts and the correct form of the present perfect.

1 he / already / achieve / his ambition .
He's already achieved his ambition.

2 I / just / upload / the file .
I've just uploaded the file.

3 she / not / leave home / yet .
She hasn't left home yet.

4 they / already / destroy / half of the rainforest .
They've already destroyed half of the rainforest.

5 you / finish school / yet ?
Have you finished school yet?

6 she / post / any photos online ?
Has she posted any photos online?

3 Complete the sentences with *for* or *since*.

1 I haven't drunk anything since breakfast!
2 They haven't flown for three years.
3 She's played soccer since she was six.
4 I've had these shoes for four years.
5 We've recycled plastic here for over two decades.
6 They have studied science since they were ten.

4 Write questions and answers using the prompts and *for* or *since*.

1 Q have a skateboard? How long has he had a skateboard?
A a year For a year.

2 Q work in a café? How long has she worked in a café?
A February Since February.

3 Q be married? How long have they been married?
A last summer Since last summer.

4 Q study math? How long has she studied math?
A 13 years For 13 years.

READING

1 Read the text quickly and check (✓) the correct answers.

1 What's the article about?
- ◯ Silicon Valley, California
- ✓ new technology in Africa
- ◯ the problem of old technology

2 What's a technology hub?
- ✓ building or buildings where technology companies work together
- ◯ city with a lot of technology companies
- ◯ country with a lot of technology companies

Africa's tech hub success

If someone asked you where the newest technology came from, what would you reply? If you answered "Silicon Valley, California" you'd be right, of course, but did you know that Africa is also helping to develop some of the next generation of technology?

A lot of this new technology is the result of technology hubs which are starting up all over Africa. A technology hub (or tech hub) is a place that has developed to help small technology companies achieve their goals. It can be one building or a group of buildings, but the idea is that people from different tech companies come together to share their ideas as well as their equipment. Many of these tech hubs are in the countries of Nigeria, South Africa, and Egypt, but they are present in a lot of other countries across the continent. They are mainly in the bigger cities but also in some of the smaller ones.

So why have these tech hubs started up in recent years? One reason is that Africa has a very young population. Over 75% of its people are under 35. Young people are often interested in innovative technology and they're not afraid of it. They're also generally very good at it.

Another reason is that parts of Africa already benefit from recent technology. Other areas of the world are still using systems that they developed ten or fifteen years ago. In parts of Africa, they didn't have the previous generation of technology and they're now using the newest and most advanced systems.

In future, the technology in our phones and our computers may well come from a technology hub in Africa.

2 Read the text and write *T* (true) or *F* (false) next to the statements.

1 New technology doesn't come from California. F
2 Some new technology comes from Africa. T
3 A lot of technology hubs are in three countries in Africa. T
4 The hubs are only in the big cities in Africa. F
5 Africa has very many young people. T
6 Parts of Africa have more advanced technology than other areas of the world. T

3 Write answers to the questions.

1 What two things can companies share in a technology hub?
They can share ideas and equipment.

2 Which three African countries are many of these tech hubs in?
Many of these tech hubs are in Nigeria, South Africa, and Egypt.

3 How many people in Africa are under 35?
Over 75% of people in Africa are under 35.

4 What does the writer say young people are often interested in?
Young people are often interested in innovative technology.

5 What are other parts of the world still using?
Other parts of the world are still using systems that they developed ten or fifteen years ago.

8 WHAT'S IMPORTANT TO ME?

LANGUAGE REFERENCE

Present Perfect vs. Simple Past

Unspecified Time in the Past	My grandad **has achieved** a lot in his life. Ice cream is my favorite food. I**'ve** always **loved** it. They**'ve lived** there for a long time. We**'ve visited** them **several times**.
Specific Time in the Past	I **worked** hard **yesterday** and **achieved** a lot. I **loved** ice cream **when I was little**. They **lived** there **from 2015 to 2021**. We **visited** them **last year**.

If there is a word/phrase saying when the action happened, for example *yesterday*, *last year*, *two days ago*, we don't use the present perfect.

Subject and Object Questions

Subject Questions	Object Questions
What **wakes** her so early in the morning?	Why **does** she **get up** so early?
Who **bakes** the cookies?	What **does** he **bake**?
How many people **came** to the party?	How many people **did** you **invite**?
What **happened** to the trees?	When **did** they **cut down** the trees?
Who **called** Nicole just now?	Who **did** Nicole **call** just now?

Phrases with *Do*, *Have*, and *Make*

do your best
do physical activities
do the shopping
do volunteer work
do well
have an opportunity
have time
have trouble
make decisions
make a difference
make mistakes
make money

Verbs + Prepositions

belong to
care about
deal with
fight for
suffer from
work for

VOCABULARY

1 Complete the sentences with the correct form of *do*, *have,* and *make*. Then match images a–f with sentences 1–6.

1 The students ___had___ an opportunity to ___do___ some volunteer work last spring. ___b___
2 She was ___having___ some trouble with a few girls at school. ___d___
3 He ___made___ some mistakes. He didn't read the instructions properly. ___e___
4 Try to find time to ___do___ some physical activities. ___a___
5 They always ___make___ a lot of money when the weather is hot. ___c___
6 Amanda ___did___ the shopping last weekend. ___f___

a

b

c

d

e

f

2 Complete the text with the correct form of *do*, *have,* and *make*.

The last two years have been so busy with exams – I really haven't [1] ___had___ time for anything else. For example, last year I [2] ___had___ an opportunity to do some voluntary work at a bird sanctuary and I'm really interested in birds, but I finally decided not to do it. I always find it hard to [3] ___make___ decisions but it was the correct one. I was able to study hard and [4] ___do___ my best – I [5] ___did___ really well in my exams. And the future? I don't want to [6] ___make___ a lot of money. I want to [7] ___make___ a difference – probably working to protect the environment. That's the plan!

3 Circle the correct options.

1 Ella belongs *with* / ***to*** a running club.
2 The environment is our future. We should all care *with* / ***about*** it!
3 She fought ***for*** / *about* women's right to vote.
4 He suffered *for* / ***from*** a very rare disease.
5 We've had to deal *about* / ***with*** so many problems recently.
6 James works *to* / ***for*** a company that makes office furniture.

4 Match 1–6 with a–f.

1 She fights ___d___
2 I don't have time to deal ___c___
3 Sam and Luke both work ___a___
4 He was suffering ___e___
5 My sister belongs ___f___
6 I know my parents care ___b___

a for the same company.
b about me and want me to be happy.
c with the contract today.
d for girls' right to education.
e from cancer at the time.
f to a book club.

GRAMMAR

1 Circle the correct options.

1 You swim very well now! You *have really improved* / *really improved*!
2 Their children *left home* / *have left home* many years ago.
3 She *finished* / *has finished* school last July.
4 I *lost* / *have lost* my headphones. Please could you help me look for them?
5 He *arrived* / *has arrived* in Mexico in 2020.
6 Julia *has known* / *knew* George since they were five years old.

2 Complete the dialogue with the correct present perfect or simple past form of the verbs in parentheses.

José When [1] did you come (you come) to London, Paolo?
Paolo I [2] arrived (arrive) here two years ago, but before that, I [3] lived (live) in Germany from 2017 to 2020.
José So you [4] have been (be) in Europe for several years?
Paolo Yes, that's right. What about you?
José I [5] have lived (live) here for a year. I [6] started (start) a job at the university last June.

3 Read the sentences and write *S* (subject questions) or *O* (object questions).

1 Who told you it was my birthday? S
2 What did Thomas Edison invent? O
3 How many museums did you visit? O
4 What did Gemma say? O
5 What happened to this vase? S
6 How did you get to the beach? O
7 Who took this photo? S
8 What persuades people to buy things? S

4 Write a subject question (SQ) and an object question (OQ) for each sentence.

1 Carmen painted an amazing picture.
SQ: Who painted an amazing picture?
OQ: What did Carmen paint?
2 Rebecca made Manuel's birthday cake.
SQ: Who made Manuel's birthday cake?
OQ: What did Rebecca make?
3 The festival started three days ago.
SQ: What started three days ago?
OQ: When did the festival start?
4 Sylva won the gold medal.
SQ: Who won the gold medal?
OQ: What did Sylva win?

READING

1 Read the text quickly and check (✓) the correct answers.

1 What's the interview about?
- ○ two teenagers' relationships with their parents
- ✓ the most important people in the lives of two teenagers
- ○ why friends are more important than family

2 What do Arthur and Isabella mention?
- ○ family
- ○ friends
- ✓ friends and family

As part of our "focus on teens" feature, Wilson Field spoke to Arthur (15) and Isabella (14) about the people in their lives that are most important to them. Their answers were interesting. Below is part of the interview.

Wilson So, Arthur and Isabella, tell me about the most important people in your lives. Who do you value the most?

Arthur My mom, definitely. She's amazing. She works really hard, but she's always had time for me. When I had some trouble at school and I needed someone to talk to, she was there for me, even when she was very busy. She's really cool.

Isabella And for me, friends are super-important. I can talk to them about things that I can't discuss with my mom or dad. And I really enjoy hanging out with them. Of course, my parents are important, too. Whatever mistakes I make, they still love me. That's not true for many people in your life, even your best friends!

Wilson Very true! And who has influenced you most? Arthur, I understand you're an artist – a very good painter. So, who noticed that you could paint and encouraged you to do it? Was it a parent or a teacher?

Arthur No, it wasn't, actually. It was my best friend's dad – he paints fantastic murals. I was drawing a picture at my friend's house when I was seven or eight and he said something nice about it. I knew he was an artist so it really gave me confidence. And he's been interested in my art ever since then. Just last week, I showed him one of my paintings and he gave me some really good advice. So he's definitely made a difference to my life. Yes, he's been important to me, too.

2 Read the text and check (✓) who says these things.

	Arthur	Isabella
1 Their mother is the most important person in their life.	✓	
2 They had problems when they were younger and needed to talk about them.	✓	
3 They can't talk about some subjects with their mother and father.		✓
4 They enjoy spending time with their friends.		✓
5 If they do something bad or silly, their parents won't stop loving them.		✓
6 A friend's parent has been important in their life.	✓	

3 Write answers to the questions.

1 What two adjectives does Arthur use to describe his mom?
He says she's amazing and cool.

2 Which person doesn't mention their father?
Arthur doesn't mention his father.

3 Who are the most important people for Isabella?
Her friends and her parents are the most important people for Isabella.

4 How old was Arthur when someone noticed that he was good at drawing?
He was seven or eight when someone noticed he was good at drawing.

5 Who has had a very strong influence on Arthur's art?
His best friend's dad has had a very strong influence on Arthur's art.

WELCOME UNIT

Track 0.01

1 play in a band
2 eat out
3 go to a concert
4 watch series

Track 0.02

1 fashion designer
2 actor
3 musician
4 chef
5 athlete
6 engineer
7 nurse
8 dancer

Track 0.03

1 It was really cold here yesterday and a blizzard hit the city in the morning.
2 We arrived in Madrid during a heatwave. It was really hot in the afternoon.
3 A forest fire can start quickly in a summer with no rain, when the country is very dry.
4 Because of the flood, everything downstairs in our house got wet.
5 There was a big thunderstorm in Perth last night. Look at the incredible photo my cousin took!
6 The hurricane caused terrible problems for people living on the coast.

Track 0.04

Olivia is at the shopping mall. She'd like to buy a new jacket, but she can't afford it. She spent almost all her pocket money last weekend, and she can't use her debit card because she doesn't have enough money in the bank.

Track 0.05

1 Many tourists like to buy souvenirs at street markets.
2 Everyone danced and laughed a lot at Grandma's party. The atmosphere was great!
3 Crowds of people enjoy the Carnival at Copacabana.
4 Women wear traditional dresses in dance shows in India.
5 Fireworks are a popular way to celebrate the New Year all over the world.
6 According to the reviews, PopParty Fest was one of the best music events of the year.

UNIT 1

Track 1.01

1 finish school
2 get a job
3 leave home
4 go to college
5 take a course
6 take an exam
7 graduate
8 get married
9 have children
10 retire

Track 1.02

M = Man
V = Verónica
W = Woman
D = Daniel

Learn&Live English

ABOUT US

M: We offer a variety of English courses for teenagers (12 to 17) in different countries.

W: Let's welcome our new students Verónica González and Daniel Ribeiro!
Verónica, 14
From: Mexico
Likes: video games and sports

M: Why Malta?

V: Some years ago I saw a video about the Maltese coast and I loved it! When I learned that English is one of the two official languages in Malta, I thought, "I want to study English there."
Most people speak English and Maltese here. I can't speak Maltese but I can read the street signs – because they use English, too!

M: Expectations

V: I think I'll have a great time here in Malta. I'm going to take a four-week English course. Later, who knows? Will this experience help me get a job in the future? Maybe. I'd love to become a game developer, so maybe I'll make games about Malta!

M: Daniel, 15
From: Brazil
Likes: languages and big animals

W: Why South Africa?

D: My parents wanted me to study English abroad before I go to college and my dream is to go on a safari, so we decided that South Africa seemed like the perfect place.
I found out that there are over ten official languages in South Africa. English is one of them and most people actually speak English as a second language here.

W: Expectations

D: I'm very excited about this course. We're not going to sit in a classroom all day. Tomorrow our instructors are going to take us to a local village. We're going to help build a school there. How cool is that?

Track 1.03

T = Teacher

T: Hello everyone and welcome to this video class. Today we're going to give you some study tips to help you make progress in this course and, um, well, any other course you take really. So here you'll listen to what last year's students have to say. OK, get yourselves ready for great tips!

Track 1.04

T = Teacher
M = Melody
A = Alejandro
F = Fernando
R = Raquel
C = Cataline

T: Hello everyone and welcome to this video class. Today we're going to give you some study tips to help you make progress in this course and, um, well, any other course you take really. So here you'll listen to what last year's students have to say. OK, get yourselves ready for some great tips!

F: My tip? Take a break every thirty minutes or so. It's impossible to concentrate after working for hours and hours. You need to give yourself some time to rest.

M: Use the Internet to practice your skills. English is everywhere, and you can read, listen, write, and speak online.

R: Use cards to review vocabulary. Write the new word on one side and its translation on the other. Use them often.

A: I give myself a lot of time to prepare for an exam. Don't try to do everything the night before.

C: Do you want to get a good grade in this course? Here's a tip that I learned from a friend. She recorded herself reading the new words after every class. I did the same, and I learned things faster that way.

Track 1.05

1 make progress
2 take a break
3 practice
4 review
5 prepare
6 get a good grade

Track 1.06

Maori Teenager Becomes Language Influencer
By Lawrence O'Brien
HASTINGS, NEW ZEALAND
You look at Turei Rarere and you see a cheerful teenager like many others. When you talk to him you understand why he is an influencer. Turei is smart, creative, and motivated.
"Two years ago, there was a party in my family and I realized my younger cousins didn't speak Maori," he explains. "And worse – they didn't think that was a problem! I was really surprised. Didn't they understand that Maori is part of our cultural identity?" This question motivated Turei to create an online group for indigenous teenagers to discuss how they felt about their native languages.
Three years later, Turei's group has hundreds of members. It is not only a group for discussion, but also a place to learn and practice indigenous languages from around the world. "We use English to talk to a large number of people, but we use our native languages to post videos or audio with traditional stories or songs."
Alexandra Silva, a 15-year old Brazilian from the Terena people, says she feels more connected to her community now. "I grew up speaking Portuguese. Turei's group helped me understand why Terena is important. I can understand my grandparents' stories now."
Turei is certain about his plans for the future: "My aunt is a Maori teacher in our local school. I'm going to follow in her footsteps. I'm planning to go to college to study linguistics and I'll always support people who want to teach or learn indigenous languages."

Track 1.07

V = Vanessa **M = Martina**

V: This is so cool! I think I'll study robotics when I leave school.
M: Oh really? Is that how you see yourself ten years from now? Making robots?
V: Definitely! I know I'm good at this, and I love it. What about you?
M: Well, I'm not sure. I don't really know much about robotics, but yeah maybe I'll go for it, too.

Track 1.08

1 definitely
2 I'm not sure
3 maybe

Track 1.09

I'll study robotics in college.
People will use robots at home.

Track 1.10

1 I'll take a Spanish course in the future.
2 My brother will go to college next year.
3 I'm not sure they'll be at home this afternoon.
4 English will be useful when I get a job.
5 Will I get married? Yes, I think I will!
6 We'll review our work before the exam.

UNIT 2

Track 2.01

1 bake cookies
2 make jewelry
3 take singing lessons
4 do gymnastics
5 play board games
6 build models
7 go skateboarding
8 do yoga
9 take a walk
10 watch the sunset

Track 2.02

G1 = Girl 1 **B = Boy**
G2 = Girl 2
The Teen Oracle
The place for no-nonsense advice *from* teens *to* teens

G1: I'm sooooo tired – I feel sleepy every day, all the time. I have a lot of responsibilities – besides school from Monday to Friday, I bake cookies to raise money for our class trip at the end of the school year and I help at an animal shelter on Saturday and Sunday. I hardly ever see my friends and never have time to go skateboarding, the only physical activity I really enjoy. I love studying, baking, and helping animals, and I don't want to disappoint others. What should I do? The thing is, I simply don't have time to relax anymore.
B: In my opinion, you're doing too much. If you're feeling tired and your health is OK, it's clear you should reduce the number of activities in your routine. How about asking for help? Your classmates should bake all of the cookies for a change. And maybe you should go to the animal shelter only on Saturday or Sunday. That way you'll have some time for yourself.
G2: When I feel I have too much on my plate, making a list of activities helps me decide on priorities. Maybe a relative or your best friend can help you with that. One important thing: you shouldn't stop exercising, even if you just take a quick walk. Should you go skateboarding? Yes, you should! Being active will definitely make you feel better.

Track 2.03

1 go for a run
2 stay fit
3 work out
4 reduce stress
5 prevent diseases
6 make friends

Track 2.04

E = Emma **G = Girl**
PT = PE teacher **B = Boy**

E: Hello! I'm Emma Madison and this is HealthyTeens. We all know that when we work out, we stay fit. But you also feel good after exercising, don't you? For this episode, I talked to some teenagers about the mental benefits of physical activity. This is what they said …
E: Excuse me … Hi … I see you really enjoy running … How does it … make you feel?
G: Going for a run makes me happy. It helps me sleep well and relax before school exams.
E: It's a nice way … to reduce stress … isn't it?
G: Yes, it is! Gotta go now! Bye!
E: The girl at the park is right – studies show that exercising helps you feel better. For some teens exercising at school is an obligation, something they don't like to do. We can't escape PE, can we? But can sports at school help teens feel good?
PT: Time out!
E: Hi! You really like playing basketball during PE, don't you? It's a great activity to stay fit … can you think of other benefits?
B: Well, these guys are my best friends. I was new here and didn't know anyone. I was feeling awful before I joined the team.
E: So, basketball helped you make friends and feel better, didn't it?
B: Yeah!

Track 2.05

G = Girl **B = Boy**
Can making art make you happy?

By David Hurley March 12

Art classes are usually fun, aren't they? Well, experts tell us that there are good reasons for that.

- Making art increases activity at the front of the brain, which makes us feel positive. And just looking at works of art can release the "feel-good" chemical called dopamine in the brain.
- Making art is a way to express emotions. When you create any piece of art, you have an opportunity to understand your feelings and deal with emotions.
- Working with art also helps you to focus on the moment. Some people mention that when they are creating art, they don't feel tired or hungry – they lose sense of time.

We talked to two teenagers about how art helped them in difficult times.

G: "Last year I moved away from my hometown. The art teacher in my new school noticed how sad I was and invited me to her art workshops with other students after school. Creating art definitely helped me feel better. I especially love to model clay and make sculptures. Every time I work on a piece, I feel relaxed and peaceful."
B: "When I was going through a hard time last year, my mom bought a coloring book and pencils for me. At first, I found the idea ridiculous – she didn't think I was a little kid again, did she? But she persuaded me to give it a try. When I started coloring, I found that I could 'turn off' the outside world and only focus on filling the forms with color. And my problems didn't seem that bad when I got to the end. Coloring calms my mind when I'm anxious."
Lucas, 14

Track 2.06

G = Girl **B = Boy**
Narrator: The Teen Oracle
The place for no-nonsense advice *from* teens *to* teens

G: Hi, everyone! I'm here because I need help. My brother Jake feels sleepy all the time. He doesn't play any sports and eats junk food. I want to help him, but I work long hours and I don't see him much. What should I do?
B: Well, I don't think you should worry too much if Jake often wants to sleep. We need a lot of sleep when we're teenagers – it's part of growing up, I guess.
But I know that physical exercise helps me feel more energetic, even during boring classes at school. Maybe you should invite him to take walks with you – that way he can be more active and you two can spend time together. My older brother works long hours too and, believe me, I miss him!
Jake's eating habits are bad. He should include fruit and vegetables in his diet. Why don't you cook some healthy meals or snacks together? Eating well will help him have more energy and you will have another moment to talk and be together.

UNIT 3

Track 3.01

1 advertisement	6 influence
2 advertise	7 attract
3 product	8 headline
4 persuade	9 logo
5 value	10 promise

Track 3.02

Smart Teen
A blog for smart teenage consumers
Four things we must not forget about ads
By Mason Carlson
Do you sometimes decide to buy a product just because of an advertisement? Well, we all do. But here are some things to remember when we read or watch ads.

1 **People produce ads to influence you**
Behind all ads there are professionals who know what techniques will persuade us to buy. Even the funniest and most creative ads have one basic aim: to sell us something.
2 **Ads want you to think you have to buy something – now!**
Ads make you think you must act urgently: there's something fantastic out there and everybody else is enjoying it. And they also say it's easy to get it. Look! This burger is the "best" and "only" costs $3.99!
3 **Ads use your emotions to get what they want**
Are you worried about your friends thinking you're not attractive and cool? Ads show you beautiful, successful people having fun. Their idea? You buy what they advertise and you'll feel great, like the people in the ads.
4 **Ads use famous people to attract you**
Advertising companies pay a lot of money to celebrities. They know that fans will buy the product, not because they need it, but just because they love the star.

Comments
Teenage girl: mei
I sometimes feel I have to buy something after I watch an ad. I buy it, I'm happy for a while, and then I want to buy something else.
Teenage boy: Blogger Boy
Ads don't influence me. You don't have to buy what they advertise.

Track 3.03

W = Wilson **D = Diego**
W: Hey, Diego … I think I'll buy these sneakers.
D: But do you have to get them now? Didn't you buy another pair last week?
W: Yeah, I did. But I love this cool logo you know …
D: You're funny … Does everything you own have to be from a big label?
W: Well, I like big labels … And I have some money to spend and these sneakers are on sale …

Track 3.04

W = Wilson **D = Diego**
W: Hey, Diego … I think I'll buy these sneakers.
D: But do you have to get them now? Didn't you buy another pair last week?
W: Yeah, I did. But I love this cool logo you know …
D: You're funny. Does everything you own have to be from a big label?
W: Well, I like big labels … And I have some money to spend and these sneakers are on sale …
D: You buy and buy, and you're never happy with what you have.
W: Ha ha, you sound like my parents: "Do we have to buy everything that's on sale? No, we don't."
D: But they're right. You should save your money for something important. Like a vacation. Or college. Or invest your money in something.
W: What do you mean?
D: Well, I'm going to buy car cleaning products. Then I'll be able to clean other people's cars and make and save some money.
W: I never thought about that … Er … I'm not sure about car cleaning. But you know what? I could buy some materials and make some motorcycle models … And I could sell them online.
D: Well, model making materials will cost you more than cleaning products, but yeah, that's a very good idea.

Track 3.05

1 sell	4 on sale
2 own	5 cost
3 label	6 invest

Track 3.06

Rethinking Waste: Lessons From Japan

Some years ago, people in a Japanese village called Kamikatsu had the idea to go "zero waste." For this to happen, all residents would need to collaborate in important ways. A central idea in the project was the creation of a waste center where the residents had to take all their trash.

At first not everyone welcomed the idea because it involves a lot of work. Before going to the center, residents have to wash their non-organic trash, including plastic bags and bottles. At the center they have to put their waste in separate containers for different materials. There are 45 different categories of waste: for example, different places for different kinds of metal like aluminium and steel, and seven containers for paper, including newspapers, cardboard, and paper tubes. There are special places for toothbrushes, pillows, and furniture.

Nowadays, however, most people agree that the waste center is a great idea. Recycling makes money for the village. The fact that all waste is separated and cleaned adds value to it because it's easier to recycle. People also enjoy going to the *kuru-kuru* store in the center (*kuru-kuru* means "circular" in Japanese), where they can leave clothes, plates, or other useful items they don't want anymore. And a person who wants something from the store can take it away for free.

The village now recycles more than 80% of its waste but the project isn't only about recycling. As one of the organizers explained, "People have to avoid buying things that will go to waste. We must also avoid unnecessary packaging and try to use our own containers when possible." In other words, we must think about waste not only **after** we use something. We have to do it **before** use as well.

Track 3.07

H = Helen **E = Emilio**
H: Hey Emilio. It's Cristian's birthday tomorrow. We have to buy him a present.
E: Ah, OK, so let's go to the mall!
H: Well, you know, I was thinking we could go to the secondhand store downtown.
E: What?
H: Yeah, why not? We don't have to get an expensive present. I bet we'll find something special there.
E: Yeah, OK, I guess … Maybe sports clothes or stuff like that …
H: Great. Let's go.

Track 3.08

1 Ah, OK, so	3 Yeah, OK, I guess
2 Well, you know	

Track 3.09

have to
We have to buy him a present.

Track 3.10

1 I always have time for my friends.
2 The students have to review for the exam.
3 Liz doesn't have a lot of furniture.
4 We have a lot of cousins – what about you?
5 This is awful! We have to do something about it.

UNIT 4

Track 4.01

1 recycle	6 protect
2 cut down	7 reduce
3 turn off	8 destroy
4 waste	9 throw away
5 pollute	10 reuse

Track 4.02

This is How Your "Green" House Will Look in 2040!

We all know we need to take action now so that we still have a planet in the future. And we can start at home! According to experts, houses in the next decades will be greener and more efficient. Check out some features:

A Houses will have a "living wall" – a wall covered with plants. If a living wall is 20 m^2, it converts 46 kg of carbon dioxide into oxygen per year! If you have a living wall in your house, you will help to clean the air.

B A living wall will also work as a vegetable garden to supply fresh, healthy food for the kitchen.

C Houses will have a water tank to collect rainwater for the garden and the toilets. If people use less water from the public water system, they will save money and help the local ecosystem.

D Garages will provide electricity for the family car – in fact, experts predict that 57% of cars will be electric in 2040. If this really happens, we will have much less air pollution.

E We will use more electricity than today because many people will work from home. This new lifestyle will demand office spaces at home with the latest technology.

F People will control the whole house from their smartphones or tablets. And if you forget to turn off a light, sensors will do that for you!

G People will use recycled wood and glass to build their houses.

H All the energy will come from solar panels on the roof of the house.

Track 4.03

I decided to become a vegetarian because the future of our planet depends on reducing the use of animal products.

But how do vegetarians help to protect the environment? Well, they help in different ways. Keeping animals for food uses a lot of resources and pollutes the air. People cut down trees to have grass for cows or to grow other food for animals. Cows, pigs, and chickens need a lot of water – did you know that we use more than 15,000 liters of water to produce one kilogram of beef? I worry about climate change and I know we need to save water.

Becoming a vegetarian isn't difficult, but you have to watch your diet. You should pay attention to what you eat and you might need extra vitamins. You may find it hard to stop eating animal products, but if you succeed in making this change, I think you'll soon enjoy your vegetarian diet.

I believe in change. We need to take care of our planet and eat food that doesn't destroy the environment. At first, your meat-loving friends and parents might not agree with you, but being vegetarian is a great way to help the planet.

Track 4.04

1 depend on
2 worry about
3 pay attention to
4 succeed in
5 take care of
6 agree with

Track 4.05

Poetry and the Environment: Haikus

Invented by the Japanese, haikus became popular in the Western world in the 20th century. Nowadays people all over the world read, write, and love these short, but powerful poems.

Haikus have three lines, but their organization is not so simple. Traditional haikus must have exactly 17 syllables, like this:

- Line 1 – five syllables
- Line 2 – seven syllables
- Line 3 – five syllables

They are usually about nature and combine powerful images in a few words, to connect to one of our five senses: sight, sound, smell, taste, and touch. Haikus often have a *kigo* – a word or phrase that has a connection with a period of the year. Look at the English translation of two classic haikus by Matsuo Basho:

An old silent pond ...
A frog jumps into the pond,
splash! Silence again.

None is traveling
Here along this way but I,
This autumn evening

Modern haikus, however, don't always have such rigid structure, but are still organized into three lines. If you want to write a haiku, you don't need to worry about the number of syllables, but you may like to stick to nature themes.

Meet Basho, the Haiku master

Matsuo Basho (1644–1694) was a samurai in his early days, but spent most of his life traveling around Japan, writing and teaching poetry. His haikus gained popularity all over Japan during his lifetime. He wrote about nature and the environment and expressed strong feelings through beautifully clear, simple images.

Haikus for the environment

We asked our readers to send their haikus about the environment. Look at two poems we selected for this article (you can read all the haikus in our online magazine).

We cut down the trees
They sadly fell to the ground
Birds are silent now
Julia, 15 – Brazil

Men burn ancient trees
Melt glaciers, raise oceans
There's no Planet B
Santiago, 14 – Colombia

Track 4.06

I think that this house of the future is a joke! In my opinion, there's nothing we can do, as individuals, to stop climate change. I strongly believe that governments and politicians should take action, not teenagers like us.

Track 4.07

I don't agree with SkepticalTeen at all! I loved the infographic about the house of the future, and many of the ideas presented in it are already available – they're just too expensive for our houses at the moment! I'd say that most people might not live in that type of house in 2040, but there's so much more we can do now! I'm certain that we can all find the time and energy to do some of the things below:

- Recycle plastic bottles.
- Turn off lights and save energy.
- Reuse things instead of throwing them away.

It's our responsibility to take action to help save our planet. If we don't act, we won't have a planet to save.

UNIT 5

Track 5.01

1 crazy
2 freezing
3 brilliant
4 useless
5 weird
6 ugly
7 silly
8 huge
9 shocking
10 spectacular

Track 5.02

MS = Marion Smith
EM = Eduardo Morales
SG = Sophie Graham

MS: Should schools allow cell phones in the classroom?

Around the world, more and more teenagers have cell phones and use them often. Cell phones can bring excellent learning opportunities, but they can also cause problems. Some countries (for example, France, Israel, and parts of China) don't allow any use of cell phones while students are at school, but this debate is very much alive.

Posted by: Marion Smith

EM: I'm a high school teacher. Students wouldn't be able to concentrate if they had phones in the classroom: they would check their social media all the time. Some people say that cell phones can make it easier for students to share information and ideas in class, but I think that's ridiculous! Teenagers already spend too much time on their phones: if we allowed cell phones in class, students would spend even less time in face-to-face interactions. It's important to learn to work with people, not with electronic screens. Allowing cell phones in class is a crazy idea. If it was a good idea, most schools would allow them.

SG: I'm a principal. But before that I'm a teacher. I know a cell phone can bring huge benefits for students: they can use their phones as calculators and cameras, they can go on the Internet to look for information, read news stories, use a dictionary. However, studies show that most students use cell phones in class to do other things not related to schoolwork. That's why we don't allow them in our school. If students didn't spend time texting and playing games, I wouldn't be against cell phones in class.

Track 5.03

1 password	5 search
2 download	6 post
3 upload	7 tweet
4 file	8 screenshot

Track 5.04

T = Teacher **H = Hannah**
B1 = Boy 1 **B2 = Boy 2**
G = Girl

T: Morning, everyone. This is Hannah Jones. Hannah was in this class, your age, three years ago. She's here today to talk to us about online activity. Hannah?

H: Thanks. Well does anyone know what "digital footprint" means?

B1: Erm ... information we leave online? About what we do, where we go?

H: Exactly! When you text or tweet, download or upload a file, when you search for something … you always leave a trace online.

B2: What about when I like something?

H: Same.

B2: Even with strong passwords?

H: Well, that's certainly important. But nothing gives you complete protection.

G: What about chats that disappear after a short time?

H: Well, someone can always take a screenshot of these chats. And they can post it somewhere else …

G: Um, I see.

H: How would you feel if I told you I didn't get a job because of my digital footprint?

B1: Really?

H: Someone in the company searched for my name online. And he found something I posted four years ago – it wasn't very nice.

B2: But ... um ... is there anything we can do to avoid problems?

H: Well, never forget: your online activity is permanent. Always ask yourself: how do you want people to see you online – now and in the future? This is something we all have to ...

Track 5.05

Taking a Break from Social Media
Fernando Alves, Brazil

Until last month I never paid too much attention to comments like "Teenagers are always on social media!" or "Too much time on social media can make you depressed." But then we had a school project: to find some facts about how Brazilian teens use the internet and to compare the results to our habits. Here's a summary of what I discovered.

Facts and comparison

82% of 9- to 17-year-olds are on social media. My class: 100%

Brazilian teens check their social media 63 times a day on average. Me: 71 times

Over half of teenagers in a study in Brazil said they almost always had a smartphone or tablet with them during meals. My class: 80%

The project made me think: did I use social media too much? Did I feel anxious if no one liked my posts immediately? And I wondered: how would I feel if I didn't use social media for five days? So that's exactly what I did.

<u>Day 1</u>

I woke up and went straight to my phone. It was weird: no social media! During the day, I felt disconnected.

<u>Day 2</u>

I'm still anxious: did my friends like the photos I posted the day before yesterday? But I'm trying to keep busy with other things. In fact this evening I learned how to make sushi!

<u>Day 3</u>

Stress levels are lower. I texted some friends and enjoyed the one-to-one conversations. It felt personal.

<u>Day 4</u>

I spent my free time exercising and hanging out with my friends at the park. I left my phone at home. I realized I don't depend on it to keep me happy.

<u>Day 5</u>

I decided to close some social media accounts and keep just two. I'll try to open them only twice or three times a day in the future. I think I'll feel happier that way.

Track 5.06

M = Mother **S = Son**
F = Father **D = Daughter**

M: Breakfast's ready! Phones down please.

S: Why do we have to put our phones down? Dad's on his computer.

F: I'm working.

D: And we're talking to our friends.

F: I know, but that's not the same. I have something urgent to do.

S: Sure, but I need to post this comment.

D: Yeah, and my friends are important, too.

M: You know, that's a really good point, but it's family time now. Two minutes. And then ... no one uses a phone or computer!

Track 5.07

1 You know, that's a really good point, but …

2 I know, but …
Sure, but …

3 Yeah, and …

Track 5.08

/ʌ/
I have **so**mething urgent to do.
I **wo**nder why we have to put our phones down.

Track 5.09

1 b much	They don't have much.
2 a some	Some ads are smart.
3 a cut	Cut the carrots.
4 a run	I can run fast.
5 b son	Who's your son?

UNIT 6

Track 6.01

a [country music]	f [jazz]
b [hip-hop]	g [reggae]
c [classical music]	h [heavy metal]
d [rock]	i [R&B]
e [pop]	j [techno]

Track 6.02

a 6 – country music	f 9 – jazz
b 1 – hip-hop	g 7 – reggae
c 10 – classical music	h 8 – heavy metal
d 4 – rock	i 3 – R & B (rhythm and blues)
e 2 – pop	j 5 – techno

Track 6.03

BTS Rocks Green Alliance Arena for a Memorable Night!
by Leticia Harris

If you don't know the guys in the photo, they are the South Korean band BTS, the most popular Korean pop (or K-pop) group in the world. The seven bandmates have attracted millions of fans from Bangkok to Brazil. Their music is basically pop, but it has always included elements of hip-hop and rock.

I've seen some great concerts, but the one I went to last Saturday was one of the best. BTS didn't disappoint their devoted fans at the Green Alliance Arena. More than 55 thousand teenagers (and some parents) sang and danced to the band's greatest hits. It was an unforgettable concert.

The boys first went on stage to sing the most popular song from their recent album and then sang hits from previous ones. Their performance of ballads was amazing – Jungkook, V, Jimin, and Jin showed all their vocal power. After that, it was RM, Suga, and J-Hope's turn to show their talent with rap.

After two hours of incredible music, the concert came to an end with the boys singing an old favorite, *Mikrokosmos*. The audience held up their phones, using them to light up the dark stadium. It was a great end to a great concert!

BTS Dad:

I was one of the parents at the concert last Saturday, with my daughter. I've never been a fan of K-pop, but BTS is great!

JaneT:

My son has never been to a concert. There's another BTS concert this Friday. Will it be safe for him to go with his friends?

Leticia Harris:

It's safe! But tickets have sold out. Sorry!

Track 6.04

1 violin
2 keyboard
3 guitar
4 trumpet
5 flute
6 drums
7 saxophone
8 French horn

Track 6.05

1 [drums]
2 [flute]
3 [guitar]
4 [keyboard]
5 [saxophone]
6 [violin]
7 [French horn]
8 [trumpet]

Track 6.06

J = Jake **K= Kate**

J: Welcome to Songs&Lyrics, your talk show about music. Our guest today is songwriter Kate Queen. Hi, Kate!
K: Hello!
J: People know you as a writer of ballads. But you're also a musician. What instruments do you play?
K: Well, I play the guitar, the drums, and the flute.
J: That's amazing! Has music always been important in your life?
K: Yes, it has, but I didn't write my first song until I was 14. It was a song about love and broken hearts.
J: Interesting. Was it about a specific person?
K: Not really … I just saw my friends falling in love, feeling sad and everything, and that inspired me. I used my keyboard to write the song.
J: Ha! The keyboard! Another instrument to add to your list. But have you ever fallen in love?
K: Yes, of course I have! But I don't want to talk about it.
J: OK, OK … but speaking of love songs, many of yours have been number one in the music charts.
K: My most successful songs have been about love but I've written a lot of songs about different subjects, too.
J: Sure, how many songs have you written?
K: Oh, I guess I've written more than a hundred songs.
J: Wow, that's incredible!

Track 6.07

The Early History of Hip-Hop
Hip-hop is a cultural movement that started in the 1970s, in African-American and Latino neighborhoods in New York. Its main art form is rap music, but hip-hop also involves DJing, graffiti painting and breakdancing. Rapping – speaking words rapidly in rhythm – is the way hip-hop artists perform most of their songs. Check out some important events in the movement in the 20th century:

1973 – "The father of hip-hop," DJ Kool Herc, aged 16, DJs a party for his sister's birthday in the Bronx, a poor neighborhood in New York.

1977 – Hip-Hop spreads outside poor areas, with rappers performing all over New York.

1979 – Sugarhill Gang records the first commercial hip-hop song, *Rapper's Delight.*

1981 – A national news magazine program reports the "rap movement" for the first time.

1982 – Hip-hop arrives in Hollywood! *Wild Style* is the first movie to show hip-hop and graffiti artists.

1986 – Run-DMC, a famous hip-hop group, records *Walk This Way*, a classic from rock band Aerosmith. Run-DMC is the first hip-hop group to be nominated for a Grammy.

1990 – Hip-hop hits the popular TV screen with *The Fresh Prince of Bel-Air*, a series starring Will Smith.

1992 – Artists from California start to dominate the hip-hop scene. Dr. Dre, one of the most famous West Coast rappers, records his first solo album.

1998 – Jay-Z and Eminem release albums and increase the popularity of hip-hop.

1999 – Singer Lauryn Hill's album *The Miseducation Of Lauryn Hill* is the first hip-hop album to be Album Of The Year at the Grammy awards.

2000 – Hip-hop is the most popular type of music in the United States and a global phenomenon.

Track 6.08

Somewhere Over the Rainbow

Singer: Judy Garland

Year of recording: 1939

Judy Garland sang *Somewhere Over the Rainbow* in the 1939 movie *The Wizard of Oz.* She played the role of Dorothy in the movie when she was only 16 years old. Garland sang it with the orchestra of the movie studio, which was usual in musicals at that time. The performance and the beautiful lyrics about hope and optimism make *Somewhere Over the Rainbow* one of the greatest songs of the 20th century. Hundreds of other artists have recorded the song.

Cover singer: Ariana Grande

Year of cover recording: 2017

Ariana Grande sang *Somewhere Over the Rainbow* for the first time in the *One Love Manchester* charity concert in England, in June 2017, 11 days after her earlier concert in Manchester ended in tragedy. Her performance is very emotional, and includes elements from jazz, with just a keyboard as a musical instrument. The song has had millions of downloads and has raised millions of dollars for charity.

UNIT 7

Track 7.01

1 production
2 achievements
3 development
4 discovery
5 construct
6 organized
7 survive

Track 7.02

1 achieve – achievement
2 develop – development
3 discover – discovery
4 construct – construction
5 organize – organization
6 produce – production
7 survive – survival

Track 7.03

Looking For Innovation? Here's Africa For You

A large and young population that wants change. Countries like Rwanda and Ethiopia, examples of the world's fastest growing economies. Many problems to solve. These ingredients make Africa the perfect place for innovation. In fact, some recent African developments have already surprised the world.

Smart Gloves for Sign Language

Roy Allela's niece was born deaf and has to use sign language. Because no one in Allela's family could communicate with her, he designed a translation glove: his niece wears the glove and connects it with a phone. The phone then translates her hand movements into an audio message. Allela's dream is to see these gloves in all Kenyan schools that have deaf students. He hasn't achieved this objective yet, but he's working hard on it.

3-D Printers from e-Waste

Electronic waste from around the world is one of Africa's big problems. Afate Gnikou from Togo has decided to do something with it: he has constructed 3-D printers using parts of old computers, scanners, and other electronics. He now works with a lab which has given these printers to local schools. In the future, Gnikou wants to use these printers to make medical equipment to help disabled people.

Water from the Air

There is six times more water in the air than in all the rivers on Earth. During a drought in 2016, when Kenya had almost no rain, Beth Koigi had a brilliant idea: her Majik Water invention uses a chemical process to take water from the air and convert it into drinking water. She has already produced a prototype of her invention.

Track 7.04

Hi and welcome to Dlamini Pod, your favorite movie podcast. This is Pete Dlamini and today we're talking about *Skimboarding Pro*, the new movie about a skimboarder by Sofia Vieira.

Track 7.05

Hi and welcome to Dlamini Pod, your favorite movie podcast. This is Pete Dlamini and today we're talking about *Skimboarding Pro*, the new movie about a skimboarder by Sofia Vieira.

As you know, Sofia is famous for her documentaries about Angola. I've been a big fan for many years. Her new movie is about Pedro, a teenager who was interested in surfing. He often went to the beach to watch the surfers but he couldn't afford a surfboard. He was tired of watching so he got a piece of wood and used it like a skateboard in the water.

Pedro didn't know about the sport called skimboarding, but that's what he was doing. In 2019 there was an international skimboard competition in Angola and some professional skimboarders saw Pedro in action. They immediately recognized that he was very good at it. After that ... well, you have to watch the movie.

It's been in movie theaters for a few weeks now, and it's received excellent reviews since the opening night. One critic said, "Sofia's success has two main ingredients: she's really proud of her country and she isn't afraid of trying new techniques to tell her stories."

Let's say hi to Sofia to see what ...

Track 7.06

1 tired of
2 good at
3 famous for
4 afraid of
5 interested in
6 proud of

Track 7.07

The Himba

The Himba almost disappeared in the 1980s because of war and drought. Since then, their population has grown. People think there may be more than 25,000 Himba in Namibia today.

Himba ways

In Himba society the men make political decisions and look after the cows and goats. The women milk the animals, carry water to the village, cook, and build their huts.

Himba women and men are famous for their complex hairstyles. Girls, women, older boys, and men all wear their hair in plaits, but in different styles. Some young girls wear plaits over their faces and older girls start wearing a headpiece made of goat skin, which looks like three leaves. After getting married or having a child they wear a different headpiece. Himba women also cover their bodies with butterfat – the fat from cow's milk – and red coloring.

Good thinkers

The modern world hasn't had much influence on traditional Himba culture. That's why scientists are interested in studying the Himba. One of the questions scientists want to answer is: "Do the Himba think in the same way as people in other societies?" The results of some studies have shown that the Himba are better at finding creative ways to solve problems. Also, their attention to detail is amazing and they achieve better results in tests like the Ebbinghaus illusion than many other people.

Tradition and modern life

Since Namibia's independence in 1990, some things have changed for the Himba. Some young people have already left their villages to get a job or go to school. Some haven't come back. In the villages, some Himba think integration with the modern world is necessary, while others think it will destroy their culture. Time will tell.

Track 7.08

Hi, I'm Rafaela and welcome to my music channel. OK, so for a long time I've wanted to find a way to hear the best of new African music. And guess what? I've just found out that there's the perfect app – it's called Music&More. Basically, you choose the country or type of music you like. Then the app shows what teenagers around the world have listened to and liked recently. This is how it works ...

Track 7.09

1 basically, ...
2 guess what?
3 I've just found out ...

Track 7.10

/t/ liked
/d/ listened
/ɪd/ wanted

Track 7.11

1 searched. Have you searched for information yet?
2 posted. My friends have already posted their comments.
3 lived. How long have you lived in this city?
4 played. My cousin and I have always played video games together.
5 walked. Have you walked to school or did you take the bus?
6 decided. My parents have decided to live abroad.

UNIT 8

Track 8.01

1 do volunteer work
2 do the shopping
3 make a difference
4 do physical activities
5 have time
6 have an opportunity
7 have trouble
8 make decisions
9 do well
10 make money
11 do my best
12 make mistakes

Track 8.02

Dilemma Teens

In this fun game, you and your friends try to suggest solutions to dilemmas that teens might face. Do you think you know your friends well? Play **Dilemma Teens** and find out!

Check out some dilemmas you will face in **Dilemma Teens**!

D1

Your best friend has had a jewelry business for a few months – she uses beads to make necklaces and bracelets. You have always thought her pieces are awful, but you have never said anything.

Yesterday, she asked you to write a review of her jewelry for her blog. You agreed to do that.

What do you do? Do you lie in your review?

D2

You did volunteer work at an animal shelter last year. Although you love animals, you decided to leave after six months because the coordinator always shouted at everyone.

She called you yesterday asking for help. All the other volunteers have stopped working there. She was very insistent on the phone.

What do you do? Do you go and help at the shelter?

D3

You're a "study buddy" at school. A student has had a lot of trouble with math and she didn't do well last semester. You helped her study for a math test, but she still made a lot of simple mistakes the day before.

The teacher gave the test scores yesterday and this student got an A. You think she cheated on the test.

What do you do? Do you tell the teacher?

You can play **Dilemma Teens** face-to-face or download the app and challenge your friends anywhere, anytime!

Track 8.03

M = Mika **G** = Girl
B = Boy **W** = Woman

M: Excuse me ... I'm interviewing people about volunteer work for a college project. Could you both answer some questions?
G: Sure!
B: Yeah ...
M: Great! So have you ever done volunteer work?
G: Yes, I have. I worked for the local food bank. I've been a volunteer there since I was 14.
M: What made you decide to do that?
G: Unfortunately, there are a lot of poor people in our city. Some people have to go to the food bank because they don't have enough money for food.
M: That's true. Who inspired you?
G: My parents. They've always done volunteer work. They fight for everyone's right to education and they really care about other people.
M: Great, thanks! What about you?
B: Me? I was a volunteer at a retirement home for a while. I read books to the residents. My great-grandmother suffered from dementia and lived there for two years. But I stopped going there last year.
M: That's terrible to suffer from dementia. What happened last year?
B: My great-grandmother passed away last December. It was difficult for me to deal with that.
M: I'm sorry to hear that ... Thank you for your time. ... Er, excuse me, can I ask you some questions about volunteer work.
W: Yes, OK.
M: Er, have you ever been a volunteer?
W: I don't think so ... I belong to a book club, but that isn't volunteer work, is it?
M: No, I'm afraid not.

Track 8.04

1 work for	4 suffer from
2 fight for	5 deal with
3 care about	6 belong to

Track 8.05

Where do the happiest teenagers in the world live?

The answer is they probably live in the Netherlands, a country in Europe that is famous for its tulips and windmills, and smaller than most states in Brazil. With 17 million people, the country has succeeded in giving its teen inhabitants an optimistic view of life that contrasts with other rich countries, such as the UK and the United States.

What is the secret of Dutch teens' happiness? As for any complex question, there are several answers.

- The Netherlands is a wealthy country that takes care of its young people. According to a report from UNICEF, 95% of Dutch children are happy with their lives.
- The Netherlands Institute of Social Research states that Dutch teens in general have positive relationships at home, at school, and with friends. Parents encourage their children to be independent and teachers are not authoritarian. Teenagers feel they can trust adults.
- Dutch teens are generally healthy. Over 80% of them have breakfast every day and only 8% of the teen population are overweight. Most students ride their bikes to school every day (in fact, cycling is a normal form of transportation for people of all ages in the Netherlands).
- There is some bullying in Dutch schools, but according to studies, it doesn't happen as often as in other countries 86% of Dutch teenagers say their classmates are helpful and kind.
- Although they have experienced more pressure from homework and exams in recent years, Dutch teens are still happy at school. One of the reasons is the school system, which allows high school students to change study programs or even repeat a year if they are not happy with their academic progress.

Track 8.06

Interviews

Kenno Appelhof is 15 years old. He has friends, goes to school, and argues with his parents sometimes, as most teenagers do. He also lives in the Netherlands, one of the countries where teenagers are the happiest in the world.

WSM Kenno, what makes you happy?

Kenno Oh, so many things. My dog Buddy makes me happy, my friends make me laugh and are an important part of my life.

WSM Who gives you help if you need it?

Kenno My family and close friends. They're people that I can depend on.

WSM How do you like your school?

Kenno I love going to school and I know getting a good education is important for my future.

Most of my friends are from school, so that's where I see them every day.

WSM What's the most important thing in your life?

Kenno I love school and spending time with my friends, but the most important thing in my life is my family. They really support me and care about my happiness. It's great to know there are people you can always trust.

Track R.01

An Inspirational Teenage Inventor

Hannah Herbst was nine years old when she started writing to Ruth, her penpal in Ethiopia. After four years of writing to each other, Hannah learned many things from Ruth. One of the things that surprised Hannah the most was that many people in Ethiopia lived with limited access to electricity and running water. Hannah, from the US, had access to electricity and water every day. It made her sad to hear that many people were living in this situation. She decided she wanted to invent something to help solve the problem of energy poverty, even though she didn't know much about engineering and she didn't have a strong interest in math or science.

When Hannah was thirteen years old she started designing a prototype called BEACON – *Bringing Electricity Access to Countries through Ocean Energy*. Inspired by the ocean where she lived in Florida, she had the idea to create electricity using the energy of the ocean currents and store it in a battery.

Hannah didn't design the prototype alone, she had different mentors who helped her. The mentors taught her that often the best solutions are the simplest ones. Before making a final design, her mentors encouraged her to change the prototype and develop her ideas. Her mentors also encouraged her to share her ideas in competitions. That's when she entered the competition called the 3M Young Scientist Challenge, and won the title of America's Top Young Scientist in 2015. The invention created many opportunities for Hannah, such as presenting the idea to the US President at the White House.

Hannah graduated from Atlantic University in 2020 where she studied Information Systems and Business Analytics. She loves to inspire students to study math and science and try to come up with inventions to solve the world's difficult problems.

Track R.02

A Report on a Green City

Name of city: Ljubljana

Country: Slovenia

Population of city: Over 288,000

Language: Slovene (or Slovenian)

Interesting fact: Ljubljana's aim is zero-waste

Introduction

Ljubljana, the capital of Slovenia, is the first European capital with the aim of "zero-waste." The city separates, collects and recycles 68% of its waste. It wants to get to 78% over the next few years, but that's not going to be easy.

Problem

Before 2004, most of the waste in Ljubljana went to a **landfill** or incinerators. The people of Ljubljana now produce only 115 kg of non-recyclable trash per person per year. That's amazing, but 115 kg of trash is still a problem. Why? We now know that burning or **burying** our trash creates health problems. It's also a terrible waste of our natural resources to use things just once and then throw them away.

Solution

So how did Ljubljana change in such a short time? The first step was to collect separated waste from **door to door**. People started to feel responsible for their waste and they began to separate it better. If you separate used glass, cardboard, plastic, and organic trash, you can recycle them. But when you throw different kinds of trash away together, you create waste.

Ljubljana has **recycling bins** downtown and there are two waste recycling centers where people can take their trash. They also try to encourage people to reuse things that people throw away. At one of the recycling centers, they check, clean, **fix,** and sell things at low prices. And there are even classes to teach people how to fix broken things.

Conclusion

Ljubljana is a good example of a green city, because people recycle and reuse a lot of their trash. Creating cities that are zero waste is important because if we reuse and recycle trash, we can save money and protect the environment and people's health.

Track R.03

How people communicated in the past

The way we communicate with each other now is very different from the early forms of communication. Sending a simple message could take many days or even weeks in the past.

Smoke Signals

Smoke signals are the oldest form of visual communication. The Chinese used them first in 200 BCE to send messages along the Great Wall of China. In 150 BCE, the Greeks also used smoke signals to represent the alphabet so they could send messages easily to each other. Later, many countries around the world used smoke from the top of a hill to signify danger. Simple but effective!

Carrier Pigeon

The Egyptians used pigeons for long-distance communication from the 12th century AD. The pigeons carried messages from Egypt to cities that were hundreds of kilometers away. Then the Romans and Greeks used pigeons, and later, many European countries used pigeons during World War I and World War II to send messages that helped save many people's lives.

Human Messengers

In the Middle Ages and before, cities, countries, companies, and rich people had their own human messengers to send important messages as quickly as possible from one place to another. Some messengers travelled by horse and boat and spent many days travelling across countries and seas in order to deliver a message safely, while messengers in some mountainous regions had to walk or run. Messengers were usually men who were fit and healthy. Sometimes it was a dangerous job and some messengers even worked as spies.

The Telegraph

Early forms of communication were dependent on geographical location. That all changed with the invention of the telegraph. The telegraph was a machine that sent electric signals along wires from one place to another and the signals translated into a message. In 1844, Samuel Morse sent the first telegraph message in Morse code, long or short clicks, each combination of sounds representing letters in the alphabet.

Suddenly, humans could send messages over hundreds of kilometres almost instantly. This was the start of telephones and even the Internet!

Track R.04

The Yoruba: Great Artists

The Yoruba are one of the largest ethnic and cultural groups in western Africa and the Yoruba people have lived in urban societies since the 5th century AD. Ile-Ife in Nigeria was the ancient capital city of the Yoruba. Originally, the Yoruba worked as farmers, **traders**, and artists. Nowadays, the Yoruba live in a special cultural region called Yorubaland in the different countries of Nigeria, Benin, and Togo.

The Yoruba have a long tradition in art and many Yoruba people are amazing artists. Their wooden sculptures and terracotta **figures** show animals and people from all levels of society. Yoruba art also includes **pottery**, textiles, and metalwork.

In the Yoruba culture, the head is seen as the center of **power** and many ancient head sculptures made of bronze and teracotta still survive today. The heads are naturalistic in style and have a serene expression. These sculptures may represent kings and queens.

Most Yoruba art has a meaning or purpose. Some items are connected to their **beliefs**, while others are for celebrations. The Yoruba wear different traditional masks and costumes during festivals and ceremonies that can last for days. These masks and costumes are an important part of Yoruba culture. In the Egungun ceremony, the Yoruba make special Egungun masks and costumes, and perform traditional dances to honor their ancestors.

Traditionally, women and men in Yoruba culture are involved in different artistic trades. The women often make the pots used for cooking and eating, and more unique pots for special occasions, such as ritual bowls. The men are responsible for leather and beadwork. They use animal skins to make things like bags and sandals, and they decorate clothes and crowns for important people with bead designs of human faces, birds, and flowers.

Yoruba art and artists have influenced many artists around the world, and you can see many examples of ancient Yoruba art in many museums.